The
Chinese
Cultural
Revolution

JEAN ESMEIN has travelled extensively in China. From December 1965 to June 1968, he was a press attaché in Peking, and witnessed the Cultural Revolution first-hand.

The
Chinese
Cultural
Revolution

Jean Esmein

Translated from the French by W. J. F. Jenner

Anchor Books
Anchor Press/Doubleday
Garden City, New York
1973

The Chinese Cultural Revolution was first published under the title *La Révolution Culturelle Chinoise* in 1970 by Éditions du Seuil, Paris. The Anchor Books edition is published by arrangement with Éditions du Seuil and André Deutsch Limited.

Anchor Books Edition: 1973

ISBN: 0-385-05098-4
Library of Congress Catalog Number 73–79206
Copyright © 1970 by Éditions du Seuil, Paris
Translation by W. J. F. Jenner
Copyright © 1973 by André Deutsch Limited and
Doubleday & Company, Inc.
All rights reserved
Printed in the United States of America
First Edition

TO CHARLES HAGUENAUER

Contents

Contents

Introduction

China today is a land without legal codes, where human conduct is governed by principles rather than regulations. In this situation there is virtually no distinction between political and moral control. The advice given by the Party press amounts to sermons, by which all who accept the prevailing ethic try to live.

In normal times information is monopolized by the central government. Rather than giving a selection of news about current events the Chinese press carries a message, and it makes up for the shortage of news by its wealth of ideological and tactical education. Through it the Party puts out examples for its cadres to publicize, and exhortations for them to pass on.

With the spread of the Cultural Revolution, all kinds of new sources of information appeared. They varied in value and could not be used uncritically. While some of the texts printed in the revolutionary press—speeches by national leaders, for example—were apparently checked before publication, the rest were polemical. Posters and leaflets had to be read with reserve.

What counted most was that, taken together, this supplementary source of news gave far more facts than the official press generally did.

Using one type of source to fill in the blanks left by the other, one can more or less put the story together in terms

of facts, dates and ideas. Although often vague, and in
need of keys for its interpretation, the official press remains
the most reliable basic source. Comparison with other
contemporary sources can explain the meaning of the
official press. And the papers themselves had a history of
their own, insofar as they were objectives in the struggle
for power.

The exposed positions of the press, from which examples
and ethical principles were transmitted, kept changing
hands. Although it would have been too much to expect
prolonged debates in their columns, some did manage to
develop.

The Chinese are inveterate exaggerators. Posters calling
for the Minister of Petroleum to be 'burned alive' did not
mean that the revolutionaries were getting the stoves
ready. The wish to 'smash' a minister's 'dog's head' generally amounted to no more than a demand for his suspension. The story is full of surprises: political figures
thrown out of some organization were often later summoned to its meetings. People supposedly discredited for
all time reappeared beside Mao Tse-tung on top of the
T'ienanmen rostrum on ceremonial occasions. The revolution may have given rise to exceptional measures, but the
regime tended to preserve its opponents.

This approach, combined with the patience of the leadership in the face of growing disorder, has led some people
to believe that the Cultural Revolution was an organized
movement; and it was still possible to hold this view when
the regime was taking precautions to prevent the workers
and peasants from being contaminated by the students.
The initial plan for the Cultural Revolution was perhaps
only for a micro-revolution. But those who wanted to run
things in the usual way were isolated in their ivory towers
when revolutionary detachments seized power in the cities
under the cold January sun.

But was something more than a deep arousal of the
masses intended? When the propaganda chiefs were asked,
by the Chinese themselves, 'Does the movement involve
reorganizing the masses?' they answered that 'it was not
a question of the reorganization of the masses, but of their

self-education and assistance'.[1] There is no key to explain this reply, which was inevitably ambiguous. An organized revolution would have taught the people nothing. All the same they had to be helped to make revolution.

Who, in the last resort, was able to control the people completely? The Party soon lost the privilege of being feared or respected. When Liu Shao-ch'i's wife proudly stood her ground at her public trial and said, 'As a Chinese woman, as a Chinese woman Communist, I am independent,' her interrogator replied, 'What sort of Communist are you? You are a class reject, drawn into the Party by Liu Shao-ch'i.'[2] Her accuser may even not have been a Party member himself. The Party aristocracy was stripped of its complacency. Its leaders learned, to their cost, how the masses could sentence to political death without recourse to hanging or killing. The struggle, waged by a tiny number at first, embraced a whole section of China, especially the cities. It had its fanatics. The movement for a personality cult of Mao Tse-tung struck one even as a distant observer. There were also realists. 'If you are to seize power, you cannot be lifted over the obstacles. You have to make a big jump,' said Chou En-lai to the young revolutionaries. 'If you are not made head of the department on the spot you will have failed.'[3]

It is surprising that few new leaders emerged. Did the men, old men for the most part, who had wanted and brought about this struggle, come forward with so much enthusiasm and experience that they eclipsed the younger men who joined forces with them? It is hard to believe that the Cultural Revolution can have raised nobody to the side of Mao Tse-tung but some old faithfuls: soldiers, his own wife, and two younger men, of whom one is his son-in-law.

[1] 'A reply to false principles.' Interview given by An Tse-jen, editor of the *People's Daily*, and other revolutionary cadres, and recorded by the Red Guards of the secondary school attached to Peking University, February 10, 1967.

[2] *Current Scene*, vol. VI, no. 6, April 15, 1968, p. 15.

[3] 'Leaders at the Centre discuss the Seizure of Power,' *Yu-tien Fenglei* (revolutionary journal) February 10, 1967—Chou En-lai's words.

It should also be added that the Cultural Revolution has not been the purge that has generally been supposed. It was intended to give the country a rejuvenated Party with strengthened cadres. Care was taken to keep all those who could be won over to Maoist politics. The congress that brought it to an end gave two-thirds of the places on the Central Committee to newcomers.

1. The Roots of the Cultural Revolution in Mao Tse-tung's Ideas

Much of the imagery of the Cultural Revolution, the names of the Red Guard organizations and sometimes their arms—spears with red tassels, shields, and even straw sandals—were borrowed from the history of the revolutionary bases in Kiangsi and Chingkangshan thirty-five years earlier. The Chingkangshan mountains in particular, where Mao had retreated with his troops in September 1927, were given new publicity. They were a symbol, a base from which revolutionary fighters set out to conquer a recalcitrant or hostile world and within which a new society was created.

From 1966 to 1968 speeches and papers, whether or not of Red Guard origin, often drew their examples and exhortations from the experience of the areas governed by the Chinese Soviets. They were invoked in order to revive the relationship that had existed between the people, the Party and the army in the Communist zones. Coming at the time when the Thought of Mao Tse-tung was at its height, these symbols and references served to remind the people of how much Mao's thinking owed to his earliest experiences and decisions as a revolutionary leader. Moreover, the leaders of this new revolution, now being mounted by the government of the dictatorship of the proletariat, looked to past experience as their guide-line.

The Thought of Mao Tse-tung is grounded throughout on ideas formed when he took the initiative militarily and had to play the role of a leader—before long the most important one—of a revolutionary group within the Chinese Communist Party that wanted a territorial base, political power, and an army.

Ten days that shook the world

In December 1967 an article appeared which recalled Mao Tse-tung's retreat to Chingkangshan. Its title was borrowed from John Reed's book on the Russian Revolution.

'It was September 18, 1927,' it began, 'ten days after the Autumn Harvest Rising . . . ten days that shook the world.'[1] But in 1927 the world had ignored this event, concentrating instead on developments within the national government.

The national government at Wuhan[2] had been created after the successful offensive by the forces of the Kuomintang and the Communists, who were still allies. It soon split. Although some of the Communists were aware of the dangers that threatened them, the Soviet emissaries at Wuhan advised them against acquiring their own armed forces.

During the Northern Expedition many peasants had risen in revolt, freed themselves, and formed peasant associations in the occupied provinces. The Communist Party was divided over the question of what support the armed peasant bands could give the revolution. Mao Tse-tung was convinced that the Party should rely on them, as the movement would educate them as it freed them from ancestral tutelage, and peasant forces would ensure the Party success.

The Autumn Harvest Rising was a military defeat for

[1] *Chiehfangchun Wenyi* (PLA Literature and Art), printed in *China Reconstructs*, December 1967.

[2] See J. Guillermaz, *Histoire du Parti communiste chinois*, Payot, Paris, 1968, esp. pp. 157 ff.

the rebels and their Communist generals.[3] They committed four separate fighting units, made up mainly of peasants. Only one of these achieved some local success, but had to withdraw before reaching its principal objective. The attempt ended in failure, and it should have left nothing behind but disappointment and death. But Mao chose to back the lost cause. On September 18th he assembled the retreating insurgents in the small town of Wenchiashih and decided to lead them to Chingkangshan, the 'Ridge of Wells,' which lay in the middle of the great Lohsiao Range.

In November 1927 Mao Tse-tung was censured by the Party's Central Committee, losing his seat on the committee and his membership of the Political Bureau. But he stood by his ideas. In the summer of 1928 he was rehabilitated by the Party's Sixth Congress, which only approved of the peasant movement with reservations. Mao Tse-tung has written that the Sixth Congress was not sufficiently aware of 'the importance of the rural bases and the protracted nature of the democratic revolution.'[4] It is our belief that in referring to the protracted nature of the democratic revolution he had in mind the task—which was even then being tackled—of teaching men to administer their affairs on land held in common.

*A new society in a closed world; unified control;
criticism and self-criticism*

The job thus taken on was a very hard one. The men who had taken cover among the peasantry thinly scattered over this impoverished region included many derelicts, rootless vagabonds, and even former bandits. First, two small bases were formed, where two bands of local brigands were in-

[3] It began on September 8, 1927, in Hunan. An unsuccessful ambush allowed news of it to escape prematurely, and one unit was destroyed through treachery. See Roy Hofheinz, Jr., 'The Autumn Harvest Insurrection,' *China Quarterly*, no. 32 October–December 1967.

[4] Mao Tse-tung, *Selected Works* (Chinese edition), vol. 2, p. 961.

corporated with some difficulty into the ranks. A shared
attitude had to be found that would reduce the differences
within the group and bring it together, so as to get the
most from voluntary cooperation.[5]

Although the rising was a military failure, the para-
phrase of John Reed quoted above celebrated the creation
of a new society, something that went beyond the defeat.
The experimental new society, though small in scale, was
to be established completely free from outside interference
under the protection of its own armed force.

Mao Tse-tung had no monopoly on the idea that the
Party needed an army. It is an idea that crops up whenever a political revolution is in progress over a very great
area; and it also draws on the old Chinese tradition of
rebels—small communities of outlaws and 'honourable
bandits'. Mao's originality lay in the idea, born perhaps in
the little town of Wenchiashih, of bases under military
protection in small and completely isolated societies where
men would be trained to live quite differently from before. He also saw that such a society could last, and that
people could be persuaded to live there for a long time
cut off from the outside world except through fighting.

It could be said that for the next two decades Mao Tse-
tung never left the little world he had created for his companions. While many of the Communist leaders lived in
Shanghai, Tientsin or elsewhere during this period, making
the compromises that were necessary in order to survive,
Mao Tse-tung had a simpler problem: defending his ideal
society with his army and educating his people.

The Party was numerically very weak in its base areas.
Few Party members had accompanied the rebels to the
mountains. If the Party was to play its part among the
people, the army had to help. The army itself had to remain under the ruling power and respect the unity of
command. In addition to protecting the frontiers of the
base areas, it was also used within them, and was entrusted by the Party with guidance of the peasant Soviets.

[5] See *Ajia Keizai Jumpo*, no. 732, 1968, pp. 25–26 for the
Chingkangshan Land Law of December 1928.

But it did not rule the country; it represented the unified command.

The army's role allowed the small group of political leaders—men of the people and educators of the people—to extend their rule right down to the level of local administration, although the Party had so few members. It was a case of what mathematicians call transitivity. In the Maoist system this is a property of the army, but it can be just as well applied to other institutions. Later on it will be important to understand that revolutionary committees did not have powers of direction: they embodied the unified leadership and had to be open to suggestions from above. One tendentious demand for full powers for the committees almost cost the Communist Party the successful outcome of the Cultural Revolution.

With power exercised through intermediaries, the risks of misinterpretation of policies, abuse of power, and deviation from the party line were great. In the interests of the system, criticism from the rank and file had to be allowed an expression. It was also essential that those in executive positions should be allowed to correct what faults they might have committed and be reinstated. Hence the reason for self-criticism. Criticism and self-criticism were the means whereby an illiterate populace could be educated, the cadres kept straight without recourse to sanctions, and a small number of political leaders at the top could be in a position to know everything that was going on. One of its intended aims was to make society transparent, which also seemed to have had the effect of accelerating political awareness among the people and keeping the authorities up to the mark. 'Be specially careful to sweep away any dust which might obscure them from the masses.'[6]

[6] 'All's well with the revolutionary committee,' *Hungch'i*, March 30, 1968: 'All those involved in the work of the revolutionary committee must closely follow Chairman Mao's proletarian line, carry out his recent directives to the letter, practise severe self-discipline, and behave towards themselves and the masses with correctness. They must frequently practise criticism and self-criticism, and be specially careful to sweep away dust which might obscure them from the masses.'

Criticism and self-criticism were only useful as long as they remained a living method.

The mass line and collective education

This method, by which the masses were urged to make their criticism, and which involved washing dirty linen in public rather than carrying out a purge behind closed doors, has led recently to the reopening of the Marxist controversy on revolutionary spontaneity. Lenin doubted whether one could rely on the spontaneity of the masses, weakened by bourgeois education. Rosa Luxemburg disagreed. 'Unless the masses of the people,' she wrote, 'all participate, socialism is created by decree, bestowed by a dozen intellectuals meeting round a green baize table. . . . The only way to a rebirth is the school of public life itself.'[7]

Which of these views one accepts is a matter of temperament. Both reckon that 'the practice of socialism demands a complete spiritual upheaval for the masses, degraded by centuries of bourgeois rule.'[8] But only one of the two thinkers was an optimist.

As has often been observed, Mao is an optimist at heart. He stresses his confidence in the masses, who will only discover the right policies by coming into political life. He is not afraid of provoking crises: 'Proper limits have to be exceeded in order to right a wrong, or else the wrong cannot be righted.'[9] He urges others to organize themselves rather than simply making laws and plans about them.

But while in the Thought of Mao Tse-tung the spontaneity of the masses was a necessary prerequisite, it was not the sole one. 'Our comrades should not imagine that the masses understand nothing of what they themselves have not yet understood . . . neither should they believe that the masses understand all that they themselves

[7] Rosa Luxemburg, *Oeuvres,* vol. 2, Maspero, Paris.
[8] *Ibid.*
[9] 'Report on an investigation of the peasant movement in Hunan,' *Selected Works,* vol. 1, p. 29.

do.'[10] To wish to make the masses act when they are not yet 'aware' would be adventurism, a blind alley, forcing them to do something against their wishes.

It is thus essential to know what the masses understand and want before one acts. The way of doing this is through an 'investigation.' In March 1927 Mao Tse-tung himself wrote up his investigation into the peasant movement in Hunan as an answer to the debate within the Party on whether or not it was advisable to mobilize armed peasant bands. Through investigation a planned action can be corrected or postponed if one finds that revolutionary enthusiasm has not yet been aroused. It can also hasten action when it reveals that the Party cannot see something of which the masses are already aware. This optimism has its other side. In the chaos of the Cultural Revolution all Chinese had to be guided exclusively by the Thought of Mao Tse-tung, although doubtless they did not all understand it. This was a chance for settling private scores, getting one's own back, abusing one's position, and even the pursuit of pleasure. The state lost heavily on millions of free journeys; work stopped; and cadres suffered. The cost of all this must have been heavy.[11] The apparent absence of any clear plan in the first months of the Cultural Revolution led several foreign observers to be critical of Mao Tse-tung.

Practice and progress

Some have seen in the Thought of Mao Tse-tung the message that the way to reform lies through sacrifice and austerity, an idea strengthened by the use of such slogans as 'building up the country through diligence and frugality' and 'relying on one's own efforts and persevering in struggle.' In fact the belief in 'self-cultivation' as a way of enabling the Party as a whole to make progress was a doctrine of Liu Shao-ch'i's group, not of Mao Tse-tung's.

Maoism makes few moral homilies. Instead it encour-

[10] 'On coalition government,' *Selected Works*, vol. 3.
[11] See Asahi Shimbun Chōsakenkyūshitsu, *Mō Takutō no Chōsen*, Tokyo, 1968, p. 17.

ages the spirit of scientific experiment that was one of the
'Three Red Flags' in the Socialist Education Campaign
of 1963–64.[12] There was no question of telling the people that self-sacrifice would enable them to accept the
standard of living that this century has inflicted on the
Chinese; instead they had to 'acquaint the people with the
facts of world progress and the bright future ahead.'[13]
The careful application of well-laid plans, and the idea that
planning and execution went together, were to help the
cadres to lead the masses along the hard road to a brilliant
future.

Frugal use of resources is one of the conditions of progress. Relying on one's own strength is a stage of socialist
transformation leading toward the withering away of the
state.

There is also a spiritual element. As will be seen below,
it complements dialectical materialism. Its role is not to
make man stronger than material forces, but to enable
man to control material forces. In the parable of 'The
Foolish Old Man Who Moved Mountains,' Mao Tse-tung
puts these words into his hero's mouth:

'High as they are, the mountains cannot grow any higher
and with every bit we dig, they will be that much lower.
Why can't we clear them away?'
He went on digging every day, unshaken in his conviction. God was moved by this, and he sent down two
angels, who carried the mountain away on their backs.
Today, two big mountains lie like a dead weight on the
Chinese people. One is imperialism, the other is feudal-
ism. The Chinese Communist Party has long made up its
mind to dig them up. We must persevere and work un-
ceasingly, and we too will touch God's heart. Our God
is none other than the masses of the Chinese people.[14]

[12] The two others were the class struggle and the struggle
for production.
[13] 'On the Chungking Negotiations,' October 17, 1945. Mao
Tse-tung, *Selected Works*, vol. 4, p. 59.
[14] *Selected Works*, vol. 3, p. 322.

II. MAO'S THOUGHT—THE REJECTION OF MECHANISTIC MATERIALISM—CLASS STRUGGLE

Organized disturbances

One axiom in the *little red book* (p. 222 of the English edition), infallibly attracts the reader's attention:

> While we recognise that in the general development of history the material determines the mental, and social being determines social consciousness, we recognise— and indeed must—the reaction of mental on material things, of social consciousness on social being, and of the superstructure on the economic base. This does not go against materialism; on the contrary, it avoids mechanical materialism and firmly upholds dialectical materialism.
>
> 'On Contradiction,' August 1937.

The first coherent explanation of the Cultural Revolution given by those actually involved was on the need to make a revolution in the superstructure, probably because of the reverse action to which Mao Tse-tung referred. The superstructure—the sum total of all the cultural constructs above the economic base—comprised the information media, statute-law and the judiciary, education, philosophy, literature, the arts, leisure activities, social conscience, and the preferences of the intelligentsia. This is where the bourgeois spirit could entrench itself after socialist revolutionary principles had been applied to the economy but before the superstructure itself had been transformed.

The academic curricula, intellectual climate, and social structure could continue to imbue new generations with traditional, capitalistic ideas based on the conception that the fruits of progress were for the benefit of a few privileged groups. If there was any chance of reaction this would be the source of the counter-revolution. If, on the other hand, the whole superstructure became the focus of the proletarian ideology that would in its turn affect the whole society.

This is not the only point calling for comment in the quotation cited above, which amounts to a denunciation of mechanistic materialism, and gives the mental factor a role by comparison with the material that upsets the theory of dialectical materialism. Such free thinking provoked passionate criticism from more academic Marxist theoreticians. When the Cultural Revolution developed in China, Soviet theoreticians regarded it as a distortion of materialism.

Some Red Guards were happy to take issue with them. They did not confine themselves to quoting from the Thought of Mao Tse-tung, though they doubtless claimed it as their inspiration, but applied their rationale to concrete situations, with revealing results. For instance, the Kehsuan revolutionary group in Shantung wrote a refutation of an article entitled 'Marxism and Maoism' by Fedoseyev, Vice-principal of the USSR Academy of Sciences. According to this group, Fedoseyev believed that in the last resort it is economic conditions that determine who is to have power, and that to advise violent revolution amounted to ignoring economic imperatives. But Fedoseyev, they said, was unaware that war enabled contradictions to be resolved, and did not understand the changes wrought by the passage from peace to war and from war to peace, changes that Chairman Mao had analyzed and explained. Struggle and the end of struggle created discontinuities within systems that would otherwise be determined by economic conditions.[15]

In this article the Maoists adduced revolutionary action to show that materialism could be turned aside from its mechanistically determined course, but they did not contrast the mental and material factors to show how they were united in the materialist dialectic. One example of an attempt to do this is drawn from an early (December 1966) poster criticizing the People's Daily; this was a time when all kinds of thought and criticism, even of the

[15] People's Daily, August 29, 1967.

most official bodies, were permitted in order to get closer to the Thought of Mao Tse-tung.[16]

The title of the editorial, 'Grasp Revolution, Promote Production,' was one of the most enduring of all the Cultural Revolution's slogans. It meant that the political struggle to rebuild society according to the Thought of Mao Tse-tung had to go hand in hand with working hard at one's job. In the eyes of the young critics this was a revisionist editorial because it said that socialism should be built in China on two different fronts: the spiritual one, by remoulding old-fashioned ideas in order to increase the people's awareness in the socialist revolution; and the material one, through the transformation of the environment and the development of the socialist economy.

The authors of this poster were probably right in thinking that the Thought of Mao Tse-tung rejects any material-spiritual dichotomy, and they rejected it in this case. They demanded that separate teams should not be formed for running the Cultural Revolution and production, even under a unified control. They wanted the Red Guards to be free to go among the workers and peasants to reform them and at the same time their political and social world, thus provoking a disturbance that the workers and peasants themselves could exploit.

Class struggle

The main point that the revolutionaries, quoted above, had in mind when they spoke of the passage from peace to war, in contrast to the principle of pure economic determinism, was class struggle. The theme is a familiar one: class struggle is a perpetual ferment that never stops. At the time of the revolutionary bases actions required by class struggle were aimed above all at bringing new peasants, determined to fight against the landlords and the local authorities, over to the side of the Communists.

When the common people of the bases had learnt over the years to live according to the standards of a new

[16] *People's Daily* editorial, September 7, 1966.

society, the scale of, and the protagonists in, the class struggle both changed. The Communist Party had won. It now occupied the vast territories of China, an area immeasurably greater than the bases. The members of the homogeneous little society found themselves in the minority amid the new mass. The consequent dilution underlined the gravity of the 'contradictions among the people,' especially as after the absorption of capitalist areas some members of the Party came under the influence of the society that now was theirs.

As the press has frequently reported, Mao urged at the Plenum of the Party's Central Committee in 1962, 'Never forget class struggle!' He was warning his comrades that if they lost the vision of a community besieged by the forces of private property, the ideal little world that had been built for them in the old days would be lost forever.

Economic development

To be ceaselessly vigilant in the class struggle, and to anticipate the reaction of the superstructure on the economic base, involved a vision of long-term evolution that had no room for the conventional development theories of professional economists. As national planners are well aware, revolutionary disturbances occurring within a given period entail the downward revision of production estimates made for that period. Such disturbances can be allowed for, but they are generally unforeseeable, and it would be arbitrary to make a 10 per cent or 20 per cent discount for work stoppages or extra consumption arising from social struggles over a period of five or ten years. Economists generally prefer to make a plan making no allowances for such risks. The simplest approach for them is to envisage continuous growth. They are optimists for technical reasons.

The political leader, who keeps class struggle in reserve as one of the methods at his disposal, naturally rejects the hypothesis of continuous growth. Po Yi-po, however, a deputy premier and head of the State Economic Commission, wanted to 'launch the incorrect policy of continuous growth' in 1960,[17] and was criticized in terms of Mao Tse-tung's ideas. This condemnation showed that in Maoist thought none of the 'primacy of politics over economics,' would be conceded, even for long-term development. A development programme drawn up in such a way as to rule out interruptions by political events would create an atmosphere seriously inhibiting political action.

Po Yi-po was also accused of wanting remuneration given in accordance with work done, and of opposing Mao Tse-tung's wish that wage differences should be narrowed. He had lost the ideal of the simple living and thrift that had made the revolutionary bases a little world remembered as a golden age.

One aim of the Thought is that all sections of the population—city dwellers, country people, workers, peasants, soldiers—should eventually have similar life-styles. For the time being local collective organizations were urged to spend less state money and learn to get by on their own resources. The spirit of economy fitted in well with the need to adapt public services to the real needs of the masses, putting them on a much bigger scale and standardizing them.

> One of the reasons why the older cadres enjoy poor health is because they are too well looked after as regards clothing, food, accommodation and transport. Our medical insurance is copied from that of the Soviet Union, and medical specialists work as ordinary doctors. It is bad for them not to see all kinds of disease more often.[18]

In his wish to have the masses educated and organized into collectives to increase production, Mao Tse-tung did not seem to have been concerned with their vast numbers and their demographic growth. Would the Cultural Revolution have been more cautiously handled if he had been

---

[17] 'The 130 crimes of Po Yi-po' in *K'o-chi Hung-ch'i* (*Science and Technology Red Flag*), February 18, 1967.
[18] 'Mao Tse-tung's talks with Vietnamese visitors,' June 24, 1964.

seriously worried by this situation? It does not seem very probable.

In addition to the leadership of the Party, a decisive factor is our population of 600 million. More people mean a greater ferment of ideas, more enthusiasm and more energy. Never before have the masses of the people been so inspired, so militant and so daring as at present.[19]

Besides, the class struggle could not be put off. Disorder was not something terrible, and good could be expected from it. Above all, the structure of production had to be transformed *before* the productive forces could be developed: this was one of the lessons of Leninism.

III. COMMUNES AND DEFENCE

The advantage of starting from scratch

Full of health and energy, Chairman Mao walked with confident steps among the poor and lower middle peasants tending the fields. Warmly he shook each one's earth-stained hand, and listened to the peasants and the cadres reporting on their work. They told him that they were planning to merge their agricultural producers' co-operatives into a big farm. It was then that the Chairman revealed his vision of the future when he said: It would be better to set up a people's commune. In this way, industry, agriculture, commerce, education and military affairs can be combined, thus making the task of leadership easier.[20]

This episode took place at Peiyuan, in the Shantung district, on August 9, 1958. It shows that Mao Tse-tung

[19] 'Introducing a co-operative,' April 15, 1958. *Selected Readings from the Works of Mao Tse-tung* FLP, Peking, 1967, p. 403.
[20] 'Tremendous Changes in Peiyuan' *Peking Review*, 1968, no. 38, p. 26.

was envisaging the transfer of economic, educational, and military functions to the level of the basic cell in the countryside. It was around this same cell that, even before the outbreak of the Cultural Revolution, the most vigorous arguments were to rage, and the fiercest battles were to be fought, between conservatives and radicals.

The Chairman had previously initiated many projects on basic agricultural units. He expressed this eloquently in a text recently revived and reprinted in large type, filling the whole front page of a paper that was several times the Cultural Revolution's leading journal.[21] It was a letter about an agricultural co-operative in Honan that had distinguished itself for its revolutionary spirit at the beginning of 1958. Mao Tse-tung held it up as an example to the nation.

> The backward sections of the masses are exerting themselves to catch up with the advanced, which demonstrates that the economic socialist revolution in our country (in those places where the relations of production have not been completely transformed), the political revolution, the ideological revolution, the technical revolution, and the *Cultural Revolution*[22] are going ahead at full speed. . . . Apart from their other characteristics, the outstanding thing about China's 600 million people is that they are 'poor and blank.' This may seem a bad thing, but in reality it is a good thing. Poverty gives rise to the desire for change, the desire for action and the desire for revolution. On a blank sheet of paper, free from any mark, the freshest and most beautiful characters can be written, the freshest and most beautiful pictures can be painted.
>
> 'Introducing a co-operative,' April 15, 1958.

There is an advantage in starting from nothing. But can one imagine how many drawings have been scratched out on blank sheets of paper?

[21] The Shanghai paper *Wenhui Pao* celebrated the tenth anniversary of Mao's letter by devoting the whole of its front page to 'Introducing a co-operative,' April 15, 1968.

[22] Author's italics.

*Complete autonomy for the communes to speed up
socialist education*

In 1958 a long war of words began when a conference,
held in Chengtu under the patronage of Mao Tse-tung,
issued its views on the question of agricultural mechanization. The ramifications of this question are important because here many areas of policy overlap: agricultural projects, state investment, the technical education of the
masses, the centralization or decentralization of Party and
government, the speed of economic development, the
problem of how to divide development between town and
country, and defence preparations.

The Chengtu conference recommended that the co-
operatives should 'rely basically on their own efforts in
mechanizing agriculture.' Specifically, it proposed that:

> Multi-purpose agricultural machinery and small tractors
> should be purchased by co-operatives for their own use.
> Medium-sized tractors should be put to service in co-
> operatives, either as state property for the use of the
> co-operative, or shared among the members them-
> selves.[23]

Nine years later the Revolutionary Rebels of the Eighth
Ministry of the Machine Industry[24] criticized the policies
that had in fact prevailed. Mao Tse-tung's line on agricultural mechanization, they wrote, which had been approved by the Chengtu Conference, had simply been
sabotaged by 'China's Khrushchev' and his followers, who
wanted state agricultural machinery stations or specialized
groups under their own control.[25] After the Chengtu reso-

[23] 'The need to wipe out the wicked crimes of China's Khrushchev and Co in sabotaging agricultural mechanization.' Com-
mentary by the editors. *Nungyeh chihsieh chishu* (Agricultural
Machine Technology), 1967, no. 5, August 8, 1967.

[24] Responsible for agricultural machinery.

[25] *Nungyeh chihsieh chishu*, no. 6, September 18, 1967.
'Sweep away the state monopoly and promote large-scale
mechanization through relying on one's own efforts' by Revolutionary Rebels in the Eighth Ministry of the Machine Industry.

lution machines were indeed given to the communes, who owned 70 per cent of all the tractors in the country at the end of 1958. But 'China's Khrushchev' and his acolytes had maliciously exaggerated the faults of this system, which were due solely to the inexperience of the communes in their maintenance and use. They took the machines back from some communes and set up pilot centres; then transferred the control of these centres from the local offices of the Ministry of Agriculture to tripartite organs subordinate to central government ministries.

Naturally they stressed technology, the higher returns obtainable when the machines were in the hands of specialists, and the better upkeep of the equipment under the control of an industrial ministry. If this interpretation of what the Eighth Ministry's Revolutionary Rebels meant is correct, the followers of 'China's Khrushchev' wanted the system integrated into the government, whereas Mao Tse-tung wanted the units of collective agriculture to be given the greatest possible freedom. The tractor stations ended up by being treated as economic enterprises. According to the same critics:

In August 1963 the exponents of the bourgeois revisionist line in the Agriculture, Water, and Forestry Ministries proposed that in two years' time all tractor stations that had not been able to make up their losses and were still in deficit should be dissolved, while those making a profit should continue to expand.[26]

As long as the problem was confined to agricultural mechanization, it seemed to be simply a question of professional training and investment.

The supporters of Mao Tse-tung held that people would acquire a better training if they were really responsible for everything they used in their work and life; only when peasants combined the roles of workers, administrators, and farmers would they be able to reach urban living standards. On Liu Shao-ch'i's side it was said that China was not yet rich enough to supply everyone with machin-

[26] *Nungyeh chihsieh chishu,* no. 5, 1967.

ery, and that the countryside would suffer from its lack of experience. Liu Shao-ch'i was attacked in the usual way:

> Seeking 'theoretical' grounds for his opposition to the agricultural co-operative movement, China's Khrushchev had recourse to the out-worn weapon of 'the theory of productive forces' taken from the revisionist arsenal of his predecessors, Bernstein, Kautsky, Bukharin and their supporters. He claimed that only after the nationalization of the industry could large quantities of machinery be supplied to the peasants, and only then would it be possible to nationalize the land and collective agriculture.[27]

Liu was worried that if collectivization took place before the mechanization of agriculture instead of at the same time, as had been intended, the considerable efforts to raise production through working collectively would give them a premature loathing for collectivization. This was what he meant by 'confusing contradictions between ourselves and the enemy with contradictions among the people.'

From the point of view of economic development, as a Western expert would see it, nothing is to be gained by increasing investment in machines if the personnel using them cannot maintain them, and the equipment has a short life. Nor is there much to be gained by sharing investment equally among all the communes. A great deal will be gained, on the other hand, by putting all investment into industrial centres and specialized groupings. In other words, development will be speeded up by putting as much as possible into the growth leaders.

To Mao Tse-tung such a policy was revisionist. It ignored the chief aim of reducing the differences between town and countryside. But what made it worst of all was that, when investments were concentrated, the chance was

[27] 'Conflict of Views in China's Agricultural Policy,' editorial in the *People's Daily, Red Flag,* and *PLA Daily,* November 23, 1967. The quotation is from a speech at a conference on propaganda work of May 7, 1951 (see *Peking Review,* 1967, no. 49, p. 14).

lost of teaching the rural communes to form themselves into small units capable of feeding, running, industrializing, and defending themselves, thus making themselves ready to answer the needs of peace as well as of war.

Military thought

Mao Tse-tung said before the Cultural Revolution that agricultural mechanization was linked to preparation for war.

At the beginning of 1966, when China's third Five-Year Plan should have been adopted, the Party leadership was divided on many issues. Chairman Mao travelled round the provinces and addressed himself to the local officials. This should have been taken as a warning that things were about to happen.

'In February 1966 our great leader Chairman Mao visited several provinces, municipalities and regions to lay the foundations of a plan for five, seven or ten years based on the decentralization of activities,' reported the revolutionaries of the Eighth Ministry of the Machine Industry. The idea was to 'extend mechanization step by step, starting from a few experimental areas, and to bring about the general mechanization of agriculture over a period of twenty-five years.' In March, Chairman Mao sent a letter giving specific instructions on the methods to be used in 'decentralizing activities':

> This objective should be linked with *preparation for war* and famine, as well as for the people's benefit. Otherwise it will not be carried out enthusiastically even if all the necessary conditions are there.[28]

The question of agricultural mechanization thus involved matters even more important than centralization, mass education and economic development. In the eyes of the Chairman, who was looking for ways of giving the new five-year plan a striking appearance, the demands of over-all defence took priority over those of growth.

[28] *Nungyeh chihsieh chishu*, 1967, no. 6, *op. cit.* Author's italics.

Over-all defence is no overstatement of Mao Tse-tung's view. It was a matter of organizing the countryside for resistance. 'Not only do we need a powerful regular army,' wrote the *People's Liberation Army Daily*,[29] 'but it is also vital to have a militia. Thus the enemy will be without collaborators if he enters our country.' The fear of collaboration with the enemy, which it was eventually found necessary to invoke, called up the ghosts of Wang Ching-wei and of Chen Kung-po, who fought with Kuomintang and the Communist Party in the early stages, but then became puppets of the Japanese during the occupation.

The Chinese leaders indicated more than once during the Cultural Revolution to Red Guards and even to foreign visitors their anxiety at the prospect of another Wang Ching-wei emerging if China were invaded by foreign forces. If whole districts and regions were not to be abandoned to collaboration—and the danger was one to be taken more seriously in the countryside, where political consciousness was less advanced—it was necessary to reinforce morale and also provide the means with which to organize resistance.

If a country is highly centralized, the rural areas are dependent on their administrative centres, and districts are dependent on the big cities, so enemy occupation of the administrative nerve centres soon puts paid to the outlying districts' ability to operate autonomously. If, on the other hand, the whole country consists of independent units with soft tissue between them, through which the invading armies could pour, but each representing a hard nucleus with an autonomous capacity to provide food, manufacture arms, carry out hit-and-run operations against the enemy, and make occupation impossible for him, then the country could keep up a very long resistance.[30] Decen-

[29] *PLA Daily*, August 1, 1967, special supplement for the militia.

[30] At the beginning of the Cultural Revolution a film called *Tunnel Warfare* was distributed. This showed how, during the Japanese War, some villagers went underground to organize themselves secretly, deceive the enemy, and harass him from the rear. This was one of the few feature films, perhaps ten in all, that were shown throughout the whole movement.

tralization, industrialization spread out at the lowest possible level, and the technical training of small agricultural communes (as, for example, through learning how to repair agricultural machinery) were thus all part of the preparations for resistance.

> In combating an imperialist war of aggression, no matter what weapons the enemy may use, if they dare to go deep into our country, we will enjoy the maximum initiative, give full play to our strong points and advantages, use various methods to deal them blows, vigorously demonstrate the magic power of people's war, and make sure that the aggressors will never go back alive.[31]

The people had no need to fear the enemy's weapons. Mao Tse-tung flew in the face of strategic orthodoxy, based as it has been since 1949 on the balance of terror, by refusing to be afraid of nuclear weapons. Like Clausewitz, he stressed the superiority of defence over attack.[32]

The military thinking of Mao Tse-tung was placed on a pinnacle by the Cultural Revolution, especially after August 1, 1967, the fortieth anniversary of the founding of the People's Liberation Army. It has been said that Marx was the thinker who gave Marxism its basic doctrine and economic ideas, Lenin contributed the political ideas, and Mao produced the military ones at the decisive moment when the struggle between capitalism and socialism was going to take the form of extended war.

Mao's military thinking did not hold absolute sway in the Party before the Cultural Revolution. The divergences that existed can be measured by looking at the different positions taken over decentralization of command and the creation of regional forces. Liu Shao-ch'i wanted the enemy contained. 'It would be bad if the enemy broke through,' he said.[33] Lo Jui-ch'ing, still chief of the General

[31] *Peking Review* no. 48, November 24, 1967, 'Basic differences between the proletarian and bourgeois military thought,' p. 15.

[32] See André Glucksman, *Le Discours de la guerre,* L'Herne, Paris, 1968.

[33] *Peking Review,* 1967, no. 24, 'Basic differences between proletarian and bourgeois military thought,' p. 14.

Staff at the time, reckoned that the right method was 'to dam the flood.'[34]

To describe the Thought of Mao Tse-tung as one of the peaks of contemporary military thinking inevitably strikes us Westerners as surprising. The Thought of Mao Tse-tung does not seem suited to the defence of integrated twentieth-century states. The more specialized a country is in its regions, mining centres, ports and intercommunicating industrial complexes, its areas of specialized trade or single crop culture, and its administrative centres, the more its life depends on the links between the centre and the various complexes. The more integrated and vulnerable its systems, the longer the range at which its defensive weapons have to act against attacks that could paralyze at very long range the links between the systems. This is why nations of this sort provide themselves with complex weapons systems and make complex strategic dispositions, aimed at giving long-range protection.

Mao Tse-tung would seem to view the problem differently. We have seen above how he excludes polarized development on political and social grounds. If extensive integrated systems are also impossible to defend, the simplest solution is to reduce their number and size. With this simplification, the problem reverts to the organization of resistance in the smaller areas, so that they can rely on themselves in the event of an invasion and organize themselves for survival. They may be scorched by the invaders as they pass, they may suffer losses, but they will never yield.

The decentralization of industry in the countryside is essential to a strategic defence based on such a cellular structure. The North Vietnamese were to show how it could be done. In the period just before the Cultural Revolution they had not yet undergone the heavy American bombings, but later on they invented *sotanization*, the transport of the industrial equipment of the cities to caves and to places where it had cover, albeit precarious. Thus

[34] *Ibid.*, p. 15.

the Vietnamese were able to make up for shortages in supplies of any kind and cope with cut communications.

Organs of popular participation in local affairs

Political organization below the level of the Party was logically needed to correspond to the localized organization of defence. In the Thought of Mao Tse-tung this was to be found at the level of the peasant associations. All signs suggest that the revolution has now tried to bring this about.

But the revolutionary committees of the towns have been the institutions of the Cultural Revolution longest in the news. At first the revolution stopped at the edge of the countryside, either because its abrupt introduction would have been rejected by the masses and condemned by powerful leaders, or else because the authorities did everything in their power to prevent it coming in. Rural revolutionary committees emerged more quietly than the urban ones, though they were the subject of a propaganda campaign in March 1968.[35]

The press went to great lengths to underline what was different in the new formula for government: the system should not be made up of outsiders. Its members were to keep close to the grass roots and get things ready for economic development and war preparation.[36] Local revolutionary committees were made up of three elements—peasants, young revolutionaries, and cadres won over to the revolution. This was a formula for a triple alliance without the army. The place of the army itself was taken by the militia, who were not regular soldiers.

Many revolutionary committees would have been formed earlier if all the necessary elements had been present to take part. It was hard to get the revolutionary masses to participate in large numbers, as Chou En-lai himself

[35] Probably after discussions among top leaders at conferences held between February 20 and 27, 1968.

[36] See especially the April 6, 1968, New China News Agency dispatch on the P'ingku Revolutionary Committee.

complained in his speech of February 2, 1968, to representatives of committees in various sectors of government.

To bring about the representation of the revolutionary masses in local institutions, Mao Tse-tung set about reviving peasant associations in 1964, an idea that went back to the risings of 1927. The poor and lower-middle peasants' associations founded in some places in accordance with the scheme contained in the Central Committee directive of June 1964, had above all to be independent of the Party and the government.

According to Clause 3 of the scheme, all the poor and lower-middle peasants belonging to the rural people's communes who made a personal application could be members of the association if approved by a general meeting of their production team. Membership was, to this extent, voluntary. Members of the associations had full rights to elect and recall delegates to their own level and higher levels, as well as the right of making criticisms 'even in the case of mistakes and shortcomings on the part of leading members.'

One might almost be reading a document from two years later, when Shanghai and Peking wanted to form themselves into 'communes' on the lines of the 1871 Paris Commune. 'If members suffered reprisals because they had criticized actions of the production teams or brigades of the people's communes, or had criticized their leaders, they had the right of appeal to all organizations affiliated to them.'

The role of the associations was in particular to 'Respond actively to the call of the Party and Chairman Mao,[37] to be exemplary in complying with and executing the policies and commands of Party and state, and to persist in the direction of socialism.'[38]

The peasant associations were thus to constitute another

[37] Author's italics.
[38] Full text in *Ajia Keizai Jumpo,* no. 681, Tokyo, 1967, p. 24 ff. (Full English translation in R. Baum and F. C. Teiwes, *Ssu-Ch'ing, The Socialist Education Movement of 1962–1966,* Berkeley, 1968, University of California, Berkeley, China Research Monographs no. 2, pp. 95–101—translator.)

network in addition to those of the Party and the government.

It was virtually made clear that their function, apart from guiding collective agriculture forward, was to hold themselves ready to respond to appeals from Chairman Mao and propagate his thought. But by all indications these June 1964 directives never got beyond the stage of being a trial scheme. Associations of this sort were only set up in some places, notably in southern provinces, and this was not always done in the spirit in which they were originally conceived.

There is a fascinating similarity between some of the provisions of this 1964 scheme and certain propaganda documents distributed at the beginning of the Cultural Revolution. (Later programmes for the revolution were marked by the contradictions that developed among the people as it proceeded.) It could be said that the movement which led to the founding of the poor and lower-middle peasant associations was comparable in its organic and social aims to the Cultural Revolution, with the big difference that this time the operation was intended to proceed either with the Party's agreement or at any rate without coming into conflict with it. Is it possible that the collapse of this agreement was the reason why the Party had to be challenged directly?

2. The Polarization of the Communist Party

The period from 1959 to the outbreak of the Cultural Revolution was one of clashes and secret conflicts inside the Communist Party from which no appeals were made to public opinion. Some of the leaders wanted draft schemes regarded as settled when they had been examined by higher authorities but not yet fully approved. Other leaders dragged their feet over the publication of schemes that revived earlier more advanced programmes of collectivization or socialization; alternatively they truncated schemes, only issuing the non-revolutionary parts to their subordinates, or changed the texts, on the grounds that these were still in draft form. Their opponents angrily tried to make known their real points of view instead of the mutilated versions, but this was against Party rules.

The political struggles always followed this sort of scenario, with the authorities in the Party machine taking the part of conservatives and the mass-liners as radicals.

The radicals were aggressive. Whenever they could they made their views heard at the highest levels, and in their criticisms they showed as little consideration to their friends as to their enemies. They were more interested in stating their views than in widening their connections, and showed no apparent regrets for strength lost and alliances wrecked. The main conservative tactic was inertia. They only acted when respect for the correct forms or the pressure of a sector of public opinion influenced by the radicals forced them to put on a show of acting. There was no majority in favour of bringing about new socialist transformations.

The majority of them felt, sincerely perhaps, that the transition to socialism had been in the main achieved. They reduced radical schemes to minor reforms that stayed at the project stage. The radicals then tried to stir up public opinion. If the debate was over collectivization and the political role of the poor peasants they visited the countryside. Another concern of theirs was the return of 'Right opportunists' to political life, and as these latter held key positions in literature and the arts, the radicals launched Marxist literary criticisms, making the most of the freedom of the press available to them and trying to win positions in the world of journalism.

Needless to say, all the issues dividing the two sides were important questions on which all Communists had to take a stand, and the split was gradually spreading right through the Party.

The organization and working of the Party

The numerical strength of the Chinese Communist Party was not very high, comprising only some twenty-five or thirty per thousand of the population, with a much lower proportion in the countryside than in the towns. There was nothing unusual for a commune brigade of 1,500 people to have only three to five Party members. This was a tiny handful with which to arouse the masses, particularly in view of the size and number of the tasks before them. This may have encouraged the Party's representatives in small communities to make too much of their personal authority.

The Party's structure was like that of all other Communist Parties, and its institutions worked on the principle of democratic centralism. In principle, important decisions had to be put to the vote of delegates elected directly or indirectly from the basic levels, and it was to these that the authorities entrusted with their execution were responsible. Decisions once taken had to be strictly carried out.

The Party's highest executive body was the Central Committee, which was in principle elected for a five-year period by the Party Congress, though at the time of Cultural Revolution the Central Committee had been in existence for almost a decade. According to the Party Constitution it was supposed to meet in plenary session at least twice a year to re-elect its executive agents: the Political Bureau, the Standing Committee of the Political Bureau, and the Secretariat. One result of the splits within the Party was that 'work conferences' were called instead of plenary sessions.

Local and national government rested on a system of people's congresses and 'people's committees' parallel to that of the Party. Party committees guided the 'people's committees' of the same level, right up to the level of the State Council or Cabinet. Within the Central Committee's bureaus were specialized departments guiding the ministries. The key organs and bodies in the country—ministries, army units and staff departments, offices, factories, banks, newspapers—in effect were run by the collective leadership of their Party committees. These were known as the Party committees of the 'unit.'[1]

The most influential figures tended to hold concurrent positions in the Party committee and 'people's committee' of each level. Each committee had its standing committee or central group—in the case of the Central Committee's Political Bureau it was its own Standing Committee—and a secretariat responsible for the day-to-day work under the guidance of the standing committee. The secretary of a committee was a key figure, and Mao Tse-tung always laid great stress on the training of the men who filled it.

A party committee has ten to twenty members; it is like a squad in the army, and the secretary is like the 'squad leader'. It is indeed not easy to lead this squad well.

[1] A factory, a department store, an agency, or a people's commune, for example, are 'units.' The term 'system' is used for a whole nationwide network of services under a single political and technical leadership: industry, communications, finance, commerce, agriculture, forestry, foreign relations, etc.

. . . To fulfil its task of exercising leadership, a Party committee must rely on its 'squad members' and enable them to play their parts to the full. To be a good 'squad leader' the secretary should study hard and investigate thoroughly. . . .[2]

What is true for the secretary of a unit's committee is even truer for the secretary of the Central Committee. The Secretary General, Teng Hsiao-p'ing, and the Second Secretary, P'eng Chen, had considerable power. The Second Secretary in particular included among his functions that of confirming the appointments of cadres to positions in the Party. This gave P'eng Chen influence and capabilities which went far beyond his responsibilities as mayor of Peking.

The pre-1969 Party Constitution provided for sanctions against its members in order to allow for errors to be put right. They ranged from a warning to suspension from one's position in Party organizations. An accused member might be put on probation for a period not exceeding two years. He had the right to speak in his own defence, and could in the last resort be expelled from the Party. Decisions concerning him could only be taken by higher authority in the Party, and the masses did not have the right to judge him.

The provisions for suspension and probation, which could be for periods as short as ten or fifteen days, explain the absence of certain personalities during the Cultural Revolution which often attracted attention, followed by their reappearance shortly afterwards.

The average age of the leaders was old in 1966: over sixty for members of the Central Committee, and not much below this figure for candidate members. Several younger, dynamic men, such as Teng Hsiao-p'ing, P'eng Chen and T'ao Chu, seemed capable of replacing the historic leaders. Events spared none of them.

Foreigners used to regard the leaders at the Centre—the common abbreviation for the Central Committee, its com-

[2] 'Methods of Work of Party Committees' (March 13, 1949), *Selected Works,* vol. 4, p. 377.

missions and central services—as united. In September 1964 the *People's Daily* listed Liu Shao-ch'i, Chou En-lai, Teng Hsiao-p'ing, P'eng Chen and Lin Piao as Chairman Mao's closest companions in arms.

Campaigns before the Cultural Revolution: the Great Leap Forward, the People's Communes, and 'Readjustment'

The most famous of the rectification campaigns carried out to give the Party a 'popular treatment' was that of 1942. Mao Tse-tung decided to put right all sorts of bad habits among the cadres: authoritarianism, dogmatism, pedantry, mystification, dullness, unintelligibility, alienation from the masses. Other such movements took place in 1947–48 and in 1950 to encourage non-communists to express their views on the Party's work, so as to invigorate the united front between Communists and noncommunists.

In 1956, a year of great importance because during it the Eighth Party Congress was held, a great open-door operation was carried out. The news media were reformed, and the Chinese were urged by propaganda to express their views. This was the Hundred Flowers campaign. Although the intellectuals did most of the talking, the campaign was also aimed at the workers and peasants.

This movement for free criticism came to an abrupt halt. Probably most of the Party wanted the criticisms stopped. In any event, the Party had its own interpretation of a speech that Mao Tse-tung had just made, and it made the most of it. Edgar Faure, who has observed the cyclical nature of such movements as the Cultural Revolution since 1957, has noted tactics used by the Party machine.[3] A passage from Mao Tse-tung's report 'On the correct handling of contradictions among the people' was revised before being incorporated into an editorial that appeared in the *People's Daily* on April 14th.

[3] Edgar Faure, *The Serpent and the Tortoise*, Macmillan, London, 1965.

In this passage the theory of contradictions was brought into the campaign for rectifying ways of working. It was made commonplace. While affirming that mass struggles were not yet entirely over, he was quoted as saying that 'large-scale class struggle between ourselves and our enemies has, in the main, ended.' There remained contradictions among the people, mainly due to mutual misunderstanding between the people and the leaders. The Party therefore had to put itself right, and that concerned nobody but the Party itself. 'Was there at this point a conflict of views with concessions by Mao, or was this simply general agreement to resort to a tried formula, a good publicity gambit?'[4] In any event Teng Hsiao-p'ing, the Party's Secretary-General, left no room for doubt over how the clause in the new Party constitution on disagreements was to be interpreted: 'The right of disagreement applies in day-to-day questions, but never over principles, or in practical activities. The basis of the Party is a unified ideology.'[5]

On June 14, 1967, perhaps on the pretext of the rather serious incident of June 12th at the Party offices in Hanyang (the modern industrial suburb of Wuhan), the movement for self-criticism and submission to the Party by which atonement was already being made for the Hundred Flowers, became a very tough campaign against Right deviationists.

From 1958 onwards a new five-year plan was mounted, and political questions tended more and more to be seen through the prism of economic development. At the second session of the Party Congress in May 1958 Liu Shaoch'i called for intensified efforts in rapid industrialization and modernization. The congress adopted the general line of building socialism to obtain 'more, better, quicker and more economical' results. The leap forward was to begin in the industrial enterprises. Mao was concentrating more than ever on the countryside, doubtless believing

[4] Faure, *op. cit.*, p. 111.
[5] Robert Guillain, 'Que fleurissent cent fleurs, que cent écoles révalisent,' *Le Monde*, March 7, 1957.

that the spirit of economic progress could be used to intensify rural collectivization.

The first people's communes were founded on the initiative of agricultural co-operatives in Liaoning and
Honan. Then, rather hastily, a Central Committee work
conference at Peitaiho decided to generalize these experiments by adopting on August 29, 1958, the 'Resolution on
the establishment of the people's communes.' This resolution was expanded in a number of basic articles in the
theoretical organs that tried to go more deeply into the
matter; but most of the articles thus produced could
scarcely conceal the extent to which they had been improvised.[6] This was in contrast to the 'Resolution on agricultural co-operatives' adopted at the end of the first
session of the Eighth Party Congress.[7] Such vital questions as the number of households to a commune, the re-
tention of private property in the form of individual plots
of land, collective dormitories, and the time span over
which the communes were to be organized were touched
on only vaguely. One is left with the impression that the
main point on which agreement was reached was that an
example—that of the Weihsing (Sputnik) Commune—
should be popularized. The position taken by Liu Shao-
ch'i and his supporters on agricultural collectivization
emerged later in official press commentaries during the
Cultural Revolution. If these are entirely to be believed, it
is not surprising that it was hard to find a majority in the
Central Committee in 1968 to support Mao Tse-tung's
revolutionary schemes. A 1967 article comments on the

[6] The text of the resolution, two editorials in the *People's
Daily* and three in the *Red Flag*, all published between August
and October 1958, were published together with the rules of
the Sputnik People's Commune in the pamphlet *People's Communes in China*, Foreign Languages Press, Peking.
[7] The result of a report by Mao Tse-tung ('On the question
of agricultural co-operation,' *Selected Readings from the Works
of Mao Tse-tung*, Peking, 1967, pp. 316–39—translator) made
on July 31, 1955, in which Mao argued with all the skill and the
force of his conviction, but which was not published until
October 11th. (See Gilbert Etienne, *La Voie Chinoise* PUF,
Paris, 1962, chs. 10 and 19.)

observations Liu Shao-ch'i is supposed to have made at an earlier period on a resolution from Shansi about mutual-aid teams.

> However, working behind Chairman Mao's back, China's Khrushchev wrote the following vicious comments on a report: 'After the land reform, the peasants' spontaneous tendency toward capitalism and class polarization began to find expression in economic developments in the countryside. Some comrades of the Party have already expressed fears of such a spontaneous tendency and class polarization, and have attempted to check or prevent them. They cherish the illusion that this tendency can be checked or prevented by means of mutual-aid teams and supply and marketing co-operatives. Some people have already expressed the opinion that steps should be taken gradually to shake the foundations of private ownership, weaken it until it is nullified, and raise the agricultural mutual-aid organizations to the level of agricultural producers' co-operatives as a new factor for 'overcoming the peasants' spontaneous tendency.' This is an erroneous, dangerous and Utopian conception of agricultural socialism.[8]

This text shows that even when different leaders made the same diagnosis they were pursuing different courses of action.

The people's communes, 'a form of economic, administrative, cultural and military decentralization . . . an attempt at popular self-government and local organization of the whole of social life,' were nevertheless confirmed by the next plenary session of the Central Committee (November 28th–December 10th, at Wuhan). But the Committee set at fifteen to twenty years, if not longer, instead of three to six years as at Peitaiho 'the period of transition

---

[8] *People's Daily, Red Flag,* November 23, 1967: 'Conflict between two policies towards China's rural areas.' (See *Peking Review,* 1967, no. 49, p. 13—translator.) The comment was on a 1951 report from the Shansi Party Committee called 'Raise the mutual-aid organizations in the old liberated areas to a higher level.'

from collective ownership to that of ownership by the whole people.' And it accepted Mao Tse-tung's proposal that he should give up the Chairmanship of the People's Republic, an act of the greatest importance, and keep only the Chairmanship of the Party.

It was to be a long time yet before regulatory documents confirmed the institution of people's communes. Although a very large number of communes were formed in the first flush of enthusiasm, 'containing 90 per cent of the rural population at the end of 1958,'[9] it was only in 1961, after the change of social and economic policies known as the 'readjustments,' that texts of constitutions appeared, and these were still provisional and not backed up by legislation. In the circumstances it is not surprising that the texts, drafted, redrafted, and drafted again, and distributed three times, one after the other, did not show all the radical enthusiasms of the original intentions.[10]

Meanwhile the plenary session of the Central Committee at Lushan in August 1959 spelled out certain details of the organization of the communes[11] and thoroughly refuted a letter from P'eng Te-huai, the Minister of Defence, criticizing the mistakes made in the Great Leap Forward and the policy of collectivization. P'eng Te-huai and certain other figures were condemned as Right opportunists, which may have restored the unity of the Party but probably made its splits worse in the long run.

Liu Shao-ch'i was not convinced that P'eng Te-huai's attitude merited so serious a condemnation. 'The Great Leap Forward in 1958 and 1959,' he said, 'only made us increase our numbers and lose time. And at the Lushan

[9] Marthe Engelborghs-Bertels et René Dekkers, *La République Populaire de Chine: cadres institutionnels et réalisations,* vol. 1, p. 21.

[10] May 1961, draft; June 1961, revised draft; September 1962, revised draft. The text of the second draft is in *Ajia Keizai Jumpo,* no. 691, Tokyo, 1967, p. 22.

[11] Confirmation of the system of the three levels of production—production team, production brigade, people's commune. The production team corresponded to a group of households or a hamlet. The brigade had a thousand or more members.

meeting Mao Tse-tung treated anyone who did not agree with the Great Leap Forward as a Right opportunist.'[12]

Chou En-lai himself had felt doubts, as he later acknowledged. 'I too have my share of responsibility for the resistance to the Great Leap Forward in 1956, but I have made my self-criticism.'[13]

In the event he defended the Leap even when it met with difficulties.

In his April 1959 report to the standing committee of the National People's Congress, Chou En-lai declared that one should not in any way underestimate the mass campaign launched last year for the production of iron and steel, or fail to see the importance of the huge numbers of little furnaces for the future production of iron and steel.[14]

The Ninth Plenary Session of the Eighth Central Committee, held in January 1961, recognized that the Great Leap Forward had met with relative setbacks in some areas. It decided to reduce the scale of basic investment and to 'readjust' the rhythm of economic development.[15]

It is almost certain that these decisions were taken at the direction of Liu Shao-ch'i; and it is said that Mao Tse-tung was not present at the meeting. After this the government adopted new financial policies, stressed productivity, approved rewards for increased output, made concessions to the peasants, and reinforced 'vertical control' in a reaction against the tendency of decentralization in the previous period. When later on revolutionaries investigated the events of this period, it was a meeting known

[12] *Mōtakutō no Chōsen*, Tokyo, 1968, p. 119.

[13] *Hsinghua Chantoutui* of the Second Faculty of the Peking University of Engineering, in a poster quoting a meeting of Premier Chou with the State Economic Commission and the State Planning Commission on April 6, 1967, in Peking.

[14] *'L'industrie sidérurgique chinoise.'* Documentation by the Presidency of the Council, Paris, November 12, 1959, in *Notes et Études documentaires*, no. 2591, p. 22.

[15] *Red Flag*, 1961, nos. 3 and 4.

as the 'Meeting in the Western Building' that drew most of their anger.[16]

Those present at this meeting, held in Peking at the beginning of 1962, included Liu Shao-ch'i, Teng Hsiao-p'ing, Ch'en Yün, and Po Yi-po, another member of the standing committee of the Political Bureau who was also an economic expert. Ch'en Yün's report presented the conclusion that stocks were exhausted, factories were being badly run, with an excess of manpower and excessive production costs, and a monetary inflation was provoking a flow of funds back to the countryside, thus involving the risk that the peasants would have nothing to buy with their money. The meeting therefore approved the system of temporary labourers to stimulate production, an increased number of technicians 'in defiance of the popular line,' and the strengthening of direct control by the Central Committee.

In the countryside some land was returned to peasant ownership in the form of individual plots; it was learned later that in some places up to a third of the arable land was redistributed in this way. Free markets were restarted almost everywhere. It was agreed to set production norms on a household basis. This was the period of *san tzu yi pao:* 'Three freedoms and one contract.' The freedoms were those of the private plot, the market, and small-scale private enterprise, and the contract was to deliver agricultural products to the collective. The last draft rules for the working of the people's communes appeared in September 1962, when an article of sixty clauses was distributed to local committees. According to this the production team was to be the smallest autonomous decision-making unit, and it was also decreed that the system should not be changed for the next thirty years.

The production team was more or less equivalent to

[16] At least two Red Guard papers bear witness to this: *Tung fang hung* of the Second Red Guard Headquarters, January 27, 1967, in an article by the Red Guards of the Peking Institute of Aviation; and *Shoutu Hungweiping* of the Third Red Guard Headquarters, January 7, 1967, in an article by the Red Guards of the Central Institute of Finance and Credit.

the village. For the Chinese peasants, who have always had forms of association among the inhabitants of a village or a neighbourhood, or among the hands working for the same farmer, it was following time-honoured custom to become a group, sharing a cart and a bicycle. In re-establishing a type of collective ownership that was as close as possible to that of a family group, and in guaranteeing the peasants' personal incomes from the work-point system, their own sales and their handicrafts, an attempt was being made to carry out a policy of social peace. A blind eye was turned to class differences.

After the Tenth Plenum of the Central Committee

The Central Committee met for its Tenth Plenum in September 1962. One can well imagine that at this point Liu Shao-ch'i and his political friends were primarily concerned with closing the Party's ranks, while Mao Tse-tung and his supporters kept up the struggle to have their ideas accepted. All references to this meeting indicate that it was a dramatic one.

When Mao Tse-tung launched his appeal, 'Never forget class struggle!' it could be seen, said one commentator, that a fight was on, and that it 'inevitably was reflected in the Party.' The two rival factions may have already envisaged that a purge would be needed, the one wanting to overthrow the other, while the latter wanted to strengthen its authority in the Party.

Soon afterwards the leaders drafted the campaign of the 'Socialist education movement' from which both were to draw advantages in the years that followed. While one group saw it as a step forward towards genuine people's communes and power for the masses, their rivals used it to strengthen the Party's position. At the beginning of 1963 the movement had probably not yet been given either its name or its definitive slogans, only its aims. The slogans were to be taken from a note written on May 9, 1963, by Mao Tse-tung on 'Seven well-written documents from Chekiang province on the participation of cadres in manual labour.' These were class struggle, the struggle for produc-

tion, and scientific experiment.[17] The movement was given
the same name as that of a 1957 one with more didactic
slogans.[18] In the months that followed, precious time
slipped by while the secretariat of the Central Committee
appeared to do nothing. Mao Tse-tung took up a plan that
had been drafted by his supporters for April 1, 1963, on
the application of the socialist education movement to the
countryside, rewrote it himself, and had it put on record
by a meeting of leading members of the Central Committee
that met in somewhat obscure circumstances on May 20,
1963. This document, the 'Draft decision of the Central
Committee of the Chinese Communist Party on certain
problems in our present rural work,' is generally known as
the 'Earlier Ten Points.'[19] It was only to be officially
adopted by the Central Committee at its Eleventh Plenum
in August 1966, when the Cultural Revolution was in full
flood. It took thirty-eight months for these ideas to be accepted by the majority of the Party's highest body.

However, three successive versions of the Ten Points
were to appear. Could it have been that the Party machine
diverted their ideological aims by switching them into questions of social morality, thus running counter to the intended direction of the programme for socialist education
on which the leaders had agreed in September 1962?
Special emphasis was put on the 'Four Clean-ups' movement. At first the four matters to be set right were account books,[20] property, the work-point system of pay-
ment, and the running of the collective granaries. In a

[17] See *Peking Review*, 1968, no. 51, p. 3. 'Peasant experts
and the Revolution in Agricultural Education' (from *Red Flag*,
no. 5, 1968).
[18] 'Respect the laws, understand the relationship between
the workers and the peasant, and understand the relationship
between the individual and the mass.' See *Ajia Keizai Jumpo*,
no. 692, Tokyo, 1967, p. 1.
[19] See *Ajia Keizai Jumpo*, no. 701/2, Tokyo, 1967, pp. 19
and 34, for the text and commentaries. (See also Baum and
Teiwes, *op. cit.*, pp. 58–71 for a full English translation—
translator.)
[20] Formerly accounts were often kept by creditors, with the
object of using them as pledges on private property.

later formulation the four issues were politics, economics, organization, and ideology, which corresponded better to the political objectives of the cadres.[21] Liu Shao-ch'i was accused of having the cadres watched by informers under the pretext that the contradictions between the 'four goods' and the 'four evils' could not be cleared up without discreet enquiries, which amounted to favouring a purge of the Party rather than having it cleaned up by open class struggle.

The implication seems to be that after their first trial applications the original Ten Points were modified, for in September 1963 a second version came out with the preamble that 'the cadres have now been trained and proved by prepared tests.'[22] This second version was still only a draft, but was apparently not acceptable, since a third one was published a year later, apparently drawn up by P'eng Chen on the request of Liu Shao-ch'i. It was this final version which was the most sharply criticized two years later by the revolutionaries.

It is noticeable that, for example, instead of referring to uniting 95 per cent of the cadres and the masses in order that the class struggle be adapted to include the people, the third version required that '95 per cent of the cadres and 95 per cent of the masses' should be united, as if the one were the precondition of the other. It also advocated starting with the cadres when dealing with the problem of the 'four evils'. It seems that according to this third series of directives the whole question was to be treated as one of rectifying and strengthening the Party. In May 1967 an article criticizing Liu Shao-ch'i in the *People's Daily* stated: 'He deliberately removed the class content from the struggle inside the Party.'[23]

On January 1, 1965, Mao Tse-tung called a working

[21] *Ajia Keizai Jumpo,* no. 692, Tokyo, 1967, p. 2.

[22] *Ajia Keizai Jumpo,* no. 692, p. 8. The texts of the second and third versions are in issue no. 701/2 (and in Baum and Teiwes, *op. cit.,* pp. 72–94 and 102–17).

[23] 'The class struggle is essential to a Communist Party' New China News Agency, French language release no. 051219, 1967.

party of the Political Bureau at which he took the chair. He criticized Liu Shao-ch'i and brought the matter to a close by replacing the whole series of Ten Point directives with the Twenty-three Articles. This final document,[24] as it was now described, was not a draft but a 'digest of the minutes of the Central Committee Political Bureau's working party.' It brought back the concept that there were contradictions between socialism and capitalism within the Party and the masses. This had been eliminated by the previous documents with their stress on organizational matters.

The opposition between the ideological aims represented by the 'Mao Tse-tung line' and the organizational ones of the 'Liu Shao-ch'i line' was to be the basic theme of the later criticism of Liu over his book *How to Be a Good Communist,* generally referred to in the press during the Cultural Revolution as the 'Book on self-cultivation.'

Analysts of the following period noticed that Liu dropped all reference to class struggle from the 1962 edition of his book. Taking their criticism further, they noted that he put Party members on the sidelines of the clash of class interests, and said, 'Their different ways of seeing problems lead members of the Party to resolve them by different methods, and cause the growth of divergent views and opinions within the Party.'[25] Their special position had to be earned through self-improvement. But if Party members held themselves aloof from the struggle for socialism, did they have the right to participate in the institutions which the masses had entrusted to them for their control? Could the privileged leaders exploit the will of the masses in order to issue orders to them?

On February 12, 1966, at the dramatic moment when the Party was being split into two centres, a Maoist resolution declared that it was necessary to 'develop socialist education and let the masses know that democratic cen-

[24] 'Some problems currently arising in the course of the rural socialist education movement' (January 14, 1965). Text in *Ajia Keizai Jumpo,* no. 701/2, p. 67 ff. (Baum and Teiwes, *op. cit.,* pp. 118–26—translator).

[25] New China News Agency, *ibid.*

tralism had to be carried out thoroughly, and that all deviations from democratic centralism were evil tendencies.'[26] This resolution explained that leaders whose ideals were based on the idea of master and pupil were contravening the principle of democratic centralism. Work conferences on democratic centralism held in ministries and systems during March and April 1966 attracted attention. A fuller analysis would have revealed that this was the point at issue. However, the writings of Liu Shao-ch'i were being more widely distributed than those of Mao Tse-tung. A new, revised edition of *How to Be a Good Communist* was published in August 1962, admittedly a little after the policy of 'readjustment' came into effect. From September 1962 to July 1966 14,899,500 copies of this were printed, compared with 6,261,000 copies of the *Selected Works of Mao Tse-tung* in the same period.[27] Possibly every member of the Party had a copy of Liu, but they did not yet all have a copy of Mao.

'Readjustment' encouraged other writers to criticize the regime. Teng T'o, for example, used a historical anecdote:

> In the reign of the Dowager Empress Ming Su, the Sung government became daily more corrupt. There was no intelligent and capable prime minister at the top with assistants responsible enough to take charge of personnel and administration, so that the local officials in the lower ranks did exactly as they pleased. As a result the problem became inordinately confused.[28]

The Party machine had to fight on two fronts, against unbelievers and radicals.[29] In these conditions the machine

26 Quoted in *K'ochi chanpao*, June 2, 1967, *op. cit.* The passage is taken from a Central Committee Notice of February 12, 1966, on the publication of Mao Tse-tung's speech on January 30, 1962, at the enlarged work meeting.

27 See *Ajia Keizai Jumpo*, no. 683, Tokyo, 1967.

28 (*Peking Review*, 1966, no. 22, p. 10—translator.)

29 We have seen above how it had been forced to act on two fronts earlier: on the internal one with the article of April 14, 1957, during the Hundred Flowers, and against the critics in the resolution of the Conference in the Western Building at the beginning of 'readjustment.'

decided not only to reform itself through discipline, but also to strengthen its foundations. In late 1964 and throughout 1965 outside observers were surprised to see that political departments had been attached to such widely differing sectors of government as industry, agriculture, trade, and finance.

There was a strong temptation to see them as extensions of the system of political commissars in the army; it was as if, from now on, there could not be a good banking service or factory workshop without a political instructor. The fact that some of these newcomers were demobilized soldiers made the similarity to political commissars even stronger. They spread the Thought of Mao Tse-tung as they had learnt to do in the army. But one cannot draw the implication that the army had infiltrated them into the administration in order to propagate Mao's thought: even at this period everybody had to express their respect for the Thought of Mao Tse-tung.

This is how the paper *Takung Pao* welcomed the veterans:

> The millions of employees and workers in commerce and finance welcome the comrades from the army. Many of them do not care about politics and expect no benefit from it. It is good that some people should be against politics because they can be held up as bad examples. The newcomers from the army naturally do not know much about commerce; Why? Because, it is said, they have changed their jobs, everything is new to them, and their previous experience is of no use. This is indeed a strange opinion; all they have is the Thought of Mao Tse-tung, and they keep a firm grip on it. In fact they have not started new careers, only taken up new postings. Now they have to work in commerce and finance and learn the financial policies of the Centre and the State Council.[30]

There is a touch of irony here. No doubt some people

[30] *Takung Pao*, May 10, 1965. On this topic see *China News Analysis*, no. 581, September 17, 1965, from which this quotation is taken.

were delighted that the newcomers fell under the influence of the majority in the Party bureaucracy. Was this also an infiltration by activists, or a plan for centralization designed to stifle the machine? The answer can be found, it would seem, in the proportion of army veterans in the new political structure.

According to the *Takung Pao*,[31] 54 per cent of the new political instructors were former Party branch secretaries, 10 per cent came from the government, and only 32 per cent from the army. A large majority of them would thus have been in favour of the existing machine, which makes the hypothesis that the operation was designed to strengthen central control seem the more probable one.

Departments of this sort were installed down to the level of cities and *hsien* in order to structure commercial and financial activities. But this reinforcement was not limited to the low-level units; it reached right up to the Central Committee's bureaus, the political offices in charge of the systems. A political department was attached to each of the existing Central Committee bureaus in charge of agriculture, industry and communications, and trade and finance. This procedure showed that the new political organs in the economy were intended to come under the control of a special centralized apparatus.

All this recalls the method whereby the decisions of the Conference in the West Building were applied, for all that these were restricted to economic problems. We may conclude, then, in view of this analysis of its structure, that the Party was merely engaged in strengthening its position.

Cultural politics

Meanwhile, campaigns were periodically launched against intellectuals overinvolved in obsolete ways of thinking, some of whom sought to break free from the constraints of propaganda. The most individualistic of them wrote

[31] June 16, 1965.

in allegory, substituting historical or legendary events for contemporary situations, or telling stories with a double meaning. They took liberties with socialist morality. When the policy of 'readjustment' was adopted they became bold enough to write about more dangerous subjects.

One of them was Wu Han, deputy mayor of Peking, an historian and occasional dramatist; another was T'ien Han, chairman of the Chinese Theatrical Association.

Wu Han had written *The Dismissal of Hai Jui*, a play which described how a Ming emperor ordered Hai Jui, one of his officials, to put right the wrongs suffered by the peasants who had been stripped of their land by the gentry, and then dismissed him under pressure from landlord interests. Hai Jui had become dangerous because he took the cause of the peasants too much to heart. The play was later criticized on the grounds that it depicted a character so forgetful of his own class origins that he could seemingly serve with sincerity the interests of his own class enemies. Wu Han created a mandarin deliberately prepared to sacrifice himself for the peasants, which was a literary fiction.

The work was not condemned on academic grounds alone. The play had ulterior political motives, and the matter was more serious still because the character of Hai Jai was connected with that of P'eng Te-huai, the 'Right opportunist' who had claimed to be defending the peasants when he attacked the Party and the people's communes. Wu Han seemed to be pleading for the rehabilitation of the rightists condemned in 1959. This gave apparent support to the view that such men were about to return to active politics.

Whether he was unaware of the criticism that was to follow, or was defying it in advance, Wu Han had his play published in the January 1961 issue of the Peking *Literary and Artistic Review*, at the same time as the Ninth Plenum of the Central Committee, which formally marked the failure of the Great Leap Forward. This was enough for it to be seen as an act of defiance.

Wu Han was not the only writer to take subjects and characters from the past. 'A mass of ghost stories and

other pernicious operas were once again staged at the
Peking opera house,'[32] said Lu Ting-yi, then director of
the Central Committee's Propaganda Department. He was
not exaggerating. From 1961 to 1966 there was much
talk in China about ghost stories. These 'ghosts' were the
favourite heroes of feudal and bourgeois literature: em-
perors, generals, mandarins, and scholars, all irrelevant to
the contemporary world because they were 'politically
dead.' Mao Tse-tung did not confine himself to pronounce-
ments on the subjects of plays; he declared that much of
the control of culture was in the hands of the dead.[33]

One critic, however, did not shrink from writing a story
called 'Ghosts do no harm' in a Peking evening paper in
August 1961.[34] He was Liao Mo-sha, head of the United
Front Department of the Peking Municipal Party Committee.[35] Liao collaborated with Teng T'o, a member of
the secretariat of the same committee, and Wu Han, to
write short essays in the form of cautionary tales under
the joint pseudonym of 'Wu Nan-hsing.'

These pieces came out under the heading 'Tales of a
Three-Family Village'[36] in the municipal Party committee's
journal Ch'ien Hsien ('Front Line') between October 1961
and July 1964. Their rather insolent tone, which soon
made them popular with malcontents, must have drawn
some reaction even from within the Party committees responsible for the contents of the magazine, because after
September 1962 the 'Three-Family Village' changed its
approach somewhat. Instead of amusingly retold stories

[32] Speech of Lu Ting-yi at the opening of the Festival of
Peking Operas on Contemporary Themes (June 5, 1964). See
A Great Revolution on the Cultural Front, FLP, Peking, 1965.

[33] 'December 1963 instructions to cultural circles,' quoted in
Peiching Hungse Hsüanch'uanping, May 10, 1967.

[34] Translated text in Enzan Yawa, Mainichi Shimbunsha
Yakuben, Tokyo, September 1966.

[35] Also candidate member of the North China Bureau of
the CCP Central Committee. At the end of 1961 P'eng Chen,
with the encouragement of Liu Shao-ch'i, went through the
Central Committee's directive and Mao Tse-tung's speeches of
1958–60 and compiled a twenty-nine point 'list of errors.'

[36] Allusion to a poem by the Sung writer Lu Yu.

from the past, and observations on morals, education, and the arts, there now appeared more dramatic articles such as the 'Ode to Petroleum' extolling one of the regime's great achievements, the Tach'ing Oilfield. It was said later that the 'Three-Family Village' was covering its tracks.

Teng T'o, former chief editor of the *People's Daily* and still active in journalism, also wrote essays and fables on his own account for the *Peking Evening News* from March 1961 onwards.[37] This series lasted only until September 1962, when the leaders had it out with each other at the Tenth Plenum of the Central Committee.

During this short time he published 153 of his 'chats,' which Yao Wen-yuan later inveighed against for 'using the past to make mock of the present.' One can form one's own opinion from the following excerpt, together with the angry comments of the cultural insurgents, as quoted in a critical article which appeared early in the Cultural Revolution.

In *New Stories of Ai Tzu,* Lu Chuo, who lived during the Ming Dynasty, relates a *typical case of amnesia:* 'There was once a man in the Kingdom of Ch'i who was so forgetful that he forgot to stop once he started walking, and forgot to rise once he lay down. His wife was much worried. She said to him, "I have heard that Ai Tzu is a clever and resourceful man who can treat the most baffling diseases. Why don't you go and consult him?" "I will," said the man, and rode away on horseback, taking his bow and arrow with him. Having gone a short way, he felt an urgent need and dismounted, sticking his arrows into the earth and tying his horse to a tree. Having relieved himself, he looked to his left and, seeing the arrows, exclaimed: "Heavens! What a narrow escape! Where are these arrows from? They nearly got me!" Then he looked to his right, and saw the horse, and cried out with joy, "I may have had a bad

---

[37] They were called 'Evening chats at Yenshan' after the small mountain range northwest of the capital in the region of the Great Wall, which would have unmistakably suggested Peking to any Chinese reader. Teng T'o wrote them under the pseudonym Mao Nan-tun.

fright, but here's a horse for me." He was preparing to remount, with the reins in his hands, when he trod in his own stool. He stamped his feet and cursed, "Damn! I've trodden in a dog turd and ruined my shoes." Then he spurred on his horse and rode home. As he arrived, he hesitated before the gate, wondering, "Who lives here? Is this Master Ai Tzu's house?" His wife saw his bewilderment, realized that he had lost his memory again, and gave him a scolding. The puzzled man said, "We are not acquainted, Madam, so why are you abusing me?"

'This man certainly seems to have a bad case of amnesia. *But we cannot tell for sure what turn the illness will take when it reaches its crisis point: probably either insanity or imbecility.*

'According to ancient Chinese medicine books . . . one of the causes of amnesia is the abnormal functioning of what is called the vital breath. In consequence of this the patient not only suffers from loss of memory but also becomes *eccentric*, has great difficulty speaking, *grows irritable, insane, and finally raving mad.* Another cause is brain injury. The patient feels numb at times, and the blood rises to his head, causing occasional fainting fits. Unless treated in time, he will become an idiot. Thus if anyone finds either of these groups of symptoms present in himself, he *must take a complete rest at once, stop talking, and refrain from all activity. If he insists on speaking and acting, he will soon suffer a catastrophe.* Is there then no effective method for curing this disease? Certainly there is. For example . . . when a patient has a bad attack, *take a bucketful of dog's blood and pour it over his head, followed by some cold water to make him a little more clear-headed.* . . . According to modern Western medicine, one way is to *hit the patient on the head with a specially made club to induce a state of shock, and then recall him to his senses.'*

('A Special Treatment for Amnesia,' *Front Line,* no. 14, 1962)

Comments: The attacks contained in this article reveal the bitterest hatred of our great Party. Medical books nowhere include as symptoms of amnesia the patient's failure to keep a promise, or attacks of 'eccentricity,' 'insanity,' 'raving madness.' Still less do they prescribe such treatment as dog's blood or blows with a club. *New Stories of Ai Tzu* by the Ming writer Lu Cho are really political satires and have nothing to do with medicine. Teng T'o is talking politics here, not medicine. This cannot be denied.[38]

What must have made this piece seem all the more blasphemous and shocking were the rumours about Mao Tsetung's health that would have occurred to the reader.

Liao Mo-sha and Teng T'o, who had to make a self-criticism for the piece they had called 'Confucian morality may have its uses,'[39] were probably reprimanded. The Peking Party Committee told them to show more discretion, and in September 1962 the publication of *Ch'ien Hsien* ceased. It would have been virtually impossible to aim the thunderbolts of official criticism at such senior figures without severe repercussions. The Party as a whole turned a blind eye, which encouraged the bolder spirits at the very time when the advocates of 'readjustment' were beginning to lose ground.

Mao Tse-tung does not seem to have devoted himself to strictly cultural questions with the same tenacity that enabled him to win out on the peasant problem. Teng T'o's satirical sketches were not challenged until long after they were written. Chiang Ch'ing, Chairman Mao's wife, maintained in a 1967 statement that Wu Han had to be published before he could be criticized.[40]

The radicals therefore countered the rival movement by means of occasional criticisms, and also by example. The first festival of new operas on modern themes was held in Peking in April 1960. Peking opera, it should be said, is still popular in China. The North Chinese, espe-

[38] 'Teng T'o's "Evening Chats at Yenshan" are anti-Party, anti-Socialist double talk.' First published in *Wenhui Pao* and *PLA Daily*. Translation from *The Great Socialist Cultural Revolution in China* (2) FLP, Peking, 1966, pp. 17–19.

[39] *Enzan Yawa,* Mainichi Shimbunsha Yakuben, Tokyo, September 1966, p. 40 ff.

[40] Speech on April 12, 1967, to the enlarged meeting of the Central Committee's Military Commission reported in a Red Guard leaflet of April 1967.

cially the Pekingese themselves, are very fond of it. It would have been ill-advised to suppress this art, even though the affectation and stylization of its form were offensive to the revolutionary spirit. It was a much better idea to 'chase away the ghosts,' write more plays on contemporary issues, take themes from the revolutionary wars, 'class struggle, production, and construction since Liberation,' and bring in some socialist education. Peking opera had to be prevented, as far as possible, from being a refuge for those who sought memories of another way of life.

The job of 'workers in literature and art' was to create new operas on the themes of socialist life. There were pieces on the Leap Forward in the countryside, on the Vietnam war, on not devouring the surplus in harvest feasts, or letting privately owned ducks graze in the collective fields. But there were also *The Red Lantern* and *Shachiapang*, which could be given as examples. They were badly needed. For a critical audience prone to mockery there were too many duds among the pieces on prosaic themes produced to order by the workers in literature and art. Mao Tse-tung himself spoke twice on the subject. He issued instructions in December 1963,[41] and again in June 1964. After his first directive Liu Shao-ch'i, Teng Hsiao-p'ing, P'eng Chen, and Chou Yang[42] met on January 3, 1964. They agreed that from then on there would be a socialist literature and theatre, but that it was also necessary to preserve the traditional theatre alongside the modern one. They kept clashes to a minimum, though not without offering some provocation in the process, and kept the classical theatre alive.[43]

Mao Tse-tung's second directive was issued when the Festival of Peking operas on contemporary themes opened on June 5. He condemned the prevailing tendency, and

[41] Speech quoted above.

[42] Long regarded as a kind of Chinese Zhdanov, Chou Yang was deputy head of the Central Committee's Propaganda Department.

[43] *Peiching Hungse Hsüanch'uanping*, May 10, 1967.

said that the Party's policies had not been applied for the past fifteen years.

Mao Tse-tung had expounded his policies on literature and the arts once and for all in his *Yenan Talks*. By now he had some reason for feeling irritated. Little inspiration had been drawn from them and they were not being referred to often. One may also observe that his wife, the former actress Chiang Ch'ing, had resumed her activities and was busying herself with the productions of the Second Peking Opera Company. Through her Mao Tse-tung must have been better aware of the divergences of opinion in cultural circles.

Chiang Ch'ing had much to say. The First Peking Opera Company was unwilling to alter its style, hence her decision to fall back on the Second Company. When she wanted to adapt *Spark Among the Reeds* to make it a truly socialist piece free from compromise over class struggle—this was to become *Shachiapang*—her ideas were not accepted.[44]

Mao Tse-tung's friends still had all kinds of comments to make on the state of politics in artistic and educational circles. Young workers and peasants were always the victims of discrimination in the universities, they maintained; and schools where study and practical work were equally divided according to Party principles were neither numerous enough nor sufficiently suited to the education of the masses. While it should have been the intention to educate people who would spend the rest of their lives working in fields and factories, the aim these schools seemed actually to have set themselves was only to combine manual labour with study, for the benefit of students to whom the Party would give as good jobs as possible. Besides, the schools held up as models by Lu Ting-yi—Chiaot'ung University and the Harbin Polytechnic School—were quite simply capitalist or Soviet revisionist in type.[45] In the cinema industry weeds were springing up and the Thought of Mao Tse-

[44] On Chiang Ch'ing see Kosei Shoden in *Chūōkōron*, Tokyo, December 1967 and January 1968.
[45] See *Red Flag*, 1968, no. 3, translated in *Peking Review*, 1968, no. 37, p. 16.

tung was not being properly taught. It was reported later that in the *People's Daily* the chief editor, Wu Leng-hsi, was even giving secret instructions that the diffusion of the Thought of Mao Tse-tung was to be checked.[46]

The army spared no efforts in spreading the movement for the Thought of Mao Tse-tung—a movement it had nurtured itself—and the *PLA Daily* led all the other papers in publicizing it. So much so that to all outsiders it appeared to be pouring out without let or hindrance. The 'heroes' of the Thought of Mao Tse-tung appeared one after another: sincere, modest youngsters, persevering in their work and ready for self-sacrifice. National campaigns in their honour were organized among the army and the people by the propaganda machine. Their stories were very simple. They were of proletarian origin, had read the works of Mao Tse-tung by themselves, would go to any lengths for others, and one day died or were seriously injured to save the lives of their comrades or of children.

They were nearly always the victims of a machine or a piece of technical equipment symbolizing progress—a lorry, an oil-well in flames, a load of shells, often a railway locomotive. The modern, technical world came upon them, overwhelmed them, and continued inexorably on its course after the moment of drama in which a disaster was avoided. Perhaps the lesson to be drawn was that the younger generation should not expect any profit for itself in the building of socialism, and should not hope to enjoy the fruits of their efforts in peace. They were to sacrifice themselves for the sake of posterity.

There were fifteen or twenty heroes of this type, from Lei Feng to Men Ho, in the period from 1965 to 1968. Most of them were soldiers. One hero alone was distinct from the others: Chiao Yü-lu, the party secretary in a poor district, who despite his cancer pushed himself to the very limits of his strength to help the people protect

[46] 'Speech to the editorial and reporters' staffs of the Jenmin Jihpao, April–May, 1964' according to an editorial appearing simultaneously in *Red Flag* and the *People's Daily,* September 1, 1968. Wu Leng-hsi was editor-in-chief of the *People's Daily* and director of the New China News Agency.

their fields from floods, and to make barren land fertile.
He read both Mao Tse-tung and Liu Shao-ch'i, and was
probably conceived of by the Party machine in response
to the other heroes as a demonstration that there could
be models of a different kind, less political and more concerned with production. He went out of favour for a time
before being revived a year after the beginning of the
Cultural Revolution.

In addition to launching these heroes, some people
within the propaganda organs were already searching Mao
Tse-tung's works for pieces that could be read with profit
by the less educated. They recommended the 'Three Old
Articles': 'Serve the People' (how to devote one's life to
the service of others); 'The Foolish Old Man Who Moved
Mountains' (God helps those who help themselves); and
'In Memory of Norman Bethune' (people from outside
can also be decent and good). But even these basic vir-
tues were not spared by the mockers. Cheng T'ien-hsiang,
a member of the Peking Municipal Party Committee's
secretariat, said at a meeting of the committee that when
the workers in a transport company recited 'The Foolish
Old Man Who Moved Mountains' together as they loaded
coal on a lorry, 'far from making them work harder, it
slowed them down.'[47]

Although Mao Tse-tung was doubtless primarily concerned with problems of the communes and socialist education, it was finally on the cultural front that he allowed
the revolution to break out.

An enlarged meeting of the Standing Committee of the
Political Bureau was held in September and October 1965,
with the heads of the Central Committee's regional bureaus taking part.[48] It had been called to study the question of Vietnam, and finally agreed on the key decision that
it would have to reject a common initiative of socialist
countries to give aid to the Vietnamese war effort. It was
a very stormy meeting, and soon afterwards Mao Tse-
tung withdrew to Shanghai, abandoning the Centre. In

[47] *K'ochi Hungch'i*, February 18, 1967, *loc. cit.*
[48] 'Circular of the Central Committee of the C.P.C.' May
16, 1966.

her book, *The Cultural Revolution in China*, the economist Joan Robinson, who visited China two years later, includes the 'report' given her by a member of the Shanghai Revolutionary Committee, and in this we read that 'in 1965 the Chairman called for the repudiation of the Wu Han.'[49] He does not appear to have got it.

On November 10th an article by Yao Wen-yuan criticizing Wu Han in the strongest terms was published in the *Wenhui Pao*, a Shanghai paper that was to be on several occasions the main organ of the Cultural Revolution. Ch'i Pen-yü, another prominent activist in the Cultural Revolution, wrote later that 'Under the leadership of Comrade Chiang Ch'ing the proletarian revolutionaries of Shanghai undertook the criticism of *The Dismissal of Hai Jui*. . . .'[50] thus confirming that Yao Wen-yuan had acted not in isolation but together with Chiang Ch'ing and a small group of radicals.

The attack was clearly aimed at the Peking municipal Party. P'eng Chen, the mayor of Peking, angrily asked Yao Wen-yuan, 'Why wasn't the publication of this document announced [in advance]? Where is your Party spirit? Doubtless this criticism came from the boss.' He added, 'What's going to come of it? But all are equal before the truth.'[51]

Why did they choose this time and place to take the initiative? One reason was given by Yao Wen-yuan himself, who wrote that their enemies 'were attacking with exceptional savagery and moving the centre of gravity from politics to organization.'[52] Perhaps in the eyes of the Maoists their opponents were so strongly entrenched that the struggle could be confined to ideas alone without jeopardizing their own safety. The choice of cultural terrain

[49] *Op. cit.*, p. 50.
[50] Ch'i Pen-yü's speech on the twenty-fifth anniversary of the Yenan Talks, quoted in New China News Agency, no. 052417, French edition, May 24, 1967.
[51] *Chingkangshan* of the Red Guards of Tsinghua University, Peking, May 27, 1967, quoted in Konno, *Pekin Kono Ichinen*, Shinnihon Shuppansha, Tokyo, 1968, p. 31.
[52] 'On the Three-Family Village' in *The Socialist Cultural Revolution in China* (1), FLP, Peking, 1966.

for the attack probably owed much to the way Wu Han, Teng T'o and Liao Mo-sha were embodiments of the Peking municipality, that impenetrable 'independent kingdom.'

The Party split into two Centres

The year 1966 opened with the Party's leaders in disarray. At their last work conference they had discussed aid to Vietnam, a question that was to come up again during the visit of a Japanese Communist Party delegation. They found themselves disagreeing on the line to take with the Soviet Union over joint action. They may well also have discussed the new five-year plan due to start in 1966. Agreement on this would also have been virtually impossible, with some of them insisting on a new leap forward in the countryside while others wanted heavy industries developed, both sides becoming more and more inflexible.

There is no documentary evidence that the Third Five-Year Plan was adopted at this meeting. Occasionally the press stated that industry, agriculture, or the economy as a whole was fulfilling the first year of the Third Plan, but that is by no means the same thing. Doubtless the units suggested a plan for the year as usual to be approved with or without modification by the Party's bureaus. But this was not at all equivalent to the long-term economic programme moulded by political attitudes involved in a five-year plan.

Just as individual heroes were held up as examples, the radicals also had their economic models, principally Tach'ing and Tachai. Tach'ing, on the marshy and inhospitable plains northwest of Harbin, was one of the regime's triumphs. Starting out with scanty resources but ample courage, it had grown into a centre of oilwells and refineries. About 40,000 people, many of whom had come from the cities, worked there living in rustic shacks beside brackish lakes. The Tach'ing movement was also a campaign to encourage the opening of virgin lands.

Tachai was a production brigade in east-central Shansi which, in the face of a hostile environment, had brought fertility to the soil and cultivated the hillsides with a system of high-level terracing. Despite suffering from an alternation of torrential downpours and prolonged droughts, Tachai always managed to get by on its own resources, making constant improvements on the basis of experience and at the minimum cost to the state. Tachai had, moreover, put into effect a system of payments for collective work whereby everyone decided for himself what he had really earned. Tachai was an example of simplified administration and a model for the building of socialism in agriculture. Neither Tach'ing nor Tachai had been created in the year which had just elapsed, but the propagandists only got hold of them now; and the publicity given the two models was intended to compensate the public for the absence of a five-year plan.

Despite the split in the Centre the Party's work was not fatally hindered, since the central services were still concentrated in Peking. But the atmosphere in which Party members worked must have been bad, since it was inevitable that the split at the top was common knowledge. Even in the 'independent kingdom' of Peking some Maoist radicals recruited supporters and made difficulties. The Party machine meanwhile was doing nothing to carry out those of Mao Tse-tung's instructions with which it disagreed. According to a later inquiry, these were the means Peking used to block a study on the progressive mechanization of agriculture that Mao Tse-tung had approved in February 1966:

At this time China's Khrushchev was still resisting tenaciously, and he resorted to various tactics in order to disregard Chairman Mao's instructions. First he asked several departments and his own running dogs to 'study the question and make suggestions.' Several days later this was done, 'so that a meeting of the Central Committee could be called to discuss the question.' Having thus postponed Chairman Mao's instructions for twenty days, he made the new suggestion that a certain department of the Central Committee should 'first study differences in conditions, make a number of separate reports on the question and submit a plan for discussion by the Central Committee.' Finally he decided on his own authority that 'the document from Hupei province should not be distributed to the regions for the time being.'[53]

The first foreigners to see that something was amiss were the Japanese Communists. A Japanese Communist Party delegation, led by Secretary-General Miyamoto himself, left Tokyo on February 7th on a tour of North Vietnam, China, North Korea, and back to China. Apart from its aim of having serious talks with the CCP, the mission wanted to bring about, with the consent of the Vietnamese Party, co-ordinated aid to the Democratic Republic of Vietnam by the Socialist countries. On the eve of its departure *Akahata* published an editorial under the title 'How to strengthen the united front for joint international action against American imperialism.'[54]

On their second journey through Peking the Japanese delegation was welcomed by P'eng Chen, who said in his speech, 'Modern dogmatism must be opposed at the same time as modern revisionism.' This sentence set the visitors thinking.

When the Japanese passed through the first time the Chinese Communists raised many objections to the joint action that was proposed to them in principle, and seemed very reserved. But some progress was made at the end of March, and a joint communiqué was agreed on with the Chinese working party under Chou En-lai. Liu Shao-ch'i was abroad at the time and Teng Hsiao-p'ing was travelling in China. The communiqué, which mentioned only the points on which agreement had been reached, and was silent on the rest, was settled on the basis of a draft prepared by the Chinese, signed by both parties and celebrated at a banquet.

The Japanese delegation could have returned to Japan satisfied, but it asked for an interview with Chairman Mao

[53] *Akahata* (national paper of the Japanese Communist Party), February 4, 1966.
[54] *Chūgoku Bunka Daikakumei wo dō miru ka*, Shinnihon Shuppansha, Tokyo, 1968, p. 209.

Tse-tung and was received by him at Hangchow on March 28th.[55] Although the communiqué had been signed by both Parties, Mao Tse-tung wanted an addition to be made, that this would be an international anti-American and anti-Soviet united front. The Japanese delegation refused, and Mao Tse-tung vetoed the publication of the communiqué.[56]

This was happening at the very time when Mao Tse-tung had just violently abused P'eng Chen because of the decision of his work team on the Wu Han case. After the incidents described earlier, and the publication of Yao Wen-yuan's article in Shanghai, Mao Tse-tung apparently declared that 'The point of the play is the dismissal. Hai Jui is P'eng Te-huai.'[57] But the self-criticism of its author, Wu Han, was very mild. A work team was set up to determine the matter, and in case of need to pronounce the necessary condemnation. This was the first 'Central Committee Cultural Revolution Group.' It was later known as the 'Group of Five.'[58] Its only job had been to set out the principles later known as the February Theses. The Theses were condemned on account both of their content

[55] *Ibid.*, p. 210.

[56] See Konno, *Pekin Kono Ichinen*, pp. 20–21.

[57] *Ibid.*

[58] It seems that this group was formed by P'eng Chen and K'ang Sheng, and in addition to them to have included Lu Ting-yi, Wu Leng-hsi and perhaps Chou Yang. Six others also took part in the February 3rd meeting that produced the text of the 'Principles suggested for the press by the Cultural Revolution Group on the present academic controversies' and the February 7th meeting that adopted them. (See *Chunghsüeh Hungweiping*, May 20, 1967.) These six included Liu Jen and Cheng T'ien-hsiang, thus strengthening the representation of the Peking Municipal Party Committee.

K'ang Sheng, in charge of the Party's international relations and candidate member of the Political Bureau in the 1956 Central Committee, now ranks fifth in the Party hierarchy. In 1969 he was promoted to the Standing Committee of the Political Bureau.

Liu Jen was then political commissar with the Peking Garrison Forces of the PLA, second secretary of the Peking Municipal Party Committee, and secretary of the North China Bureau of the Central Committee.

and the manner of their distribution within the Party. As far as their content was concerned, it was a question of 'purging the academic world of all bourgeois thought, a problem that has been solved neither in the USSR nor in other socialist countries.' They watered down the Maoist cultural programme, according to which the workers should build a store of knowledge by themselves, for themselves, and of practical applications. All they promised was 'a new historical period in which workers, peasants and soldiers will themselves *master*[59] the theoretical weapons of Marxism-Leninism, the Thought of Mao Tsetung, as well as science and culture.'[60]

In any case, these Theses were discreet, asking for the maximum of caution in press criticism, and forbidding the publication of the names of the criticized. The movement was to remain within the Party, needing the approval of the appropriate bodies before a criticism was made.

This is why it is open to suspicion that these *Principles* were not transmitted in the regular way, according to the rules applicable to a document of this nature. P'eng Chen was attacked for putting them out in the name of the Central Committee without its approval. During the time the Party was split into two centres both sides avoided discussions, as this would have made a plenary meeting of the Central Committee essential and neither side would win. It is almost certain that Mao Tse-tung was told of the Principles, if not before they were published then at the same time. Konno,[61] who has gone into the problem, concludes that Mao Tse-tung did not forbid their publication.

If it is true that Mao Tse-tung saw the report on February 28th as a normally reliable Red Guard Paper maintains, his angry reaction was not immediate. It was only on March 28th that he exploded:

The Tenth Plenum has decided on class struggle, so

[59] Author's italics.
[60] According to the text published in *Peiching Jenta Sanhung* (a journal of Peking People's University) in May 1967.
[61] *Op. cit.*, p. 31.

it is said. Then why has Wu Han written pieces libelling the Party? Is there nothing the Cultural Department [of the Central Committee] can do about it? Why is it allowing a decision of the Centre to become a dead letter? . . . The big clique of academics is repressing Leftist writings and concealing anti-Communist intellectuals. The [Central Committee's] Propaganda Department is the abode of the King of Hell. It must be knocked down and the young people set free. We must raise innumerable Sun Wu-k'ungs, one after the other, and storm the Palace of Heaven.[62]

At last September's conference I saw comrades from all the regions and asked them, 'What will you do if revisionism appears in the Central Committee?' It is a considerable danger.[63]

It became clear later that at about this time another Cultural Revolution Group was taking shape as a result of the initiatives of Lin Piao, Chiang Ch'ing and their friends. But this group was itself Maoist. A 'Discussion on literary and artistic activities in the army' took place in Shanghai from February 2nd to 20th with Chiang Ch'ing in the chair.[64] On March 20th Lin Piao sent by letter an

[62] Allusion to *Journey to the West* a sixteenth-century fairy story by Wu Ch'eng-en, also known as 'The Monkey Pilgrim.' Sun-the-Monkey, the offspring of a rock, had the power to metamorphose himself in seventy-two different ways, and could cover 108,000 miles with a single somersault. He went down to the Palace of the Dragon King at the bottom of the Eastern Ocean, demanded a magical cudgel from him—the golden cudgel of Mao Tse-tung's poem—then went to Hell, where he struck his name off the register of death. The Jade Emperor who reigned in Heaven was so incensed that he sent troops to destroy Sun Wu-k'ung. After their failure the Emperor invited Sun-the-Monkey to Heaven, put him in charge of the stables, and gave him the title of Great Wonder-worker, Heaven's Equal. Mao's poem on this theme is called 'An answer to Comrade Kuo Mo-jo' (November 17, 1961). In this poem two lines are particularly well known:

The Golden Monkey raises his magic cudgel,
And the Jade Palace is cleared of dust.

See *Chinese Literature*, 1966, no. 2.
[63] Tsinghua University's *Chingkangshan*, May 27, 1967.
[64] *Chūgoku Bunka Daikakumei wo dō miru ka*, Shinnihon Shuppansha, Tokyo, 1968.

abstract of these discussions (in the editing of which Mao Tse-tung took part on three occasions), to the members of the Central Committee's Military Commission. Four days later *Red Flag*, the Party's theoretical journal, published an article criticizing certain historians[65] and signed by Ch'i Pen-yü, Yen Chang-kuei, and Lin Piao himself.[66] With this should be considered another article by Kuan Feng[67] in the *People's Daily* of March 19th. Ch'i Pen-yü and Kuan Feng were later to be members of the Central Committee's Cultural Revolution Group, an important body in the control of the uprising.

Given the strength of the Party machine, it undoubtedly needed courage for these men to insist that the editorial committees accept their articles, despite the instructions of the Group of Five, but they probably already formed a group.

Once the conflict reached the press, newspapers and literary figures who had been discredited were induced to make their self-criticisms. This may even have been done at the demand of the heads of culture and propaganda, who were trying to keep their freedom of manoeuvre by the tactic, later denounced, of 'sacrificing a knight to save a queen.' The Peking papers that had published Teng T'o and Liao Mo-sha tried to limit the discussion to academic problems as far as they possibly could, but on April 16th they published a note in which they criticized their editorial policy.

Wu Han admitted his sins in the *Takung Pao* of April 23rd. Meanwhile the famous historian Kuo Mo-jo, the head of the Academy of Sciences, made his self-criticism on April 14th to the standing committee of the National People's Congress. He did it in style, saying that all his

[65] 'A necessary critique of Comrade Chien Po-tsan's history,' *Red Flag*, March 24, 1966.

[66] Ch'i Pen-yü was a young historian known for his work on the T'aip'ing history, and an editor of *Red Flag;* Kuan Feng was a *People's Daily* editor; Yen Chang-kuei was perhaps a pseudonym.

[67] *Mōtakutō no chōsen*, Tokyo, *op. cit.,* p. 26.

work should be burnt, and declared his intention of becoming the pupil of the workers, peasants and soldiers.

The Peking Municipal Committee was attacked inside the Party on April 24th. Its leadership was 'crossed out from one end to the other with a black line,' *Red Flag* was later to declare.[68] Liu Shao-ch'i found himself forced to give up his attempt to protect P'eng Chen. Liu Jen, a key man in the municipal group as he was Political Commissar to the Peking Garrison, tried to organize a defence for it on April 17th, but without success.[69] He was dismissed at the same time as P'eng Chen, and arraigned with P'eng in the same public trial at the beginning of June.

The army had been put on the alert and its discipline strengthened since January, when Lin Piao had issued directives declaring a state of emergency in preparation for war.[70] It is unlikely that P'eng Chen and Liu Jen could have obtained the co-operation of the army, even to enter the universities, which were in such a state of agitation at the end of May. It was thus tactically essential that Liu Jen should be eliminated immediately.

There was no plan for the Cultural Revolution before the one that was put forward on May 7th, perhaps the most ambitious of all those to be formulated in the eventful period then beginning. It took the form of a letter from Mao Tse-tung to Lin Piao, almost a private document; a letter from thinker to doer, written without any heed of the Party machine.

The essential feature of this directive was that there was to be no more specialization or exclusiveness in any field of activity. Soldiers had to study politics, till the land,

[68] Editorial in *Red Flag*, no. 8, 1966, 'Long live the great proletarian Cultural Revolution.' Translation in the Foreign Languages Press, Peking, *The Great Socialist Cultural Revolution in China*, Part 4.

[69] See Fernand Gigon, *Vie et Mort de la Révolution Culturelle*, Flammarion, Paris, 1969, pp. 122–23.

[70] Article by Hsiao Hua, *PLA Daily*, January 19, 1966. See *Chūgoku Bunka Daikakumei wo dō miru ka*, Tokyo, 1968, p. 208.

and go into industry; similarly workers, peasants and students were to extend their activities to other fields, as were people working in trade, public services, Party and government. Of course, the main task of the workers was to work in their factories and of the peasants to till their fields; but by going in for kinds of work outside their usual range they would destroy the barriers between town and countryside, between workers and intellectuals. Everybody needed all-round development, leading to the growth of proletarian political awareness, which would make new Communists of them all. Mao Tse-tung's letter to Lin Piao was not published in the press until the end of July.

The man Mao Tse-tung had chosen to carry out his ideas, from now on the only man to be called his 'closest comrade-in-arms,' had unbounded faith in the leader and was apparently utterly confident about the future. At an enlarged meeting of the Political Bureau on May 18th Lin Piao said:

> Mao Tse-tung is our Party's greatest leader, and his every word sets a standard for our movement. The whole Party will settle the score of those who oppose him, the whole Party will criticize them. Mao Tse-tung has done a great deal more than Marx, Lenin or Engels. They did not direct a proletarian revolution in person. They are nothing like Mao Tse-tung. What a great role he has played in political struggles, and above all what a great role in military struggles! Lenin did not live as long as Mao Tse-tung. The population of China is ten times Germany's, triple that of Russia, and China is teeming with revolutionary experiments. In every respect China is superior. Mao Tse-tung is the greatest man in our country and in the whole world.[71]

It was at this meeting of the Political Bureau that the new Central Committee Cultural Revolution Group was appointed, and the activities of the Group of Five were brought to an end after being condemned in the most

[71] *K'echi Chanpao,* organ of the revolutionary rebels of the System of the State Science and Technology Commission, June 2, 1967.

ignominious terms by the Central Committee's *May 16th Circular*.[72]

Neither the meeting nor the circular was confined to the dismissal of the Peking municipal authorities. Both threatened all the 'representatives of the bourgeoisie who have infiltrated into the Party, the government, the army and cultural circles,' adding:

> Some of them we have already seen through, others we have not. Some are still trusted by us and are being trained as our successors—persons like Khrushchev, for example, who are still nestling beside us.

All who read the document in May—in other words, Party men of a certain rank and above—must have taken note that the Chairman had turned the revolutionary spirit against the Party and was challenging it.

The Central Committee's Cultural Revolution Group, which came directly under the Standing Committee of the Political Bureau, was soon to take over the media of propaganda which it lacked at first. Yao Wen-yuan's fulminations against the 'Three Family Village' of May 10th came out in the Shanghai paper *Wenhui Pao* and the *PLA Daily*. From May 18th onwards the latter was criticizing the *People's Daily*, thus causing many repercussions. On May 20th a programme of homage to Mao Tse-tung in a new style was broadcast on the radio.

At this point the revolution was still only cultural. It was being called a 'revolution in the superstructure.' But the press was not slow to remind its readers that the 'fundamental question in revolution is the question of power.'[73]

---

[72] Only published on May 16, 1967 (see *Peking Review*, no. 21, 1967, pp. 6–9 and correction in no. 25, p. 35—translator).

[73] 'Let us sweep away all harmful influences.' *People's Daily* editorial, June 1, 1966. See *Peking Review*, 1966, no. 23, pp. 4–5.

3. The Army During Its Period of Neutrality

The army played a very important part in the Cultural Revolution. As it had been ideologically prepared, Mao Tse-tung was able to rely on it as his main support in his dealings with the Party, whose apparatus was not yet under his control. The peasants were still too short of political awareness; and the industrial workers, as beneficiaries of somewhat opportunistic policies, had tended to drift away from politics.

Mao Tse-tung could depend on the army as a means of putting pressure on the 'authorities' in the Party and the government who, in their unwillingness to understand his ideas, were entrenched in the old order and refused to come to terms with him. He could depend on the army to prevent the country from being paralyzed if the troubles got out of hand, and could hold it in reserve while the students were active.

The army was on no account to become involved in the Cultural Revolution itself. Its reactions to what took place could not be allowed to threaten its unity. It was liable to be called upon to take over public services if the economy ground to a halt or civil war loomed; and the escalation of the Vietnam war was threatening China.

At the outset the army was not supposed to need a revolution within its ranks. It was a thing apart, dedicated to serving the people and keeping clear of the disputes of committee politics.

All these reasons probably explain why what happened within the army took place before and after the initial flare-up during which the students were the shock troops. When the Red Guards were on the rampage the army gave the impression that the disturbance had passed it by and that it maintained complete control over itself. To be sure, something had happened in its ranks before that, either because some purges were thought necessary to get the army well under control before the envisaged troubles broke out; or, more probably, because the new turn taken by the Vietnam war had brought into the open disagreements over the role the army should play in a time of crisis.

Everything changed after the initial flare-up. The army had to be called in to keep control and maintain order. Although its unity depended on an understanding among its leaders that the army would not involve itself in the struggles, it was gradually drawn into the Cultural Revolution at the request of the Maoists. Once this principle was cast aside there was a clash of differing political views, and it became very hard to restrain agitation within the army itself.

The Cultural Revolution in the provinces developed differently from Peking. The revolutionary movement was submerged by a flood of declarations of faith from all sides. Everyone, even opponents, called themselves Maoists; it was poorly organized; and it was misunderstood by many Chinese. The masses it was trying to reach had for long known only Party-run movements; it may have been difficult for them to realize that this time the Revolution was not being controlled from above.

The military leaders in the provinces must have been appalled by the news of the revolution in Peking. To many of them the young agitators must have seemed like heretics. They doubtless wanted to maintain order and preserve the Party's achievements by keeping the agitation within bounds. In so doing they drew criticism on the army from the revolutionaries and hastened the spread of the Cultural Revolution to the army.

After Korea: the peasant army's new image

The Chinese army is essentially an army of peasants. It is trained not only for 'military work'—armed combat—but also for 'ideological work' and 'productive work.' Its peasant roots are enough to explain the sympathy its men had for the Maoist movement.

In 1930 Japan also had an army of peasants; and its officers, often of the same stock as the men, reacted like the countrymen they were to the problems of domestic policies. They felt that city life was corrupt. In their eyes the political parties were either, like the Marxists, alien to the spirit of Japan, or corrupted by money, like the liberals. The Japanese army is known to have intervened in politics several times. As the leaders raised the stakes they were led to a complete seizure of power, in which the real interests of the peasants were forgotten. But the starting point had been a lively concern for a countryside suffering from the post-war crisis, and resentment at the towns, whose expansion was of benefit only to their own citizens.

It would be wrong to suggest that the situation in China was identical. All the same, with the peasantry living in backwardness while the cities enjoyed twentieth-century conditions and political awareness, peasants sent into the cities on garrison duty were greatly struck by the differences they encountered; and it was quite natural that a movement favouring austerity should win their support. Such a movement might begin by taking a critical view of urban political morality. From this point of view, an economic development strategy which concentrated on the polarization of industrial development could evoke a mass reaction strong enough to shake the power structure. This is a phenomenon frequently encountered in countries where the social status of the peasantry has historically been higher than that of other labouring classes. China did not introduce military conscription until 1955. The Chinese army underwent the ordeal of the Korean War with volunteer manpower and organizational methods inherited from the Liberation War, by which the Party committees in the army discussed strategy as well as the execution of military actions. There were no ranks as such for officers or NCOs. The system of Party committees in the army, which had survived fundamentally unchanged ever since the Sanwan Reorganization,[1] was built up from the base of a committee for each battalion and a Party branch in every company. As the little red book says[2] 'The Party branch is organized on a company basis; this is an important reason why the Red Army has been able to carry on such arduous fighting without falling apart.'

An important series of reforms in 1955[3] introduced new methods of recruitment and a regularized system of ranks and privileges for officers. The army now began to modernize its structure. There were indications that the discussions of the lower-level committees now carried less weight; but the reforms did not necessarily imply a change of attitude. This was no doubt why a compromise could be found between the supporters of Party committees in the army and those who advocated that authority should be vested in the General Staff.

However, disagreements apparently developed rapidly in 1958 and 1959 between the Party's radicals and the officers in charge of the army's organization. The latter, grouped around Marshal P'eng Te-huai, the Minister of Defence, had the unpleasant experience of being criticized by the Central Committee when it met at Lushan in Sep-

[1] October 4, 1927, at the end of the Autumn Harvest Uprising. See *Jimmin Chūgoku*, November 1967, pp. 40–41.

[2] English edition, p. 136.

[3] The 1955 documents include a law on military conscription, regulations on auxiliary services in the PLA, and a State Council order converting the security forces in *hsien* and Special Districts into armed People's Police. Fourteen ranks were created for officers and three for NCOs. It was said that the change from a voluntary system to one of conscription would bring changes in the relationship between officers and men, and that if specialists were needed for modern weapons it was as well to give them some sort of special treatment (see *Chūgoku Kenkyū Geppō*, no. 242, Tokyo, April 1968, p. 25).

tember 1959. The radicals were later to list the errors of
P'eng Te-huai:

> He gave first place to military technique and denied that
> political and ideological work is the primary factor in
> the fighting ability of our army. He attempted to abro-
> gate the absolute leadership of the Party in the army and
> the system of collective leadership through the Party
> committee, and tried instead to push through the system
> of 'one-man leadership'. . . . P'eng Te-huai opposed the
> strategic principle of active defence put forward by
> Chairman Mao. He adopted a completely passive atti-
> tude towards preparations for dealing with American
> imperialist aggression. He did not proceed from the
> standpoint of combat readiness for eventual war. In-
> stead he adopted the opportunist attitude that 'War is
> impossible, or improbable.'[4]

P'eng Te-huai and several other military leaders lost
their jobs in the army command, but not their full or candidate membership of the Central Committee.[5] Their condemnation was not unanimous. Some of their ideas were
still accepted by members of the Party and they still retained some support in the army. They were known as
the exponents of the primacy of weapons.

Lin Piao, the new Minister of Defence, undertook a
purge of the army. The systematic study of the works of
Mao Tse-tung seems to have begun in 1958 in some units.
Mao Tse-tung himself had taken up his pen when P'eng
Te-huai was condemned and on three occasions put for-
ward his point of view.[6] The movement for a general and

---

[4] Li Hsin-kung, 'Settling accounts with P'eng Te-huai . . .'
Peking Review, no. 36, September 1, 1967, p. 15.

[5] Resolution of the 8th Plenary Session of the 8th C.C. concerning the anti-Party clique headed by P'eng Te-huai, *Peking
Review*, no. 34, August 18, 1967, pp. 8–10 (excerpts only).

[6] 'How Marxism should correctly be applied to mass revolutionary struggles' (August 15, 1959). 'The history of the machine gun, the mortar, and other subjects' (August 16, 1959),
'Two letters to the editorial department of the Poetry Publishing House' (September 1, 1959). See *Chūgoku Kenkyū Geppō*,
no. 242, 1968, p. 13.

intensified study of the Thought of Mao Tse-tung was the method chosen for remedying military deviation. Particular stress was laid on the 'Four First' and the 'Three-Eight Working Style,' slogans that had been given to the Workers' and Peasants' Red Army many years earlier.[7]

Until 1958 the study of Mao Tse-tung's Thought in the army had been confined to his military ideas. From then onwards the whole of his thought was to be studied. In the development of this movement, 'the absolute authority of the Thought of Mao Tse-tung' became established in the army, in which exemplary morality, strict discipline, great austerity and a strong sense of mission were all fostered.

It is easy for a body trained to think in a particular way to become remote from the rest of the people, who do not share its demanding principles and lack its sense of mission. The army's leaders were on their guard to preserve it from risks of contamination. When the Cultural Revolution spread, soldiers were seconded to the revolutionary committees with responsibilities that were new to them. Others were put in charge of factories. Some were influenced by civilian scepticism or joined in quarrels be-

[7] The 'Four Firsts': Priority of men over material; of political work in its relation to other activities; of ideological work over other aspects of political work; and of lively ideas over academic thinking in ideological work.

The 'Three-Eight Working Style' refers to the 'Three Main Rules' and the 'Eight Points for Attention.'

The Three Main Rules were originally: Obey orders, take nothing from the masses, not even a needle and a thread, and hand all captured goods over to the authorities.

The Eight Points: Speak politely; pay a fair price for your purchases; return what you borrow; give compensation for any damage you do; do not beat or insult people; do not trample on crops; do not importune women; do not mistreat prisoners. (See J. Guillermaz, *Histoire du parti communiste chinois*, p. 188.)

The movement for the study of Mao Tse-tung's Thought later adopted the Three-Eight Working Style, formulated by Mao Tse-tung into three points and eight characters, recommending: steadiness of mind, enthusiasm, directness, flexibility in strategy and tactics, unity, energy, seriousness of purpose, and application.

tween different interest groups, forgetting their own mission.

Political cadres were aware of such risks, as 'the army does not exist in a vacuum.'[8] When soldiers were demobilized they were the objects of special attention from their comrades and the political commissars of their units. 'Fighters should be told about the problems that may arise in their families,' recommended a unit in Canton.[9] Thus the army took its own course, guided by the Thought of Mao Tse-tung but not sheltered from influences coming from the people. Its command in particular came under the influence of the Party machine, as the Party in the army was the same Party as in civilian circles, differing only to some extent in its appearance.

P'eng Te-huai and the advocates of the theory of the primacy of weapons had been removed from the control of the army, but with the support of the Party machine their resistance continued. Liu Shao-ch'i apparently said at an enlarged work meeting of the Central Committee in January 1962 that the struggle against the P'eng Te-huai group had been taken too far. In June the dismissed Minister of Defence himself produced an essay of 80,000 characters demanding that his case be re-examined.[10]

The withdrawal and reaction of the advocates of weaponry

Marshal Lin Piao, Minister of Defence since 1959, was convinced that the Maoist minority had to take action, by urging the masses to overthrow the Party machine. It is the law, he said,

> with all things, correct or incorrect, that if you do not attack them, they will attack you; if you do not strike them, they will strike you; if you do not strengthen your resistance to them, they will strengthen their resistance to you. It is therefore necessary to mobilize the masses

[8] *PLA Daily*, April 16, 1966.
[9] *People's Daily*, November 8, 1966.
[10] See *Chūgoku Kenkyū Geppō*, no. 242, Tokyo, 1968, p. 17.

for the struggle. If they do not struggle we risk being dispersed; it will then be impossible to ensure unity.[11]

Lin Piao reorganized the Central Committee's Military Commission, of which he was the first vice-chairman, and one can assume that it was still chaired by Mao Tse-tung himself even after the Wuhan Plenum. It is hardly surprising therefore that it was through the Military Commission that he was later to recover control of the government. The new Military Commission met three times in 1960, and at its third session, in September and October, it approved 'intensive, repeated and prolonged' publicizing of the Thought of Mao Tse-tung, carrying out the 'Mass Line,' and 'the expansion of democracy.'[12] In the operational control of the army Lin Piao replaced Huang K'o-sheng, dismissed at the same time as P'eng Te-huai, with Lo Jui-ch'ing. We have seen how after the Lushan Plenum of 1962 Mao Tse-tung set about reconquering lost ground. Behind him he had the army which, trained in his Thought, had struggled against the theory of the primacy of weapons and now stood, more unified than before, around Lin Piao. Next the Socialist Education Movement was launched in the countryside, and after February 1964 extended to all walks of life throughout the country in the campaign to 'Learn from the PLA.' The army put itself in the vanguard of the Party, not only for an ideological movement but also for a political campaign. A silent struggle was developing between the entrenched views of the Party machine and the radical tendencies supported by the army. The latter scored with the publication of the Twenty-three Points, dealing with the application of the Socialist Education Movement in the countryside.

11 *Tungfanghung*, Wei-Jenmin Chantoutui of Peking Engineering University, February 23, 1967. Speech by Lin Piao to a meeting of senior cadres of the whole army in February 1960. This speech also refers to the major themes of the unity of opposites of 'the division of one into two' and of activism, all of which were to be basic to the tactics of the Maoists throughout the Cultural Revolution.

12 See *The Politics of the Chinese Red Army*, ed. J. Chester Cheng, The Hoover Institution, Stanford, 1966.

But the movement was carried out in the countryside by cadres under the orders of the Party machine. The army could not do it itself. The army made exhortations, distributed tracts, found models, and planned campaigns around such heroes as Lei Feng; but the class struggle which the radicals wanted never developed on a large scale, and the 'authorities' in the Party kept their grip on the countryside. The gap between the Party machine and the army widened, while the soldiers who believed in the primacy of weapons were not yet entirely powerless, which was to lead to further purges in the future.

Documents published later revealed that the militarists had begun their counter-attack in 1964, before the big escalation in Vietnam. In that year, according to the *People's Daily* of May 30, 1968, 'Lo Jui-ch'ing formed his plan to reverse the policy adopted for the development of our army.'[13] Lin Piao reacted with his customary vigour:

At the end of 1964 Vice-Chairman Lin Piao gave the important directive that first place was to be given to proletarian policies and that ideological and political work were to be strengthened. . . . Lo Jui-ch'ing's great military plans came to nothing.[14]

Minor rectifications—i.e. a limited purge—were ordered, but 'Lo Jui-ch'ing did not permit the experiment of minor rectifications to proceed.'[15]

The army thus had a difficult time, with the Minister of Defence and his Chief of Staff at loggerheads on the question of purges. When the bombing of North Vietnam began, many Chinese expected the war to extend to their own country. As Han Suyin has written:

'China herself foresaw that the threatening and provocative *cordon sanitaire* of the previous seventeen years,

[13] 'Men Ho, a good cadre, endlessly faithful to the Thought of Chairman Mao,' *People's Daily*, May 30, 1968.
[14] 'La 9e compagnie rouge,' New China News Agency (French language), no. 050907, 1968.
[15] *Ibid.*

now aggravated by the presence on her doorstep of half a million American troops in Vietnam and an aerial armada out of all proportion to the local requirements, was the prelude to an attack on her. She accepted the challenge.'[16]

In the state of alert before a possible war military men gained more freedom of speech, and the 'weapons first' theory could now be more openly expressed. Speaking at meetings commemorating the victories over Germany and Japan, Lo Jui-ch'ing repeated the orthodox view that an 'active defence' was necessary, but added that there was no need to wait until the enemy attacked first.

Lin Piao replied on September 3, 1965, with his famous article 'Long Live the Victory of the People's War.' The general drift of this was that while no concessions should be made to American imperialism a head-on conflict was not the right way to oppose it. He did not say that troops would be sent to Vietnam, or that it would be necessary to enter the war against America in the near future. It was a question of carrying out an active strategy against America, and mobilizing all under-developed countries and oppressed peoples for the struggle. The dispute between Lin Piao and Lo Jui-ch'ing was between advocates of modern and guerrilla war, between supporters of joint action with the USSR and of independent action.

In the absence of statements of their positions by the militarists the reasons behind them can only be guessed at. There are two possible hypotheses, and surprisingly enough both pointed to a military alliance with the USSR. At first sight, the 'weapons first' advocates, allied as they were with the Party apparatus, appear to have stressed the imminence of the danger and argued in favour of taking the offensive. This would have been intended to create a tense atmosphere favourable to the declaration of a state of emergency, or at least to more power for the military leaders. As the latter believed that it was high time to strengthen the army's resources in heavy equipment and

[16] Han Suyin, *China in the Year 2001*, Basic Books, New York, 1967.

aircraft they would have been willing to act jointly with the USSR.

The other hypothesis is that, as tension grew between China and America, a military analysis of the situation confirmed the 'weapons first' advocates in their caution. While they wanted an easing of China's policy towards the USA, they were also prepared in the last resort to co-operate with the USSR if necessary. From what we know, Lo Jui-ch'ing seems to have taken the first line of reasoning and P'eng Te-huai, who was criticized for saying that war was unlikely, the second. Lo Jui-ch'ing had been criticized for saying that there was no need to wait until one was attacked before taking the offensive. P'eng Te-huai held back, while Lo Jui-ch'ing went too far. But both attitudes led towards a *rapprochement* with the Soviet Union, in the former case for the sake of power and in the latter out of prudence.

It may well be thought that the policy of Mao Tse-tung and Lin Piao led them to align themselves more firmly with Vietnam than did that of the 'weapons first' partisans.

The army reorganized and prepared

Lin Piao had the insignia of rank abolished in June 1965— a symbolic expression of his policy. Once again he decided to make a purge, not an easy thing to carry out when the threat of war put the army in the firing line. On November 18, 1965, he published his 'Directives for work in the army in 1966.' This concentrated on people's war, suitably enough for a situation in which China, finding herself encircled, was expecting an invasion of imperialist forces on her own soil.

A general conference on political work in the army met from the end of December to January 20, 1966. This conference, guided by the chief of the PLA's General Political Department, Hsiao Hua, gave 'priority to politics,' set the target of 'crushing the bourgeois line and bourgeois theories in the army,' and demanded 'a purification of the army in the political, ideological and organizational spheres.' This last item indicated a purge. When the clean-up only affected organization, it involved nothing more than an administrative shake-up; but a requirement that everyone should go through the ideological mill meant that hard trials lay ahead.

The details of the purge that was to bring the army back under control are not yet known, but it is generally thought to have led to the incident known as the 'February *coup d'état*.'

The 'February *coup*' was an operation by which Lo Jui-ch'ing, the Chief of the General Staff, would have put his underlings in the key positions in the army. The Red Guards of Peking University and Jenta (the People's University of Peking), whose investigations claimed to include the first evidence of this *coup d'état*, insisted with great emphasis that the Peking 'authorities' moved troops in from the provinces to strengthen the capital's garrison. These troops were billeted in the universities. Liu Jen, secretary of the Peking Municipal Party Committee and Political Commissar of the Peking Military Region, apparently transferred troops from Shansi, Hankow[17] and Tientsin, wanting to have them at his disposal in Peking.

The Red Guards who made the investigations and reached these conclusions clearly wanted to expose a crime by the former municipal Party committee. After these revelations at the end of January 1967 the matter was taken up again in April by the revolutionary group that had seized power in the municipal committee and the organs of the Peking Party committee. The intention this time was to investigate thoroughly the services they had just taken over. They drew up an indictment in the style commonly used in the revolutionary public meetings during the period after the power seizures:

We of the justice department have investigated the plot

[17] See Konno, *Pekin Kono Ichinen*, Shinnihon Shuppansha, Tokyo, 1968, *op. cit.* Since Hankow was not in the area under Liu Jen's jurisdiction this should perhaps be Nankow, a town strategically situated at the foot of the pass of the Great Wall.

by Liu, Teng, P'eng, Lu, Lo and Yang, and demand that they be condemned to death for their crime.[18]

Their poster ended with this peroration. But other posters which went up at the same time reported that a telephone call from the Central Committee's Cultural Revolution Group had ordered that all posters dealing with the 'February *coup*' were to be pasted over. This amounted to disowning them.

Throughout the Cultural Revolution February, like July and August, was a disturbed month. References to February always had undesirable reactionary connotations: the Group of Five and the 'February *coup*' in 1966, the 'February Counter-current' in 1967 and in 1968. Official organs were later to refer to the events of February 1966 only as the 'February attempt to settle scores,'[19] thus using the affair of the Group of Five to cover up for the story of the *coup*, the truth of which Chou En-lai himself denied.

Whatever it was, the incident of the so-called *coup* involved a conflict among the military leaders that led to a purge. If we credit the investigations by the revolutionary group who made the indictment quoted above, P'eng Chen and his followers launched a public opinion campaign throughout China in 1965 and early 1966, saying that war was about to break out at any moment and that it was necessary to prepare for it.

From March 1965 and throughout the autumn they burned many documents on the excuse of preparing for war, assembled supplies for war, organized the rear areas. . . . stockpiled material for strategic construction programmes and military factories. . . . Anticipating that Peking would be the base for a *coup d'état*, they intensified military training, selected over sixty students who had graduated from primary and secondary

[18] From posters put up in Peking after April 17, 1967, by the 'Army Corps for the destruction of the old regime' in organizations of the Municipal Party Committee. The six men were Liu Shao-ch'i, Teng Hsiao-p'ing, P'eng Chen, Lu Ting-yi, Lo Jui-ch'ing, and Yang Shang-k'un.

[19] *Pékin Information*, no. 37, September 16, 1968, p. 26.

schools, trained them in radio transmission, and supplied the militia with large quantities of munitions. They formed various military units in the universities and higher schools. . . . In October 1965 Liu Jen, putting his trust in a foreign country, set out a third line and made preparations for using foreign aid if things went badly.[20]

In addition, according to an earlier poster denouncing the 'large military clique of Lo Jui-ch'ing,'[21] Lo had conspired with a number of generals to take power in the army high command. He even wanted to instal the 'anti-Party elements' Liu Chen and Chang T'ing-fa[22] in the air force, and dared to tell Lin Piao to make way.

Was there really a plot? In February 1967 Red Guards cited statements attributed to Lin Piao and K'ang Sheng to confirm that there had been.[23] Chou En-lai thought it useful to point out that there was no need to see conspiracies everywhere.[24] The military preparations at the beginning of 1966 that had attracted attention had nothing to do with a *coup d'état*, and whatever Lo Jui-ch'ing was to be blamed for it was not that. It remains to be said that Lo Jui-ch'ing tried to kill himself on March 18th by jumping out of a window, and was condemned on April 3, 1966, either by the Centre or by the Central Committee's Military Commission.[25] The verdict against him was confirmed on May 16, 1966, which was therefore a significant date not only for the investiture of the Cultural Revolu-

[20] 'Army Corps for the destruction of the old regime,' April 17, 1967, *op. cit.*

[21] Poster of the Hsin Peita Red Guards, January 28, 1967.

[22] Both were previously assistants to the air force chief of staff.

[23] According to the Revolutionary Rebels of the No. 1 Machine-Tool Factory, Peking, cited in Konno, *Pekin Kono Ichinen*, Tokyo, 1968, *op. cit.*

[24] See *Hsin Peita*, May 7, 1967.

[25] See *Chūgoku Kenkyū Geppō*, no. 242, 1968, p. 17. The 'Report of a Central Committee Working Party on the question of the errors of Lo Jui-ch'ing' was approved on April 3, 1966, and confirmed on May 16th, probably by the Eastern Centre.

tion's new group in the Central Committee, but also for
the army.

The preparations for war that had given rise to alarming
rumours, and possibly misled the Red Guards of Peita and
Jenta, had not escaped the notice of outside observers.
That winter they saw the militia training in the fields and
sometimes even in the streets of Peking at dawn. It was
also learnt that factories had received instructions concerning the mobilization of their cadres, and that the Peking People's Committee had created a 'Third Bureau' in
1965 which was moving out supplies and building up stock-
piles in the suburbs to the north and east of the city.[26]

The condemnation of Lo Jui-ch'ing was most effective
in putting down the forces hostile to applying the ideas
of Lin Piao. It could be said that it spared the army
leadership from being split into two. The radical military
leaders established their authority in Peking almost as well
as they had done in Shanghai and Hangchow.

All indications suggest that the former marshals in the
Central Committee's Military Commission supported Lin
Piao and Hsiao Hua. They doubtless reckoned that their
line on the Vietnam war was the most reasonable one at
that time. When Lin Piao sent them what were later known
as the 'Chiang Ch'ing Theses'[27]—as opposed to the 'February Theses'—the commission treated them both as an
army document, and, acting in the name of the whole
Party, as one of general policy.[28] Thus began the custom
of addressing matters to the Military Commission instead

[26] According to the organs of the revolutionaries of the Steel
Institute, April 12, 1967.

[27] Summary of the minutes of discussions of literary and art
workers in the army. See Mōtakutō no Chōsen, p. 26. (See
also Peking Review, no. 23, 1967, pp. 10–16: 'Summary of the
Forum on the Work in Literature and Art with Which Comrade Lin Piao Entrusted Comrade Chiang Ch'ing'—translator.)

[28] However, there was no suggestion of this in the press
before the Peking Municipal Committee was overthrown. The
first references to the 'Forum' in the press date from June 30,
1966, when the People's Daily reported the working conference
of the whole army on literary and artistic creation called by the
General Political Department of the PLA.

of to the Party's other leading organs—the Political Bureau and its Standing Committee—which were now split.

As we have seen, the *PLA Daily* led the attack in the sphere of public opinion, in co-operation with the Central Committee's Cultural Revolution Group, in order that the academic discussions on the cases of Wu Han, Teng T'o and the historians should lead to intensified political struggles. The press bombardment of the 'bourgeois headquarters' opened the way to the violent phase of the Cultural Revolution. After the purge in the army, the ideas of Mao Tse-tung and Lin Piao on war in the prevailing circumstances were accepted with no further opposition. The *PLA Daily*'s May Day editorial reasserted that ultramodern weapons were powerless against men with a high political awareness, an idea that was inseparable from the conclusions drawn from it: that in politics—that is, the organization of the masses from the base upwards—China enjoyed 'an absolute supremacy.'[29]

The army during the launching of the Red Guards

The careful preservation of the army's unity made it possible for the student movement to be launched with the protection of reserve forces strong enough to disturb anyone who might have wished to resort to force in defence of the threatened Party machine. From July to December the army remained powerful and calm, present but not involved, equally ready to intervene in the country to maintain order or to intervene abroad if the Vietnamese wanted it.

After the overthrow of the Peking Municipal Committee at the beginning of June came the period of the 'work teams' (later to be the subject of controversy) which had been intended by the Party to bring the Cultural Revolution in universities and offices under control. When Mao Tse-tung came back to Peking the students reacted against the 'work teams' and the Eleventh Plenary Session of the Central Committee was held. The author was present when

[29] *Takung Pao*, quoting the *PLA Daily*, February 19, 1966.

the Red Guards were called out, and at all eight mass meetings held from August to November for students to see the Chairman 'at close quarters.'

Throughout these events the 'commanders and fighters of the People's Liberation Army,' to use the language of the official press, 'stood guard to protect the young Red Guards when they launched themselves into the community. Their presence guaranteed the right of hundreds of millions of revolutionaries in towns and countryside to hold revolutionary debates and mass revolutionary criticisms.'[30]

The army was present without arms. It kept order at the meetings of the young demonstrators; it moved them away when there were fatal crushes in which those most eager to see the Chairman were suffocated. Detachments of soldiers watched from nearby when the Red Guards hunted down the bourgeoisie.

The only references to troops being deliberately used to influence a political decision appeared in the organs of the Japanese Communist Party after it made its analysis of the Chinese Cultural Revolution in April 1967. According to these sources Lin Piao used the army to prevent some members of the Central Committee from attending the Eleventh Plenum, and also to enable some students to take part although they had no right to do so.[31]

The military figures who were the most important politically were prominent at the mass rallies. On October 18th Yang Ch'eng-wu and Hsieh Fu-chih rode with Mao Tse-tung in the first vehicle of the motorcade while Hsiao Hua and Yeh Chien-ying were with Lin Piao in the second.[32] Moreover Mao Tse-tung and nearly all the top

[30] *Peking Review*, no. 36, September 1, 1967, p. 6.

[31] See in particular the May 1967 issue of the review *Zenei*, and the *Akahata* of April 29, 1967.

[32] Yang Ch'eng-wu: Acting Chief of the General Staff after the dismissal of Lo Jui-ch'ing. According to some rumours, Mao Tse-tung was indebted to him for keeping order in Peking on July 18th and 19th, the time of his return to the capital. Hsieh Fu-chih: Minister of Public Security, later Chairman of the Peking Revolutionary Committee.

political leaders, including Liu Shao-ch'i and Teng Hsiao-p'ing, wore military uniform for the big rallies. The sense of mission and the discipline of the army were held up as examples to the Red Guards in all sorts of ways.

The army could of course help the Cultural Revolution even while standing back from it. The movement had been given its directives in the Central Committee's Sixteen Points of August 8th, and it appeared to be aimed only at the 'authorities' in the Party machine, government, administration and education. The order that the army was not to be involved in the Cultural Revolution in civilian circles was confirmed by an urgent notice from the Military Commission on October 1st.[33]

But some repercussions among the troops were inevitable, and they probably occurred in the military academies. These were the army's most sensitive spots as, after all the encouragement that students in general had been given to join in the dispute, the staff and students in these institutions could not be kept free from the contagion of the universities. Ho Lung[34] took a hard line when addressing them in a speech on November 13th:

We must neither take part in the Cultural Revolution in our locality nor interfere with it. We must not join in local bombardments of the headquarters (i.e. of the bourgeoisie), rebellion, confiscations of private property, or demonstrations.[35]

But by now this was no longer enough to prevent incidents from occurring; those that had already started had to be brought to an end. Party Work Teams had entered

[33] See Konno, *Pekin Kono Ichinen, op. cit.*, p. 121. On January 31, 1967, Liu Chih-chien, deputy head of the army's General Political Department, was accused of having added this passage to the urgent notice on his own authority.

[34] Vice-Chairman of the Central Committee's Military Commission, in charge of military education and sports commission.

[35] Speech by Ho Lung at a meeting for teachers, students and cadres from the whole PLA who had come to Peking for revolutionary exchanges. Distributed in leaflet form in Peking.

some military academies after the June incidents.[36] In
these schools protesters who had come forward had been
persecuted and labelled as 'anti-party' or 'rightists' for opposing the leaders of the Work Teams. In the next phase
they naturally tried to take forceful revenge. The Military
Commission decided to order a kind of amnesty to bring
the quarrels to an end.

The former Work Teams, Party committees in the schools
and other organic groups were urged to destroy all dossiers
of criticisms that might have provided material for further
struggles:

> All dossiers drawn up against the masses (against all
> non-Party people who had made criticisms) during the
> Cultural Revolution in the schools and universities must
> be declared invalid and burned in the presence of the
> masses . . . under the supervision of the heads of the
> leading organizations and representatives of the students
> of the schools involved.

Whether or not they had been already annulled, all files
had to be destroyed. Copying them or disposing of them
privately was forbidden, as this might 'cause errors to become ingrained.' All disputes that had arisen from these
documents had to be settled by joint consultation in the
spirit of the Sixteen Points. Discussion alone was permissible, violence never. Leading cadres who had made policy
errors during the Cultural Revolution had to be dealt with
according to Chairman Mao's policy on the correct handling of contradictions among the people. 'The ideological
aspect must be clarified and comrades reunited.'[37]

Reading this document makes one wonder whether the
Military Commission did not feel in October 1966 that the

[36] On the dispatch of Work Teams to the universities to hold
back the students and organize a Cultural Revolution that would
not infringe on Party discipline, see Chapter 4, *Students and
Red Guards,* below.

[37] Urgent directive of the Military Commission and the General Political Department of the PLA ratified by the Central
Committee on October 5, 1966. See *Tanjug News Agency* release, November 17, 1967.

Cultural Revolution had gone far enough towards its objectives, and that the time had come to put quarrels aside and return to the normal working of institutions.

But the students of the military schools could not be prevented from getting involved, Red Guard style, in revolutionary activities against those of their leaders who were being criticized. Twenty-seven organizations from military institutes rearrested Lo Jui-ch'ing on December 20th[38] in order to submit him to a public trial. A little later some regular soldiers took the rebel course. The paper *Mainichi* reported on January 14th that a PLA unit had forced a group of 'counter-revolutionaries' under the orders of Liu Chih-chien, deputy head of the army's General Political Department, to surrender. This unit also seized a large number of documents.[39]

The army's leaders also had worries on account of the armament and other industries under military control. When the Centre permitted workers to become revolutionaries, organizations appeared in the ministries that ran these industries.[40] The Seventh Ministry of the Mechanical Industry was paralyzed by a long strike that began on December 24th, and the rivalry between the two main revolutionary organizations that were formed there lasted a year. The Centre had to intervene to forbid outside elements from participating in the revolution in the ministries of the mechanical industry.[41]

In December the most radical elements in the Cultural Revolution intensified their pressure. We shall see below how organizations of 'revolutionary rebels' took control of the Trade Union headquarters from the 27th onwards. The same tactics doubtless also gave them control of some of the Public Security bureaus which had the function of

38 See *Hsin Peita*, January 20, 1967.

39 The unit was no. 750 (*Lan*). Liu Chih-chien was accused of adding the passage quoted above forbidding the army from intervening in the civilian Cultural Revolution to the October 1st urgent notice of the Military Commission.

40 Some had been formed earlier. The organizations 915 and 916 of the Seventh Ministry (in charge of aircraft construction) were so called to commemorate September 15 and 16, 1966.

41 Shanghai Radio, January 25, 1967.

police departments in the towns, and of the French gen-
darmerie in the countryside. In December many of the
Public Security cadres were labelled as 'black elements'
and replaced by soldiers.[42] Chiang Ch'ing even demanded
at a meeting of the leadership on December 18th that all
the police should be put under army supervision; and her
idea was accepted by the Minister of Public Security, Hsieh
Fu-chih.[43] But everything has its other side. As the police
had to hold the revolutionaries back in a number of incidents, the revolutionaries found themselves up against an
obstacle identifiable as connected with the army. The soldiers were thus intervening in the Cultural Revolution—but
in the eyes of the revolutionaries it was on the wrong side.
When, for example, revolutionaries wanting to arrest
Cheng T'ien-hsiang to bring him before a criticism tribunal
were unable to force their way into his home they demanded that the Public Security should hand him over.[44]
Public Security refused. According to the revolutionaries
the Peking police opposed a meeting when they were informed when and where it was to be held. In the last resort
this criticism was directed against the army.

There had been several strikes in Peking from the middle of October onwards,[45] probably in protest against the
intrusion of Red Guards into places of work. At times the
Public Security forces had to intervene. On January 30th
they clashed with a group of workers at the big Shihchingshan steel works. The incident stirred high passions in the
capital. Policemen and soldiers put up posters everywhere
demanding order and respect for the Public Security
forces.

Although the army was being held in readiness for war,

[42] Lee Pat Lo, *Far Eastern Economic Review*, August 17,
1967.

[43] Hungarian News Agency Report. See also 'The Diary of
the Cultural Revolution,' *Asahi Evening News*, Tokyo, May
1967, p. 20.

[44] This was the incident of January 6, 1967. See *Asahi Shimbun* (Japanese edition), January 10, 1967.

[45] The first was at the No. 1 Cotton Mill on October 15.
('The Diary of the Cultural Revolution,' p. 4.) Another took
place in the Wangpingtun mine at the end of November.

some of its men had already been drawn into the revolution in Peking. In the provinces, where the art of making revolution by criticizing the 'authorities' in power was taught by students back from their 'revolutionary exchanges' in Peking, the army played a repressive role in some places. It should be added that what was known of the events in Peking must have seemed scandalous in many circles.

In the thinly populated provinces containing much virgin land, such as Sinkiang, Chinghai and Tibet, where conditions were hard and government, Party and army regarded themselves as being in active service to maintain a strategic defence, guarantee lines of communication, and keep alive the 'pioneer spirit,' the local leaders had to admit that something was happening in Peking but saw no need to change anything where they were.

In Szechuan, the army's rear base for Tibet, the same attitude seems to have prevailed. Revolutionaries from Peking complained of being repressed by the army.[46] In Canton the head of the military region's Cultural Revolution Group appears to have misunderstood his role. He wanted to prevent the revolutionaries from making searches and opposed them with armed soldiers. Casualties resulted in Kiangsi, which was closer to the Centre, when serious clashes between revolutionary organizations occurred from January 9th to 12th; the victims were mostly Red Guards from Peking. The army took no part at Nanch'ang, but one of the organizations on the conservative side was a group of army veterans and demobilized soldiers.[47]

According to some posters, conservative workers from Shanghai and Wuhsi entered the city of Nanking with the

[46] 'At K'angting, Luting, and Kangtzuchou in the Southwest the army has oppressed revolutionary rebels.' Appeal by the Proletariat of the Tibet Autonomous Region's Revolutionary Rebel High Command, January 22, 1967.

[47] Nanch'ang Radio, January 22nd, and a Peking poster of January 23rd, as reported in *Asahi Shimbun* (Japanese edition). The organization was the August First Combat Group of demobilized soldiers in civilian jobs in the city of Nanch'ang.

connivance of part of the army to fight against the revolutionaries. Deaths and injuries resulted. 'The T'ao Chu
faction used the army and the Public Security forces to
make house to house searches.'[48]

This incident in Nanking, combined with the Shanghai
railway strike at the beginning of January, caused a break
in rail communication between north and south China for
several days.

Even in Shanghai, where it allowed Chang Ch'un-
ch'iao[49] to bring off his master stroke of having Futan
University militarily occupied in order to be rid of a conservative group, the army was not perhaps quite as sympathetic towards the Cultural Revolution as Lin Piao would
have liked it to be. In fact the *PLA Daily* wrote on January 14, 1967, that 'the army's leaders must learn from
the Shanghai revolutionary rebel group.' One is tempted
to see this as advice to make a better job of imitating them.

In many sectors the army was already involved in the
Cultural Revolution before the rebel high command ordered it to intervene everywhere where the left needed
support. By January the whole of China was in the throes
of struggle. On January 15th the theoretical journal
Red Flag published an article urging revolutionaries to
seize power everywhere.[50] On January 23rd the New
China News Agency reported that power struggles were
taking place in Shantung, Kiangsu, Chekiang, Fukien, Kiangsi, and Anhui. However, one ought not to suppose
that all the army units were only concerned with maintaining public order irrespective of the course followed
by the revolution. In Tsingtao it was only thanks to the
initiative of several soldiers that the new 'revolutionary

---

[48] 'The Diary of the Cultural Revolution,' *op. cit.*, p. 28.
[49] Chang Ch'un-ch'iao, secretary of the Shanghai Municipal
Party Committee, and member of the Central Committee's Cultural Revolution Group. See Neale Hunter, 'All the Way
Rebels,' *Far Eastern Economic Review*, August 3, 1967.
[50] More indirect clashes resulted from this where revolutionaries wanted to seize control of public security bureaus.
Events were particularly stormy in Changchun, Kirin province,
on January 20th and 21st. See 'The Diary of the Cultural
Revolution,' p. 42.

rebel committee' could be formed[51] and could sweep away the old committee structure.

The revolutionary command unified

In the long ordeal of these troubled days, even before it was ordered to play a political role, the army had been asked to take on such political jobs in some districts as guarding prisons, granaries, commodity stores and banks,[52] and, especially, taking control of radio stations. The January 19th order to guard prisons and depots was one of the first decisions to appear above the joint signature of the Central Committee, the Military Commission, the State Council, and the Central Committee's Cultural Revolution Group. It also came at practically the same time as the decision to unify the revolutionary command, of which more below. In Shanghai it was the order to hand over prison keys to the army that revealed who had taken them over.[53] In other words, the order took back from the revolutionaries a significant part of the power they had seized. The army's control of radio stations gave rise to the strongest of protests from revolutionaries in some places. The order was not given the same interpretation everywhere, for Lhasa Radio in Tibet was taken by the revolutionary rebels on January 16th.

Immediately after the decision giving the soldiers control over radio stations, and doubtless as part of the same series of measures, a major decision was taken: the whole army was to be subordinated to a unified revolutionary command. This decision shocked some of the army's leaders and shook its unity. The first intimation of this was when the army's Cultural Revolution Group was reorganized[54] and placed under the Central Committee's Cultural Revolution Group in addition to the Military Commission.

[51] On January 23, 1967.
[52] Central Committee decision of January 16th, reported by the Czech CTK agency, January 17, 1967.
[53] The request was broadcast by Shanghai Radio.
[54] January 12, 1967.

There was now a military Cultural Revolution group in the same position *vis-à-vis* the army as the Central Committee's group towards the rest of the Party and the government. Because of the army's special tasks and the threat of war it doubtless kept for itself a measure of independence. The group's new position in the power structure, however, meant that it was no longer able to decide to what extent the Cultural Revolution should be brought into the army.

Revolutionary events, particularly those of Shanghai, showed how urgently a single command was needed for the revolution and all other affairs of state. A reorganization took place in the Central Committee's Standing Committee, at that time divided, the Military Commission, which could not represent the Centre by itself, and the Central Committee's Cultural Revolution Group, which had become the Party's ideological body for the time being.

This reorganization was revealed on January 22nd, when Chou En-lai sent instructions to the army's Cultural Revolution Group via Ch'en Po-ta[55] and Chiang Ch'ing, the leaders of the Central Committee's Cultural Revolution Group. To explain this, Hsieh T'ang-chung, who passed on the instruction, added:

> The instructions for our millions of soldiers comes directly from the Defence High Command. The instructions of Chairman Mao and Vice-chairman Lin come from the same origin. . . . Comrades in national defence must act in accordance with the instructions of Chiang Ch'ing and Ch'en Po-ta.[56]

[55] Instructions by the Army Cultural Revolution Group on the organization of a meeting of representatives of revolutionary 'liaison posts' in units in the provinces.

Ch'en Po-ta, a candidate member of the Political Bureau before the Ninth Congress, since then a member of the Bureau's Standing Committee, and a leader of the Central Committee's Cultural Revolution Group, had long been Mao Tse-tung's secretary.

[56] See the January 23, 1967, circular of the Red Rebels of unit 160 (*Tsung*) of the PLA, distributed as a leaflet.

He was emphasizing that the command was now completely united, and that it included defence. But the army's provincial leaders did not always take full notice of this. Some of them believed that they could justify failing to obey implicitly the orders of the Central Committee's group on the grounds that it was a body with limited powers only.

> When Premier Chou and Acting Chief of the General Staff Yang said on September 26th that the Centre's Cultural Revolution Committee was the general staff of Chairman Mao's command, they attributed merely secretarial functions to it. The army command did not tell us (what it really was), and we did not see the Central Committee's Cultural Revolution Group for what it was.[57]

The new status of the army's Cultural Revolution Group meant that it had to be reorganized: its top leaders, Hsiao Hua and Liu Chih-chien, had been opposed to the change. Their hostility came to the knowledge of revolutionary organizations, who wanted to search their homes. They also wanted to search the home of Ho Lung, who probably had also voted in the Military Commission against the charges.

The revolutionaries tried to have them put on trial in public, but the leaders of the Centre opposed this.

> At an enlarged meeting of the Military Commission everyone helps each other. Besides, until Chairman Mao and Vice-chairman Lin have reached their conclusions the questions remain open. . . . Hsiao Hua's personal safety must be guaranteed, said Chou En-lai.[58]

> Some of those who have provided material against Ho Lung are honest, but others want to sow disorder in the army.[59]

[57] Statement by Ts'ai Ping-ch'en after being brought to Peking with Ch'en Tsai-tao in the consequence of the Wuhan incident of July 1967.

[58] Chou En-lai, in instructions passed on by Hsieh T'ang-chung on January 22nd (circular of Red Rebels of PLA unit 160 [Tsung] op. cit.).

[59] Quoted in *Yutien Fenglei*, February 12, 1967.

It is not a matter of knowing whether Hsiao Hua as an individual is in full sympathy with the movement. These are still internal contradictions. There is no need to enlarge the matter or extend it any further.[60]

Although the Centre took seriously the threat weighing on the army's unity, it reversed the policy of suspending the movement in the army and forbidding it from joining in the civilian Cultural Revolution.[61]

It was on January 23, 1967, that the Centre took the crucial decision to commit the army on the side of the revolutionaries when they asked for its support.[62] We have seen above how the revolutionaries had often met with an unfriendly reception in the provinces. The army was no longer to be neutral towards them; it had to help them effectively when they were down. The decision authorized the army to use its weapons to combat counter-revolutionary elements and freed it from any obligation to obey political 'authorities' who had taken the capitalist road.

The Peking troops set an example from January 22nd onwards by occupying the Fangshan[63] offices of the

[60] Peking leaflet of January 22nd: 'Directives by Chou En-lai and Chiang Ch'ing issued at 2 a.m., on January 22nd.'

[61] Liu Chih-chien was criticized for his addition to the Military Commission notice of October 1, 1967 (see above). He lost his position in the Army's Cultural Revolution Group, which was from then on headed by ex-marshal Hsü Hsiang-ch'ien with the assistance of Chiang Ch'ing and Kuang Feng (a journalist who had made his mark in the *People's Daily* during March 1966), who were already members of the Central Committee's Cultural Revolution Group. See *Mōtakutō no Chōsen*, p. 221. The membership of the army's new group was given in the *People's Daily* of January 13. On Kuan Feng see 'Diary of the Cultural Revolution,' p. 44.

[62] Other posters in Peking dated this resolution to January 20th. It was foreshadowed by a speech of Chou En-lai's on January 21st in the Great Hall of the People quoted in *Asahi Shimbun* (Japanese edition). The text of the resolution is given in Konno, *op. cit.*, pp. 227–28.

[63] Fifty kilometres southwest of Peking. The source is a leaflet by the Tungfanghung Defence Group of the Electrical Laboratory of the Ministry of Hydroelectric Power.

Party, the Public Security, and the government, putting in a joint command of revolutionary organizations. The groups they pushed aside were young revolutionaries of the power laboratories and electrification school at Liukouch'iao.

It had to be made clear to the people that the army was not a threat, and precautions were needed to prevent revolutionary criticism from developing within the army so far as to weaken it. The ideological contradictions that had almost split the High Command on January 11th and 12th also had to be reduced. Finally, the frontier provinces and regions, where the local commanders reckoned that the engagement of the army domestically risked leaving gaps in the country's external defence, posed special problems.

A directive of the four Central bodies on January 28th dealt with the first two questions.[64] It laid down that in the army the Cultural Revolution should not go beyond the limits of each unit, in order to preserve intact obedience to the command structure. It also prohibited soldiers from arresting people and disgracing them by making them wear dunce's hats, and from requisitioning or seizing goods, thus reassuring the masses on the attitude the army would take, its new involvement notwithstanding.

On January 31st the positions taken by some military leaders during the month were examined.[65] Liu Chih-chien was criticized, which made it possible to resolve the open contradiction between the decisions of October 1, 1966, and January 23, 1967, one for and one against the army's entry into the revolution in civilian circles.

Fifteen days later it was learned that Mao Tse-tung had decided that the Cultural Revolution was to be conducted differently in the military districts where difficulties had arisen. He added that there was no need for the revo-

[64] See *Agence France Presse* despatch from Peking, January 28, 1967.

[65] At the Chinghsi Hotel in Peking. See *Konno, op. cit.*, p. 121. Yang Yung, commander of the troops in the Peking district, and Liao Hang-sheng, their political commissar, were criticized together with Liu.

lution to be conducted simultaneously throughout the army; it should be done by stages instead.[66]

The decision of the central bodies clearly concerned Sinkiang, Tibet, Inner Mongolia, Kwangsi and Fukien. Indeed, it has been reported that a poster appeared quoting another directive of Mao Tse-tung's to the army which urged it to strengthen precautions against war in the provinces along the frontier with the USSR.

The army managed to achieve a balance between its internal and external commitments. But its new internal responsibility was a grave one: identifying the good revolutionaries among all those who asked for its help. This could not be done without the assistance of the Centre's intelligence services.

[66] Poster of February 15th.

4. Students and Red Guards

For several years the radical Maoist minority in the Party tried to have their ideas adopted through the ordinary methods of discussion, persuasion and example. But when their enemies seemed to have gained the upper hand organizationally they decided to move on to a new kind of action. Their tactics, which had to fit Mao Tse-tung's ideas, were to appeal to the masses by exposing scandals that would shock them into joining forces with the minority to get the discredited leaders suspended from their duties. As long as the aim was only to criticize a few leaders—the proportion was arbitrarily fixed at 5 per cent for the top ranks—it did not, apparently, seem necessary to mobilize all of the masses.

The students might be enough. The workers and peasants had not been sufficiently awakened politically under the Party's rule, so that it would have taken them a very long time to get going. Their latter participation may well have been envisaged, but this involved the danger of large-scale disorders. There must certainly have been arguments for trying to interest the workers and peasants in the debate through the example of the students, who were more easily controlled.

The Maoists had also long wanted to ensure that the third generation of communists would be, and remain, 'red.' Back in 1963 one could have read in the *People's*

Daily[1] that the imperialist world had evil designs on the young people of China, and was counting on the 'peaceful transformation' of the third generation in the Communist world. Mao Tse-tung took the matter to heart. This is confirmed in some lines that Robert Guillain wrote in 1964:

> It has been revealed . . . that Mao Tse-tung, who has not published any major political writings for a long time, has recently presented a very important document to the Central Committee: a plan for the youth of China. It has not yet been issued, but, as is the usual practice, some preliminary summaries have been released. In it the Chairman analyses the nature and the role of young people, lays down the methods by which they are to be won over to socialism, and gives detailed instructions on how they must be better trained for revolutionary struggle.
>
> The most astounding statement is that these directives of Mao Tse-tung's must be taken as applying not only to the coming generation but also to all those that will follow—five, six or even more, according to the Central Committee of the Youth League. This is how long the period of transition to Communism will take, Mao has stated.[2]

As it turned out in 1965–66, the Communist Youth League did not live up to the hope placed in it. It was, in particular, short of recruits. It is easy to think in retrospect that mobilizing the students to criticize the 'authorities' in the Party was killing two birds with one stone: bringing about mass activity, and giving the youth an educational shock. The students were given a vacation and thrown into politics. A revolution in miniature could be attempted by limiting the revolutionary masses to the students, and restricting their targets to 5 per cent of the Party's leading cadres.

But could it have been successful in stopping there, and

[1] May 4, 1963.
[2] 'Year XV of New China,' *Le Monde*, Paris, 1964, pp. 45–46.

thus keeping within limits the disorder resulting from the operation? The students were asked to express their feelings, in the first place about the university authorities who seemed to deserve criticism. During this phase student action went far beyond what had been hoped for from it, thanks to the mistakes made by the Work Teams sent by the Party to take over the Cultural Revolution in educational establishments. The students were then asked to criticize erring Party leaders outside their schools.

From the end of the Eleventh Plenum onwards, all the students took to the streets. The Red Guards were those of them who had already become organized. They hoped to play an organized political role, and saw themselves as auxiliaries to the Party or the army. But it was the *whole* student body that was called upon to arouse the masses of the people.

The organizations that were, strictly speaking, Red Guard ones, were generally very small and they varied greatly. Some were fervent enthusiasts for the ideal of free thought, while others faithfully tried to fulfil the tasks assigned to them within the Party. All factions always laid claim to the Thought of Mao Tse-tung, and Maoism was as much the banner of anti-progressive organizations as of the progressives themselves. But the revolution could not be restricted to the scale of a revolution in miniature, both because of what happened in the provinces—a phenomenon analogous to the one we have observed in the army—and because some radicals had aims more ambitious than a simple struggle among the authorities, even one resulting in a different majority within the Party.

As with many other prolonged revolutions, this one progressed by sudden leaps. The students, who had been the first to be committed to the fray, found themselves leading a movement that was changing without them realizing it. People quite at home in one phase found themselves left behind suddenly and without warning. New splits between groups were caused as the movement developed. At the outset student activists encountered the hostility of the workers and peasants. In September there was clear evidence of friction between them.

The students had long been politicized, but the leaders of the Cultural Revolution were divided over how to form the students into a political force, and thus found it hard to group them into cohesive units. The term 'Red Guards' is generally understood to refer primarily to a small number of front-line groups more militant than the rest. Yet the students had to show the way in a mass support of renovation of the Party, and had to start by establishing for themselves provisional revolutionary institutions in their universities.

Some features marked the students off from the workers and peasants. They did not have a clear-cut class origin, and often argued about how much importance to attach to their comrades' social backgrounds. They were aware of the drawbacks of their intellectual origins, and many of them, conscious of the petty bourgeois tendencies that were particularly strong among them, wanted the student Cultural Revolution teams completely integrated with the workers and peasants in production units. The leaders of the Cultural Revolution did not allow this, probably because the workers and peasants felt reservations about students.

The Cultural Revolution as we know it remained an urban phenomenon. It was in the cities that the students felt free to take revolutionary action, and where their intellectual character led them to discuss finer points of theory. And the petty bourgeois tendency encouraged an extreme left approach that was later to cause some problems.

The first political awakening

We have seen how, in 1964, Mao Tse-tung presented a paper on the training of the young to the Central Committee. His rivals in the Party machine could not let him monopolize this subject. On August 19, 1965, the paper *Kuangming Jihpao*[3] revealed that Chairman Mao and Chairman Liu had both issued important directives on

[3] The daily paper for cultural circles.

education in 1964. It is not known exactly what Liu Shao-ch'i's directives contained, unless they envisaged a double reform: first, in full-time schools where manual labour was to be included in the curriculum, and, second, in the schools where study and productive work were mixed.[4]

The leaders in Peking took some liberties with the Thought of Mao Tse-tung. Commenting on the subject of education, the Peking municipal Party review wrote:

> In normal conditions there should be more teaching than political activity. In full-time schools the teachers should spend the hours for study teaching. Comrade Mao Tse-Tung said in 1950 that schools of the old type should be changed, but not in too much of a hurry, without violence or haste.[5]

The schools adopted less rigorous time-tables. There were more extra-curricular activities, more time to spend in the library, more leisure. The student's burden was lightened. P'eng Chen's popularity in Peking was not probably in much need of a boost, but the Communist Youth League should not have neglected its own. Indeed, reports had for some time been stressing that there was a recruitment crisis.

In an organization where the members' ages were between fifteen and twenty-five 'few are under twenty and few are girls.'[6] 'Village membership makes up only 13 per cent; 10 per cent of production brigades do not have a single member and another 30 per cent have only one or two.'[7] 'If an appropriate number of new members is not brought into the League every year,' the same article continued, 'there can be only three possible consequences: as the number of new members become fewer

---

[4] See Chou En-lai's report to the National People's Congress, *People's Daily*, December 31, 1964.

[5] *Ch'ien Hsien*, Peking, 1965, no. 8. Reprinted in *Kuangming Jihpao*, May 10, 1965.

[6] *China Youth* (fortnightly), 1964, no. 14, p. 24.

[7] *China Youth News*, April 2, 1964, editorial.

than that of the leavers, the League will diminish and its
organization will be weakened; if there are many over-age
members the League will no longer be a youth organization; and it may happen that in a factory, a commune,
a *hsien*, or even in a larger area, members above the
upper age limit will form the majority.' The League was
one of the first to suffer as a result of the inauguration of
the Cultural Revolution. In fact it is significant that the
fortnightly magazine *China Youth* announced a series of
articles on the constitution of the League, starting in August 1965, that was to run to eleven pieces but was cut
short in November—about the time that the Party was
divided into two.

Although there was a difference in spirit between Chairman Mao's directives on youth and Chairman Liu's on
education, a movement to give students a bigger part in
social life and more means of self-expression had been
born. Preparations for national defence contributed to
this with militia training; and in addition students in the
big cities were urged to go among the peasants to join
in the Socialist Education Movement. Some of them were
sent to the villages from 1964 onwards to take part in
the 'Four Clean-ups.'

If this campaign was run in many places as an operation
to strengthen the Party, the students seconded to it must
have felt that they were being treated as future cadres.
The Party machine thus won new adherents. All the third
and fourth year students in universities and other institutions of higher education in Peking and several other cities
were mobilized for the movement in September 1965 and
sent to the countryside, to be followed in November by
the fifth-year students. Revolutionary students were later
to accuse the university authorities of having wanted to
get rid of the most awkward of them in this way. They
reckoned that there was more scope for political activity
in their universities than in the villages to which they had
been sent. But for many young city-dwellers this first contact with political reality, even though it took place under
Party control, was a spur to action.

Educational establishments were already excited by discussions on the value of doctrinaire teaching, student participation in work, the use of free time, involvement in the League or in better forms of political activity, and on the student role in politics, especially in the Socialist Education Movement. At this point the news of the Party's May meeting and of the circular of May 16, 1966, reached the universities. The order was given to 'criticize thoroughly all bourgeois reactionary ideas in academic circles . . . and to this end criticize at the same time all the representatives of the bourgeoisie who have infiltrated the Party, the government, the army and the cultural world.'

Seven members of the Peita philosophy department launched an attack on May 25th against the university's first Party secretary and chancellor, Lu P'ing, and a deputy, P'eng P'ei-yun. They displayed on the walls of their university the first poster of criticism in large characters (*tatzupao*) of the Cultural Revolution, signed with their seven names.[8] When the national leaders and the press called them the 'initiators' of the Cultural Revolution they became famous. At their head was Nieh Yuan-tzu. She was a lecturer in the philosophy department and the departmental Party secretary. After a short struggle in the university their *tatzupao* was broadcast on June 1st—on Mao Tse-tung's personal decision, as was later learned[9]— and held up to the whole country as an example to follow.[10]

The victory of the revolutionary staff and students of Peita was approved by the new Peking Municipal Party Committee, in which Li Hsüeh-feng replaced P'eng Chen. The first decisions of the new committee were to dismiss Lu P'ing and P'eng P'ei-yun, to reorganize the university's Party committee, and send in a Work Team.

In other universities in Peking and elsewhere student demonstrations followed the example of Peita. Other

---

[8] The public was told officially of this in the *People's Daily* of June 2, 1966.

[9] Joint editorial of *Red Flag* and the *People's Daily*, January 1, 1967. See *Peking Review*, no. 1, 1967.

[10] *People's Daily*, June 2, 1966, 'Let us acclaim Peking University's capital-letter newspaper.'

Work Teams were despatched. 'Even before June 1st the teachers and students at Nanking University responded to the call of the Centre and Chairman Mao, and threw themselves into the struggle for the great Cultural Revolution,' wrote the *China Youth News* on June 16th. Nanking's first *tatzupao* was posted on June 2nd.[11] A Work Team was forced on Sian's Chiaot'ung Tahsieh—Chiaota—on June 3rd.[12]

The Party had been familiar with the tactical device of Work Teams since the Socialist Education Movement, and long before. Teams made up of trusted cadres were sent into 'units' where they had to carry out investigations, identify the faults, make changes, or suggest punishments. The favourite method of the Work Teams was an investigation behind closed doors and a secret report. They were not popular. Moreover they did not rely much on the masses as their composition was decided upon from above.

Work Teams as such were not always regarded by Maoists as fundamentally bad. It was the Teams' actions in the schools that pushed the radicals to revolt, and constituted the worst of the offences for which Liu Shao-ch'i was condemned. Liu, as the man in control of the organs of the Centre in Peking, was the man chiefly responsible for the Work Teams.

There were Teams in universities, schools, offices, such public services as banks and newspapers, and even several ministries. Forced to work fast in a political situation they little understood, and told to carry out purges in the name of the Cultural Revolution to which the Party machine gave them no clues, they regarded their job as a 'clean-up.' Instead of getting close to the students, listening to what they had to say, or encouraging them to talk, they stood on

[11] An attack on K'uang Ya-ming, First Secretary and Chancellor of Nanking University, by the students of the secondary school attached to the university. K'uang Ya-ming was accused afterwards of having called 'reactionaries' those who took the side of the *PLA Daily* in the quarrel of the Centres. See *People's Daily*, June 16, 1966.

[12] The University of Transport and Communications, the main centre of student disturbance in Shensi.

their dignity and kept away from them, apart from holding a few public trials.

The journal *Red Flag* later published a study of the activities of the Work Team sent to Tsinghua University on June 9th. It concluded that the team had treated teachers and school Party cadres as 'deep-dyed villains' when there was virtually nothing to reproach them with, and that only a small handful of them had been defended.[13] The students for their part were disconcerted, particularly those of Peita, where the intimidatory sanctions demanded by the Work Team stunned everyone. It was later reported that the team had tried to find who had been responsible for laboratory accidents that had occurred long before the Cultural Revolution, and have them condemned to death.

The cadres of the youth organizations and the class monitors could not understand what was happening at first and held back, while the progressive students raised their voices to say that the movement was being put into reverse. By denouncing the Work Teams for misusing their authority they made themselves its next targets. Everyone, whether young cadres or progressives, wrote posters all the time—partly according to orders; apparently everyone was required to use up a certain quantity of paper and ink every week under the strict eyes of the Work Team. When all the accessible walls in the university had been covered with *tatzupao* permission was given for them to be displayed in rooms. Sometimes posters were hung on lines that divided rooms into corridors.

Work Teams seem to have been an improvised attempt to keep the Cultural Revolution as close as possible to an academic quarrel run by cadres who could rely on the solidarity of the Party machine to prevent any disorders from weakening the Party. Even leaders who later declared their allegiance to the Cultural Revolution, such as Li Hsüeh-feng, appealed then to the full authority of the Party in an attempt to protect the Work Teams. 'To oppose the Work Teams is to oppose the Centre,' he said

[13] Quoted in *Mōtakutō no Chōsen*, p. 34.

on June 26th.[14] It must be pointed out that at this point
Mao Tse-tung had not yet returned to Peking, where only
one of the Party's two Centres was to be found, and hardly
anyone had any confidence in the other one. Rare indeed were the local leaders who could have realized that
they would have to cross the Rubicon and use the mass
of the students.

However, the progressive students, baulked in their
enthusiastic attempts to apply the May 16th Circular—
in Sian, for example, they were not allowed to post notices or cartoons in the street, or to stage marches in the
town; they had to confine themselves to criticizing the
'Three-Family Village'[15]—now began to discuss the need
for reform in education.

Some groups[16] wrote to the Central Committee and
Chairman Mao condemning all the old rules and sending
in their schemes for reform over the heads of the Work
Teams.[17] One of the most famous of these was the letter
from seven students at the People's University, Jenta, insisting that henceforward the universities should recruit
their students from secondary school pupils who had proved
themselves in the Cultural Revolution.[18] There were not

[14] This error was explicitly denounced in the 'Sixteen-Point
Directive of the Eleventh Plenum' of August 8th: 'Some of
the persons in charge . . . have even advanced such slogans
as: Opposition to the leaders of a unit or work team means
opposition to the Central Committee of the Party, which means
opposition to the Party and socialism, which means counter-
revolution. . . . This is an error in orientation, an error of
line.' Li Hsüeh-feng was not, however, named.

[15] Directive by Huo Shih-lien, CCP, First Secretary for Shensi
Province, June 4, 1966, cited by Andrew Watson, *Far Eastern
Economic Review*, April 20, 1967.

[16] E.g. No. 21 Girls Middle School, Peking, and No. 4
Middle School, Peking. See *Peking Review*, no. 26, June 24,
1966, p. 4.

[17] 'Decision on improving the standard of teaching in secondary and primary schools' prepared under P'eng Chen in
1954. See *Peiching Jihpao*, April 24, 1967, article by the Chingkangshan group of Peking Higher Education College.

[18] *People's Daily*, June 12, 1966. The scheme put forward
in this letter also wanted courses in the humanities reduced to

yet, however, Red Guard organizations in the schools and universities; or rather there were none that could yet be seen from the outside.

The first time that the signature of the Red Guards appeared at the bottom of a document was in an open letter from a group of pupils at the middle school attached to Tsinghua University.[19] This document is dated two days after Mao Tse-tung's return to Peking[20] but fifteen days before the period when there was an exaggerated tendency to see a 'spontaneous emergence of Red Guards.'

Mao Tse-tung came back to Peking on July 18th, and that day marked a real revolt against the Work Teams. Chiang Ch'ing herself came to Peita to encourage the progressives. Students took for themselves the right of association, and the Work Teams were finally abolished on July 24th.[21]

It would have been logical for the progressive students to be the first to take advantage of the overthrow of the Work Teams and the winning of new freedoms. But in many places it was the children of top cadres who took the lead in organizations they created themselves, after actively helping the Work Teams to overthrow the academic leaders in the universities. At Tsinghua University the 'Provisional Preparatory Committee for the Tsinghua Provisional Red Guard Headquarters' was controlled by five students whose fathers were Party dignitaries, including the daughter of Liu Shao-ch'i and the son of Ho Lung. Tsinghua University, where the first Red Guards were formed by the children of top leaders, is a fascinating case of the Cultural Revolution at the end of the period of the Work Teams. Its Work Team appears to have been under the leadership of Wang Jen-chung, who stayed on as deputy

---

one, two, or three years, the general use of Mao Tse-tung's works as textbooks, more seminars, and more group discussions.

[19] *China News Analysis*, Hong Kong, no. 634, October 28, 1966, p. 5.

[20] See the article by the 'Group of Eleven' from the Chingkangshan organization at Tsinghua University, in *China Reconstructs*, 1968, no. 7.

[21] See Liu Shao-ch'i's first self-criticism.

head of the Central Committee's Cultural Revolution Group for some time, and was therefore presumably orthodox, whereas Liu Shao-ch'i and his wife Wang Kuang-mei offered their services voluntarily as advisers to the Work Team. The following children of top leaders were included: Liu T'ao, daughter of Liu Shao-ch'i and a student in the department of automation, who was in charge of the provisional presidium of the 'Provisional Preparatory Committee'; Ho P'eng-fei, son of Ho Lung and a student of industrial mechanization, a member of the provisional presidium of the 'Provisional Preparatory Committee' in charge of the 'Tsinghua Provisional Red Guard Headquarters';[22] Li Li-feng, son of Li Ching-ch'üan (First Secretary of the CCP Central Committee South Western Bureau) and student of engineering physics, was Ho P'eng-fei's deputy in the 'Three provisionals'; Liu Chü-fen, son of Liu Ning-yi (Secretary of the Central Committee's Secretariat) and student of automation, 'Commander-in-Chief of the Tsinghua Red Guards.' Wang Hsia-hu, son of Wang Jen-chung (who in addition to the position mentioned above was secretary of the Central Committee's Central-South Bureau) and student of electronics, was an official of the Tsinghua's 'Provisional Red Guard Headquarters' and founder of the 'Red Flag Red Guards.'[23] For a short time it was they who led and organized their fellow students.

K'uai Ta-fu, later to be Tsinghua's most famous Red Guard, appeared more as a lone protester than as an organizer. He was tireless in his attempts to raise opposition against the Work Team; he provoked it by holding forbidden discussions; he made himself famous by his letters—copies of which were circulated among the students—to the chancellor, Yeh Lin; he was imprisoned in the university, and went on hunger strike. Later, at the beginning of August, he wrote a self-criticism in which he acknowl-

[22] These three organizations were known as the 'Three provisionals.'

[23] See the article by Nogami in the *Asahi Shimbun*, December 10, 1967, morning edition.

edged that instead of uniting the greatest possible number of people he had conspired with a few individuals who shared his ideas.

When the high officials' children created the university's Preparatory Committee and Red Guards, K'uai Ta-fu led stronger attacks on them. He cast doubt on whether the Preparatory Committee was representative. He demanded elections without further delay, and insisted that the student masses should be consulted so that they could produce their own leaders.[24]

K'uai Ta-fu was a political thinker, and the distribution of his writings, together with those of several others whose positions were much the same, contributed towards the political awakening of the other students.[25] The children of high officials were acting like their fathers, creating hierarchical structures among the students so as to lead them towards predetermined solutions. Whether they realized it or not, they were working for their fathers.

The Preparatory Committee, discredited in the eyes of the majority because its origins were too closely linked with the Work Team, did not last long. Its members, and the children of other leaders, left to swell the ranks of other organizations more like the other small groups blossoming everywhere at the time. Many of these called themselves Red Guard Pickets,[26] and one of these, the West City Patrol, presented one of their armbands to Mao Tse-tung on August 31st.

When these students, who regarded themselves as makers of the Cultural Revolution, saw their fathers being criticized as exponents of the 'bourgeois line,' they had doubts about the Central Committee's Cultural Revolution Group. Some of them joined the Joint Action Committee (regarded as a reactionary body, of which more below), and

[24] K'uai Ta-fu: 'Eight Problems that Must Now Be Solved,' August 4, 1966.
[25] T'an Li-fu, later the first to be accused of Trotskyism and prosecuted for it, also seems to have been the son of a high cadre. Quotations of his writings sold by the thousands. See Nogami, *op. cit.*
[26] Chiu-ch'a-tui.

were arrested at the beginning of 1967. The first Red Guards were not to remain with the revolutionaries for long.

The purpose of the Red Guards

The withdrawal of the Work Teams was the occasion for public rejoicing which permitted the sponsors of the Cultural Revolution to seize the initiative and mobilize the great mass of the students. The first mass meetings were held in the universities, notably at Peita, on July 25th and 26th, where Ch'en Po-ta himself (the head of the Central Committee's Cultural Revolution Group) came to address the students.[27] Then the students were urged to show their strength in the city. Despite these efforts the two tendencies in the Party ended by making the great demonstration held on July 30th ambiguous: the radicals were celebrating the end of the Work Teams, Mao Tse-tung's return to Peking, and the triumph of the mass line;[28] while the Party machine had invited people to take part in a demonstration against the American imperialist bombing of the cities of North Vietnam. It brought peasant delegations into towns, and these were interspersed among the students. Then the Eleventh Plenary Session of the Central Committee was held.

On August 10th Mao Tse-tung went down into the crowd. Contrary to usual practice, he did not warn the Party's secretariat, the propaganda organs, or even the press. His appearance unleashed a storm of enthusiasm, and his presence in the Chungnanhai[29] was celebrated by an unending flood of demonstrators pouring night and day against the outer walls, their joy giving birth to unity.

[27] See *Chūgoku Bunka Daikakumei wo dō miru ka*, p. 214.
[28] *Red Flag* editorial, July 3, 1966: 'Trust the Masses, Rely on the Masses.'
[29] In some ways equivalent to the Kremlin. The offices of the Central Committee and the homes of Party and State leaders are concentrated in a compound beside the Central and Southern Seas (Chunghai and Nanhai), two of the lakes in the western part of the Forbidden City.

The students established themselves inside the city, and their delegations took part in the huge carnival together with everyone else. The Chairman's triumphant return was celebrated amid an endless din of drums and gongs. On August 18th an enormous rally of youngsters was held in T'ienanmen, in the course of which Mao Tse-tung introduced the Red Guards to the world.

The mission these latter were to give themselves was drawn from a slogan put forward by the *People's Daily* ten weeks earlier. Direction through the organs of the press follows a slow and somewhat closed-off progress, particularly when it is the masses who have to be reached. Abstract texts need to be closely examined, and passages giving instructions for action have to be interpreted to the masses by people familiar with the conventions of the procedure. On June 7th the *PLA Daily* had written that 'the essential task of the Cultural Revolution' would be 'to destroy utterly old thinking, culture, customs and ways of life.'[30] Thus it was that the students took it upon themselves to destroy what were often described as the 'Four Olds.'

The Sixteen-Point Decision adopted by the Central Committee on August 8th created an essential safeguard against the movement degenerating into a conflict whose outcome would be unpredictable: it gave the students protection from persecution by the Party machine, and from reprisals when they took the revolution into the streets. According to the seventh point:

> With the exception of cases of active counter-revolutionaries where there is clear evidence of crimes . . . no measures should be taken against students at universities, colleges, middle schools and primary schools because of problems that arise in the movement. To prevent the struggle from being diverted from its main target it is not allowed under any pretext whatever to incite the masses or the students to struggle against each

[30] 'Mao Tse-tung's Thought is the Telescope and Microscope of our Revolutionary Cause,' *PLA Daily* editorial, June 7, 1966. See *The Great Socialist Cultural Revolution in China* (3), Foreign Languages Press, Peking, 1966.

other. Even proven Rightists should be dealt with on the merits of each case at a later stage of the movement.

It was with the ground thus prepared that the first groups of activists moved into the streets of Peking, changing street names, burning old books, and smashing any words in shop signs that evoked the old society.

During the next few days radio and telephone spread the movement to the provinces. The city of Shenyang (formerly Mukden) had its name changed—on the railway station's nameboard, at least—because when written with the abbreviated character for the first syllable it could mean 'Set Sun,' an intolerable expression when Mao Tsetung was the 'sun that never sets.' The Red Guards changed the city's name to Hungyang, which meant 'Red Sun.'[31] The *People's Daily* however, kept to Shenyang throughout.

The students showed hostility in the streets to anyone wearing 'calf style' trousers—narrow and tight in the leg— or 'aeroplane' hairstyles—carefully flattened down—or 'winkle-picker' shoes, or anything else reminiscent of the 'Hongkong style.' They desecrated temples, harassed nuns —the foreign ones left Peking—and in the cemeteries they broke open the tombs of past reactionaries, including those of foreigners. The works of dead writers and artists, such as the painter Ch'i Pai-shih, were attacked. Many of the living who were still attached to family mementoes or a western way of life were persecuted, and some disappeared. Many of the objects confiscated were put on show at the Red Guard Exhibition[32] which some privileged foreigners visited in August 1967. Beside cases showing the texts that caused the split in the Party and the originals of the first documents of the Revolution, Sakagaki relates that 268 pistols were displayed, as well as 100,000 gold bars, 120,000 silver coins, Kuomintang flags and uniforms, and innumerable account books and other relics of former properties that ex-landlords were suspected of hiding to use someday as evidence of ownership.[33]

[31] See Konno, *Pekin Kono Ichinen,* p. 41.
[32] In the Peking Exhibition Centre to the west of the city.
[33] *Ajia Keizai Jumpo,* no. 696, September 1967, p. 4 ff.

As some activities degenerated into violence or banditry, Red Guard organizations made rules for themselves and posted them throughout the city. The most noticeable features of these were orders about good behaviour and warnings against false rumours. News was beginning to circulate more freely in China, though not without the exaggerations inevitable when it is spread by word of mouth. Beside posters containing criticisms were wall newspapers with news from the provinces and reports of dramatic events, telling how young revolutionaries had been killed by reactionary groups or even by the security forces. The spread of such news alarmed the population.

As for the information that the Red Guards themselves needed for organizing their operations in attack or defence, this was generally distributed in leaflets, which enabled them to concentrate their members rapidly when they were scattered throughout the city, but carried the risk of setting off a panic. The authors of the rules wanted to combat this and help establish some minimal organization. But beyond this basic moral code and loyalty to the Thought of Chairman Mao, the Red Guard rules were vague about the role of their organizations.

Should they be political bodies? What limits should be put on their activities? The national leaders themselves, who were somewhat taken by surprise by the new situation, gave rather differing interpretations when speaking to the Red Guards in public.[34] They seemed to be improvising. A little later Chou En-lai referred to Red Guards as being essentially organizations of criticism.

It would have been unwise to give them a political role in view of the chaotic mixture of tendencies represented in the organization.

In the political sphere we must regroup our forces. At present they consist of different sects. . . . Some es-

[34] Speech of December 9, 1966, in the Chungnanhai Small Hall to three organizations (Aviation Institute Hungch'i, Tungfang Commune of the Geological Institute, and Chengfa Commune of the Political Science Institute). As organs of criticism Chou En-lai allowed them to receive the special newspapers for cadres.

tablishments have been deeply affected by the suppression of the Work Teams. . . . We must give them the
chance to recuperate and wake up.[35]

A Central Committee directive laid down the form this
critical role was to take. It amounted to that of an inter-
mediary:

> Proposals on the abolition of old customs, old culture,
> old ways of life and old ideas shall not be examined and
> settled by the Red Guard units, but shall be passed on to
> the Poor and Lower-Middle Peasants Association of the
> commune (or, later, that of the *hsien* if the proposals
> are important enough), to examine what benefits they
> would bring and take a decision on them.[36]

But this was not enough to explain what strategic intention
underlay the decision to involve the whole mass of the
students in criticism of the authorities, even if Red Guard
activities did provide an opportunity for giving life to the
peasant associations. According to a study published in
1968 by the *Asahi,* Mao Tse-tung said in his closing speech
to the Eleventh Plenum that the Party's Ninth Congress
would doubtless be held at a suitable moment in the coming year. 'But I would like preparations for it to be referred
to the Political Bureau elected at the Eleventh Plenum,'
he added.[37]

Mao Tse-tung thus had the next Party congress in mind
when he mobilized the students. The point of entrusting
the student masses with making criticisms must have
been to have enough Party members suspended or expelled
to leave his supporters in the majority once more. Lacking
experience and a real social role, the students could not
play a big part in politics, as Chang Ch'un-ch'iao was

[35] *Ibid.*

[36] Central Committee Directive on the Development of the
Great Proletarian Cultural Revolution in Territorial Units Below *Hsien* level, September 14, 1966. As published in notices
posted by the Tientsin Municipal Committee on September 22,
1966.

[37] *Asahi Jyanaru,* 1968, no. 18, 'Wakagaetta tōsōshiki no taishitsu,' p. 21.

already reminding them on August 27th: 'It is very easy
to dismiss people, but then you will no longer have any
opposition.'[38] In other words, they were carrying out a
flanking movement but leaving the Party as it was, whereas
a real political reconstruction of society would need all
the elements in it.

In their struggle against the 'Four Olds' the students
had hitherto played their critical role within the ranks of
the people. It was after the National Festival of October
1st, traditionally a time of political truce, that they began
to act on the assignment they had been given to make the
heads of Party committees their targets.[39] There was an
inevitable hardening as a result, and this was called 'rebellion' on the strength of a single quotation from Mao Tse-
tung that the students preferred above all others: 'In the
last analysis all the truths of Marxism can be summed up
in one sentence: "To rebel is justified." '[40]

The rebel students were to meet with two kinds of resistance: hostile inertia in many units,[41] and the reaction of
the 'authorities.'

Student privilege

As we have seen above, the Sixteen-Point Decision protected the students from reprisals. But there was no way
of anticipating how things would develop once the students left their own world to carry the revolution into the
heart of the political administration, and then among the

[38] In a speech to Peking and Tientsin Red Guards. Leaflet
of September 2, 1966.

[39] The directive in accordance with which the students extended their criticisms to the people in power within the Party
was given by Lin Piao at a rally on August 31st, but it was
only after October 1st that student meetings decided to take
action.

[40] From a speech by Mao Tse-tung at a Yenan rally to
celebrate Stalin's birthday in 1939.

[41] 'Trying to spare one's own unit from the struggle between
the bourgeois and the proletarian roads will not be tolerated,'
said a call from the Rebel High Command of the Capital's
Revolutionary Red Guards on November 9, 1966.

workers and peasants. Friction with the two latter groups
had been prevalent since September. The leadership of
the Cultural Revolution reacted fast, making all possible
efforts to prevent any overlapping between the movement
among the students and that in the factories and the villages. Mao Tse-tung brought the matter to the attention
of the Central Committee's Cultural Revolution Group:

> Please consider this case. The situation is the same at
> Tsingtao, Sian, Changsha and elsewhere. Organizations
> of workers and peasants have been formed and are op-
> posed to the students. If things continue like this, we will
> not be able to solve our problems. The Centre must is-
> sue a directive forbidding this sort of thing everywhere.
> Then an article must be written urging workers and
> peasants not to interfere in the student movement. In
> Peking there have been no cases of workers and peas-
> ants being incited to attack the students, except when
> the People's University assembled six hundred peasants
> and set them loose in the city to defend Kuo Ying-
> ch'iu.[42] We must popularize Peking's experience and
> hold it up to the provinces as an example.[43]

Four days later the Central Committee decreed that
the workers, peasants and city-dwellers would have to be
persuaded to refrain from any interference in the student
movement; that the majority of the students were sound
and would learn through experience; and that there should
be no polemics with the students. If the local people
wanted to reply to the students' ideas they should send
their comments to the Party committee.[44] Local committees everywhere had to look into and resolve disputes
that arose; this responsibility could not be passed on to the
masses. The directive added that the heads of the local
committees should not be afraid of the students but should
talk to them in accordance with the mass line.

[42] Vice-chancellor of the People's University.
[43] Instructions of September 7, 1966, by Mao Tse-tung to
Lin Piao, Chou En-lai, T'ao Chu, K'ang Shang, Ch'en Po-ta,
Wang Jen-chung, and Chiang Ch'ing. Full text in Konno, *op.
cit.*, p. 223.
[44] *Ibid.*, pp. 223–24.

As Mao Tse-tung had asked, the *People's Daily* carried an editorial on September 11th admitting that some people in positions of authority had violated the Sixteen Points. The Red Guards were told that the workers and peasants were capable of making their own revolution. Students should leave them in peace and not interfere in production. A large number of students were, however, sent to help the peasants bring in the harvest.

It thus was decided, for the time being at least, to avoid clashes between different social groups. The students alone were allowed to move outside their own socio-political environment, the universities and schools, to criticize the Party and the government. Workers and peasants could make their own Cultural Revolution on their own territory, but they were not allowed to criticize the Centre or to turn against the students. As for the army, its discipline outweighed any movement toward revolution. It should be added that despite the students' privileges, including the right to operate throughout the whole country, the revolution's leaders sought to limit their effects; and students were repulsed when they tried to interfere in local affairs in districts where they had already established themselves.

From August 1966 onwards student journeys became veritable migrations. They were of two kinds: journeys by provincial students to Peking and other big cities, involving the movement of huge numbers of them, and Red Guard missions to the provinces.

Being able to travel en masse was another student privilege. The Centre invited all the students and some of the senior middle school pupils to come to Peking,[45] and this invitation met with extraordinary enthusiasm among the student youth of the whole country. It was a key tactical decision as it was bound to spread the movement that was already well installed in Peking: in this way the plot was really going to thicken. But for the students it was primarily a new freedom, a chance to get to know their country that had been given to few of them before. The Chinese

---

[45] The invitation was made on August 31st.

enjoy travelling, but movement is controlled in China and tickets have to be paid for, so that it is mainly cadres and soldiers who have the chance to travel through their country. Now, for a while, a whole generation of young people could travel at will.

Students were allowed on trains without tickets. All they needed were authorizations issued by school authorities and approved by committees.[46] These documents were doubtless often in fact issued by revolutionary organizations, and it became impossible to bring this under control when swarms of passengers overloaded the transport system. There were incidents. Trains were taken over and diverted from their intended routes. All available old wagons, locomotives and boats were brought back to service, and passengers were given priority over freight. Railwaymen worked till they dropped. As the cold northern winter rapidly set in, two million young people, who had not yet seen Mao Tse-tung and were still waiting their turn to do so, stayed on in their rough quarters in Peking, without winter clothes and threatened by epidemics.

Others were still arriving. The flood had to be stopped. Twice in October the authorities declared that no more students should come to Peking.[47] Appeals to physical effort, recommending marches on foot in the tradition of the Long March, were not enough to make people forsake the new and delightful pleasures of travelling freely. The disruption of transport by water and rail made urgent measures of another kind necessary. The public were told that the railways would be taking no passengers for several days while they reorganized themselves. On November

[46] A Central Committee resolution confirming the invitation of August 31st stipulated that all the students of universities and institutes, and 10 per cent of the middle school pupils and administrative personnel, could come to Peking; it also stated how the public authorities were to approve the documents. This decision was made public in official posters, particularly in Shanghai, in the first days of September 1966.

[47] Immediately after the fifth and sixth Red Guard mass rallies in Peking. The authorities tried to make each time the last and send everyone home. See 'Diary of the Cultural Revolution,' *Asahi Evening News*.

16th the Central Committee and the State Council announced the suspension of journeys 'of revolutionary exchange' until the following April, and ordered everyone trying to find transport to Peking to go home.[48]

The same communiqué revealed that up to November 20th nine million students and teachers had been passengers. There were several million still making their pilgrimages who would have to be taken home if they were not going on foot. But those who found places on trains were in no hurry to return home, and they extended their journeys to visit the warmer south. On November 16th the vacations, set at six months back in July, were officially extended: with too many students still away there was no alternative. The public services, especially in Peking, surpassed themselves in resolving the incredible problems presented by moving and looking after so many people.

The licence to travel was justified by another, quite simple, one: that of seeing Mao Tse-tung in person. Thus Peking had not only to welcome and feed students but also to arrange rallies and marches and maintain public order. There were eight rallies, each with a million participants, between August 18th and November 26th.[49] Some of them lasted several days. A brief description of the conditions in which the November 3rd rally took place may give some idea of what they were like.

On the two days beforehand the Central Committee's security office and the State Council Secretariat issued a circular to notify the students visiting Peking and to give them some instructions. In the previous rallies there had been fatal crushes round the T'ienanmen Gate because, when the students reached the stand from which the Chairman could be seen, they were unwilling to move on; while the vast ranks of those following them continued forward so as to crush against them. The instructions insisted that all groups should keep on walking at a steady pace, not

[48] Text in Japanese translation in Konno, op. cit., pp. 225–26.
[49] On August 18th and 31st; September 15th; October 1st and 18th; November 3rd, 10th, 11th, 25th and 26th.

disperse after reaching the Gate, and be on their guard against sabotage and attempts to start a panic. The carrying of arms was forbidden. Two million participants were expected to pass the stand on this occasion. As many students as possible had to see Mao Tse-tung so that they could go home, leaving room in Peking for others. The proceedings also had to be kept short to 'protect the health of the executive comrades of the Central Committee' who would be on the stand.

Despite these precautions there was a standstill in front of T'ienanmen. The Chairman tirelessly urged the students over the public address system to keep moving, but they would not shift. At 5 p.m. Mao Tse-tung withdrew. Chou En-lai finally got the crowd under way again by singing one of the new songs of the Cultural Revolution, 'Sailing the Seas Depends on the Helmsman.' Then he promised all those who had not seen the Chairman—possibly the majority—that there would be another rally.

To prevent these problems recurring, the arrangements for the last rallies were changed. On November 10th and 11th the young people rolled past in trucks, an impressive demonstration of the Chinese army's transport capacity. At the other rallies the youngsters were drawn up along the sides of roads, and the leaders drove slowly past in jeeps.

While the provincial students were coming to Peking to see the cradle of the Cultural Revolution and Chairman Mao, and then returning home with the good news—besides taking in as much of China as they could on the way back—the Peking Red Guards were travelling in the opposite direction, leaving outposts to spread the revolutionary ferment everywhere. The two movements taken together made up the 'great exchange of revolutionary experience' that was to teach those who had not taken part how the people in Peking had dared to take on the leading members of the formidable Party machine. During this exchange the students passed on tactical techniques to each other.

The Red Guards who went to the provinces were far fewer in number than those who went to the capital, but they made a much more effective contribution to the revolutionary cause. However, if they had confined themselves to the mission of the Red Guard organizations—that of making criticisms—they would have had to be restricted to commissions of investigation. In fact they often put themselves at the head of local students, to whom they gave training for the movement on the spot. This led to many incidents because the local 'authorities' condemned the interference of outsiders in the Cultural Revolution and were able to draw on the instinctive hostility of provincials for troublemakers from Peking.

On September 7th Mao Tse-tung had wanted Peking to be held up to the provinces as an example. How was it that in Peking the movement to criticize the 'authorities' had not led to the 'masses being incited to struggle against each other,' whereas civil strife threatened almost everywhere in the provinces? The explanations for this must be sought in the greater belligerency of isolated Red Guards, the lack of understanding shown by those on whom the Revolution burst fully grown, and the movement's lack of preparation.

Students versus 'authorities'

In the provinces, the Party 'authorities' did not tolerate criticism from Red Guards as they had accepted the confrontation of earlier criticism movements. It may be that persistent rumours as regards Mao Tse-tung's health during 1965 and the first half of 1966 caused a gradual change in the Party cadres' attitude to power. Perhaps the majority of them were growing less and less tolerant of disputes in which anybody could have a say, and had decided that under the new leaders criticisms and purges of the Party would be made by the Party and nobody else. When Mao Tse-tung realized that the cadres were resisting criticism by the masses he was furious. 'Something unthinkable has happened,'[50] he said at the Central

[50] *Asahi Jyanaru*, 1968, vol. 10, no. 18, '*Wakagaetta tōsōshiki no taishitsu*,' p. 21.

Committee work meeting held in Peking from October 8th to 25th, and he insisted that committees at all levels from the centre down through provinces and cities to *hsien* should sincerely accept criticism from students.

Resistance to the Red Guards was also being organized among the masses. Certain Party leaders were encouraging hostile reactions among the peasants and workers, and they had no difficulty finding people willing to resist, especially among the workers who were, with the cadres, the greatest beneficiaries of the regime as their living standards had been greatly raised. Reaction took the same forms as radical activity: forming organizations and making journeys. The conservatives sent missions to Peking to lay their complaints and criticism before the Central Committee's secretariat. They established their own outposts in attempts to obstruct the work of the Red Guards. Organizations from each side conflicted in nearly all the cities. Conservatives, like radicals, got into the trains as best they could, and when they met in Peking they heaped abuse on each other. In February and March 1967 there were groups of conservatives in the main railway stations trying to persuade the revolutionaries not to go to Peking to seek the help of the Central Committee's Cultural Revolution Group.[51] Organizations on both sides tried to interest the Centre and sympathetic groups in the capital in their cases.

The Red Guards for their part came back to Peking to ask the Revolution's leaders for support against the local 'authorities' who were repressing them; the guarantee that had been given to the students by the Sixteen-Point Decision needed to be confirmed. At a meeting on October 6th, Chou En-lai promised provincial Red Guards complaining of violence against them at Kweilin, Sian, and Yangchow that their personal safety would not be threatened when they went home. The Centre would make enquiries and the responsible members of committees guilty

---

[51] See Nogami's article in *Asahi Shimbun* (morning edition), December 12, 1967.

of violence towards students would be punished, no matter how important they were.

The solution to these difficulties took the form of a revival of radical activity. Criticism was carried out with more determination than ever. Enemies were to be 'expelled and shown to the masses,' and apathy was to be vigorously opposed. Taking part in the Cultural Revolution was now a duty.[52] The attempt to separate the Red Guards from the rest of society by confining them to criticism could be kept up no longer.

From the beginning of December onwards the Red Guards started to carry out arrests. They chose figures in the former Peking Municipal Party Committee and in top positions in the Central Committee, the cultural world, and even the army who had been denounced by the revolutionary leadership. They seized them in their homes and 'showed them to the masses,' presumably freeing them again a few days later. Photographs that appeared in Red Guard papers showed some of them being roughly held by activists, a placard with their name on it hanging from their necks.[53] In between bouts of rough treatment they were urged to account for their faults. Some revolutionary publications quoted their statements.

The first posters of criticism attacking Liu Shao-ch'i and Teng Hsiao-p'ing by name date from the same period. On December 2nd the Red Guards of Tsinghua and Peita universities jointly wrote: 'we believe that Liu Shao-ch'i and Teng Hsiao-p'ing are Number One and Number Two of the authorities inside the Party taking the bourgeois road.' The leadership of the Revolution let criticism of Liu develop in December and January, though later events were to show that they were not yet authorized to overthrow them. Nevertheless, these criticisms served to bring

[52] The Peking schools where the revolutionaries had not yet made themselves felt began their Cultural Revolution at this period. Joan Robinson tells how the Rebels in the Academy of Medicine came into the majority in November, during an occupation of the institution in the course of which their light and heat were cut off (*op. cit.*, pp. 141–42).

[53] Reprinted in the Tokyo *Yomiuri Shimbun*.

the attacks on T'ao Chu[54] and his group to a conclusion, and those in charge decided to get rid of them.

It should be noted that, especially at this time, criticism was widely extended, and in time it took in practically all of the leaders. Konno reports that around November 20th Ch'en Po-ta and Ch'i Pen-yü, established leaders of the Cultural Revolution, were being attacked in the same way as T'ao Chu, Wang Jen-chung and Chang P'ing-hua.[55] The notices attacking Ch'i Pen-yü were quickly covered over, and Ch'en Po-ta made a brief self-criticism on the matter that was being held against him. Criticisms only continued to be made against the other three. This suggests that criticisms were not controlled in any full sense of the word, but that the Cultural Revolution leadership discriminated by discouraging some attacks while letting others develop. But the initiative always came from the students, whose investigations probed into recent events, giving free play to their imagination. These were then sifted in terms of the tactical policy of the Revolution.

The Tsinghua students once again played an important part in the T'ao Chu affair. Within a fortnight they launched five sensational criticisms. They published Liu Shao-ch'i's first self-criticism[56] and a list of his 'crimes.' On January 6th they posted a kind of diagram giving their view of how the power structure worked. At the top was the Central Committee's Cultural Revolution Group, with

[54] First secretary of the Central Committee's Central-South Bureau, made director of the Central Committee's propaganda department in July 1966, and adviser to the Centre's Cultural Revolution Group. Rose to fourth place in the order of precedence.

[55] Wang Jen-chung, previously first Party secretary for Hupei, and Chang P'ing-hua, previously Hunan's first secretary, were with T'ao Chu both members of the Central Committee's Cultural Revolution Group. Wang Jen-chung had been the man behind the work teams at Tsinghua; hence the special investigations on him by the Tsinghua students that led on to T'ao Chu. From mid-November onwards these two men were out of Peking, leading the Cultural Revolution in their own provinces, probably in isolation.

[56] At the Central Committee work meeting of October 8–25, 1966.

the following comment beside it: 'T'ao Chu, Wang Jen-chung and Chang P'ing-hua have stirred up a second group of the Cultural Revolution.'[57]

T'ao Chu, the strong man of South China, had joined the Group in July when he became the Central Committee's head of Propaganda, and brought two of his chief lieutenants with him. The kind of provincial viceregal power from which he continued to draw his political strength was against the spirit of the revolutionary leadership. The leaders of the Cultural Revolution were ruling on his case at the very moment when the students were unleashing their critical assault.[58] The city of Peking reacted as if subversion of the Cultural Revolution Group had threatened the Centre: its walls were covered with notices proclaiming, 'Defend the Central Committee's Cultural Revolution Group.'

It should be remembered that all this was happening only a few days after the transformation of the army's own Cultural Revolution Group. This was the time when the revolutionary leaders were setting up a unified command.[59] Mao Tse-tung said later that T'ao Chu was no longer trustworthy.

Liu Shao-ch'i made his self-criticism (the publication of which was one of the most dramatic events of the period) to the Central Committee, whose principal charges against him related to the Work Team policy. This self-criticism was said to have been found wanting. To be more precise, it was not thought enough for Liu to be the only one to admit his faults. Otherwise Liu Shao-ch'i alone, instead of the whole Party, would have been in need of rectification.[60] Liu's self-criticism was firm in tone and discreet on the role played by other comrades, whether rivals or

[57] Konno, *op. cit.,* p. 73.

[58] See the report in *Shoutu Hungweiping,* January 6th, p. 167, on a meeting of January 5th at which Ch'en Po-ta and Chiang Ch'ing criticized T'ao Chu.

[59] See Chapter 3 on the army.

[60] Mao Tse-tung introduced the self-criticism with the words: 'It is not the responsibility of Liu alone, but of the Central Committee.' Quoted in *Asahi Jyanaru,* 1967, vol. 9, no. 37, p. 22.

friends. The dominant impression it leaves is that Liu Shao-ch'i was trying to preserve the images of the government and the Party.

Mao Tse-tung and Liu Shao-ch'i respected forms. The campaign launched by the Red Guards in December and January naturally reduced a little further Liu Shao-ch'i's standing in the eyes of the public, but it was only carried to the limit against the T'ao Chu group. It almost seemed that Liu Shao-ch'i only shared T'ao's disgrace inasmuch as he had shown T'ao too much favour.[61] When the Red Guards invaded Chungnanhai on January 26th, harassing Liu and his wife, their action was disowned.[62]

Liu Shao-ch'i was protected from the danger of being 'expelled and shown to the masses.' The big critical attacks on him were always led by leftists trying to inject more passion into the Cultural Revolution and take it to extremes. The insults to which his wife Wang Kuang-mei was subjected when she was tricked into leaving Chungnanhai were also the work of leftists.

The students as a political force

As we have seen, the students had taken for themselves the right of association. They also had the privilege of acting outside the confines of their own 'units.' They did

[61] 'My errors were discussed at the end of the Eleventh Plenum,' said Liu Shao-ch'i in his self-criticism. 'The Standing Committee of the Political Bureau was elected, and I joined with the rest in designating Lin Piao as Mao Tse-tung's first assistant and his successor.' See Konno, *op. cit.*, p. 82.

[62] On January 8th Chou En-lai said that it was correct to demand that the Liu-Teng line be reversed, but as they were still members of the Political Bureau's Standing Committee it would be wrong to expel them. ('The Diary of the Cultural Revolution,' p. 30.) In fact the revolutionary organizations of the service bodies inside Chungnanhai seem to have conspired to defy the leaders. 'The revolutionary masses of Chungnanhai struggled twice against Liu Shao-ch'i and Wang Kuang-mei in the Huanjen Hall, and once against Teng Hsiao-p'ing,' wrote a small paper produced by Red Guards from Pengpu on March 27, 1967. 'The Chungnanhai rebel revolutionary group is now compelling Liu, Teng, T'ao, and the others to go out from 9 to 10 o'clock to read *tatzupao*.'

not, however, create large and powerful organizations on the scale of the principal areas of the country, let alone the whole country;[63] they formed many little groups that resisted integration. As Ch'en Po-ta said, 'Anarchism and individualism are serious problems among secondary school students. In some schools there is a party or organization for every one, two or three people.'[64] According to Ch'en Yi:

> The Foreign Languages Institute is divided into two sections. Originally twenty-one units were formed. A week later there were over fifty, and a week after that more than seventy. Seventy units for under four thousand students. In other words, over seventy schools of thought. How spectacular! How impressive! This truly is 'a hundred flowers blooming while a hundred schools of thought contend.'[65]

The leaders went into the causes of the tendency to fragmentation. Chou En-lai suggested that the divisions among the students were in large part the result of quarrels over the Work Teams. Indeed, the successive changes in revolutionary policy—Work Teams, provisional committees, Red Guards, rebellion—must have deepened the differences between them, just as the changing policies on the Cultural Revolution threatened the army's unity.

The first combination of Red Guard organizations were the federations calling themselves 'headquarters,' which were centralized liaison bodies. In Peking there were known to be three of these, and provincial Red Guards who had declared their allegiance to the Central Committee Cultural Revolution Group rallied to them. In some places, however, particularly Shanghai, local groups had their own ideas and decided to be independent.

[63] The Third Red Guard Headquarters—on which see below —was not an association in the strict sense of the word but a liaison and communication network.

[64] Communication from Ch'en Po-ta to the middle school attached to the Further Education College, February 6, 1967. Quoted in *T'iyü Chanhsien* (Red Guard paper) February 25, 1967.

[65] Quoted in *Hungwei Chanpao*, April 8, 1967.

The First and Second Headquarters were not well-known, at least among the students. They may have been groupings of moderates; but in the provinces the name of the Second Headquarters was used to rally revolutionary workers. The Third Headquarters, on the other hand, was very active. It was the dominant influence in the student movement, and drew great benefit from the support of key political figures. Among the groups affiliated to it were several that were still making themselves felt: the 'Ching-kangshan Combat Group' of Tsinghua University, is already familiar; the 'New Peita Commune' at Peking University, founded by Nieh Yuan-tzu, a popular leader since the posting of the first *tatzupao;* and the 'Red Flag Combat Brigade' of the Aeronautical Institution,[66] in whose ranks Lin Tou-tou, Lin Piao's daughter, was active.

Besides these famous names the Third Headquarters also included groups that were perhaps even more significant—the Red Guards of the Central Drama Academy[67] and the Peking Film School. These were student organizations directly influenced by Chiang Ch'ing, Mao Tse-tung's wife, who had been concentrating on political work in theatrical circles.

It is almost certain that the Third Red Guard Headquarters took on the task of passing on the authentic instructions of the Central Committee's Cultural Revolution Group to the students. The missions it sent out to the provinces were more than mere outposts. They were nuclei round which local student groupings formed, often calling themselves the local Third Red Guard Headquarters.[68] Lines of communication with the Third Headquarters in

[66] This was the organization that put up posters of T'ao Chu's speech criticizing Liu Shao-ch'i.

[67] They captured P'eng Chen on December 4th. For the events leading up to this see *Asahi Shimbun,* December 29, 1966.

[68] The March 1968 issue of *Jimmin Chūgoku* (a Japanese-language monthly published by the FLP, Peking) was on Inner Mongolia. In it some Huhehot revolutionaries told how they launched a general offensive against the Work Teams and formed a Huhehot Third Headquarters after Lin Piao's speech on October 1, 1966, and the editorial in *Red Flag,* no. 13, 1966.

Peking were set up, which gave the leaders of the Revolution the advantage of an information service as quick as the government's. Although most of the local groups that joined up with the Third Headquarters were weak and isolated, they still felt that they had a duty to take part in public affairs, and were often involved in the difficult business of taking over provincial newspapers.

While forming federations some organizations continued with a great deal of individual activity, such as the Tsinghua *Chingkangshan* and the Red Flag of the Aviation Institute. Transported by trucks and possessing vehicles equipped with loudspeakers, they were able to intervene within a few hours wherever incidents took place, and could act quickly and decisively. The privilege of acting as shock troops was not confined to a few groups under the Third Headquarters. Other groups not affiliated to that organization could rival them in combat power. Among these were the Geological Institute Red Guards and the *Sanhung* ('Three Reds'), three allied groups from Jenta, the People's University. These were all formidable activist groups, and they took part in the incidents that occurred around the foreign embassies as well as at Peking Airport, when the families of Soviet diplomats were repatriated in February 1967.

It would be wrong to regard brawls, kidnappings, and beatings as the main activities of Red Guards and the *raison d'être* of the shock groups. Although these were organized to carry out 'power seizures' and to defend themselves against rival groups, the most dangerous of which were generally those inside the same establishments, their principal weapons were the pen and the writing brush. Their duty to criticize brought them freedom of the press to parallel their right of association.

Critical articles, results of enquiries, expressions of indignation, professions of faith, small news items, and notices from the staffs of various organizations went from the walls of the city to the pages of the Red Guard papers; or to be more accurate, were published in 'little newspapers' at the same time that they were posted. Any Red

Guard unit of any importance had its own organ, of a few pages, published irregularly and sold for two *fen*[69] to all who wanted to buy it, especially the curious who stood in line to be able to find out at last what was really happening in China.

The first of these unofficial papers came out in the summer of 1966, when *Hsin Peita* ('New Peking University'— the title was suggested by Mao Tse-tung and written in his own calligraphy) saw the light of day on August 22nd. *Shoutu Hungweiping* ('Capital Red Guard') first appeared on September 13th. There were many papers with such titles as *Tungfanghung* ('The Red East')—or simply *Tungfang–Hungch'i* ('Red Flag') and *Chanpao* ('Combat News'), differing not only in the quality of their production, and their extremist or moderate tone, but also in the reliability of their news. Some of the papers consisted overwhelmingly of polemics.

However, it was soon apparent that when these papers carried speeches by revolutionary leaders they did not give different versions. The various editorial committees published either almost identical texts of them or else similar excerpts, generally stating that the texts were based on the shorthand records of the meetings. There thus appears to have been a kind of press office under the Central Committee's Cultural Revolution Group that was responsible for giving papers the texts of statements by leading figures. Apart from these, the polemics were the work of the young revolutionaries and were uncensored, as can be shown by the leftist attacks which were long to trouble the political figures around Chou En-lai. There were often editorials and leading articles signed by the most ardent and gifted of the young leaders of revolutionary organizations, who won fame not only for their qualities of leadership but also for the verve with which they expressed their ideas. Among them one learnt to recognize T'an Hou-lan, the animating spirit behind the Chingkangshan group of the Further Education College, and Han Ai-chin, head of the Institute of Aviation's Red Flag group. K'uai Ta-fu

[69] One-third of a British new penny or one US cent.

reappeared. All three were later to be members of the leading group of the Peking Municipal Revolutionary Committee.

The most vigorous organizations and groups of activists were in opposition to other organizations both inside and outside their own establishments. At Peita and the Further Education College the groups led by Nieh Yuan-tzu and T'an Hou-lan were opposed by other groups who felt that they should take a more proletarian line and be less respectful towards the Party. The Institute of Aviation's dominant Red Flag group demanded the elimination of the eight other groups that shared their premises. Beyond this, all bodies affiliated to the Third Headquarters were struggling against all the reputedly reactionary organizations, the most famous of which were the Lien Tung and the 516 Group (May 16 Group).

The Lien Tung, or 'Joint Action Committee'[70] had been created in 1966 on the day of the National Festival, with the alleged aim of defending Liu Shao-ch'i and criticizing Lin Piao and Chou En-lai. Its members included some of the sons of high officials who had been among the first Red Guards, such as Li Li-feng,[71] the son of Li Ching-ch'üan, and a son of Ch'en Yi.[72] The foundation ceremony for this group was held in the Political Bureau's meeting room in Chungnanhai.[73] The Lien Tung slogan was: 'If the father's a hero, the son's O.K. Reactionary father, the son's a louse.'[74] This illustrates the confusion which the measures taken against illustrious veterans of the revolutionary wars caused the children of the Party.

The Lien Tung criticized the Central Committee's Cultural Revolution Group, Chiang Ch'ing and Lin Piao;

[70] The full title was 'Joint Action Committee of Secondary School Red Guards.'

[71] See above. His arrest was mentioned by the Tsinghua organ *Chingkangshan* of February 8, 1967.

[72] According to the Hong Kong paper *Ming Pao,* January 1, 1967.

[73] *China News Analysis*, no. 682, Hong Kong, October 27, 1967, p. 6.

[74] *Kuangming Jihpao,* January 14, 1967.

and it twice threatened the Minister of Public Security. It was finally denounced as a reactionary organization by the *People's Daily* on March 27th after 137 of their members had been arrested by the Public Security forces, probably for a breach of a Central Committee resolution of February 12th limiting the scope of revolutionary organizations to within a single unit—which was the first restriction of the right of association. The Lien Tung crossed regional boundaries, being particularly active in Kwangtung. Its arrested members were not held for long. Public Security released them on April 22nd,[75] after protests from other Red Guard organizations.

In the spring of 1967 the revolutionary leadership did not waste its authority in vain attempts to reduce the power of the most liberated of the student organizations. Instead it urged organizations to form alliances rather than let individualistic tendencies bring them into violent opposition to each other.

The Central Committee's Cultural Revolution Group wanted to bring about the creation of municipal and provincial revolutionary committees. These committees were meant to be based on a 'triple alliance' of mass revolutionary organizations, revolutionary cadres and the army. For this mixture to be successful, student organizations had to agree on who was to represent them on the committees. As every group wanted to be represented, new rivalries and divisions arose in place of the unity that was being sought for. In Peking a very stormy meeting took place at Peita on April 8th.[76] Groups from outside the university, supported by the militant organization of the Geological Institute, came along to dispute the political role of Nieh Yuan-tzu, who had probably been playing too prominent a part in the negotiations. Disagreements among students delayed the birth of the Peking revolutionary committee. It was said that agreement on which organizations were to represent the students on the new committee was only reached three days before its formation was an-

[75] See *Nihon Keizai Shimbun*, Tokyo, April 27, 1967.
[76] See especially *Singtao Jihpao*, Hong Kong, April 4, 1967.

nounced. As soon as it was set up, the committee tried hard to hasten the formation of unified revolutionary committees in the universities and other institutions of further education in the city. These efforts were not entirely unsuccessful, especially at the Institute of Aviation, where a revolutionary committee was inaugurated with great ceremony on May 20th. But in the majority of cases some organizations were unenthusiastic, refused to co-operate, and remained independently active. The only solution that could be found was gradually to bring the students back to the schools, thus preventing their clashes from spreading all over town, where they were a permanent source of trouble and all too often caused pressure to be put on the revolution's leaders.

The leaders themselves were probably divided on the question of when teaching was to start again. The radicals hoped to have the students as a force at their disposal until the Cultural Revolution had achieved its aims. The others wanted order restored as soon as possible. On March 11th several speakers at a Shanghai rally were in favour of a report on university reform, and called for the strengthening of revolutionary organizations.

The first proposal for a return to classes—a draft directive on education—made on January 13th had to be cancelled for the simple reason that the educational system was still in utter chaos. In February the decision was made to try to reopen primary and secondary schools,[77] and pupils were urged to come back on March 1st.[78] Those who did so found their schools in lamentable condition after being used as dormitories by Red Guards and students from the provinces.

[77] Posters put up by the Red Guards of the 22nd Middle School, Peking, on February 12, 1967. The Standing Committee decided on February 11th to reopen middle schools in March. Teaching would be primarily physical and military training. Red Guards were invited to set up organizations with revolutionary students of working-class origin as their core.

[78] February 25th in Shanghai. A Central Committee notice of February 20, 1967, instructed pupils in rural middle schools and technical schools to go back to their village by March 1st.

Universities for their part were expected to reopen on March 20th, but their premises were in such a state that the decision could not be put into effect. The textbooks—apart from the works of Mao Tse-tung—had all been destroyed and there were no syllabuses. In May the *People's Daily* urged all the students, except those granted special leave by the Centre, to return to their classes. This time the notice had some effect. At the beginning of July the authorities announced that 50 per cent of the universities and colleges in Peking had started their teaching again. But the great unresolved question of curricula remained the subject of interminable discussions.

On March 7th the official press hailed the Central Committee's decision to reopen the primary and secondary schools. Yet Ch'i Pen-yü, a member of the Central Committee's Cultural Revolution Group, was still saying to the students, 'To go back to classes after making revolution for six months would be an admission of defeat.'[79] For him political education in the classroom would have been a bore. Instead he wanted to push the revolution further by stepping up the criticism of Liu Shao-ch'i.

As many teachers were not prepared to return to their jobs there was a shortage of staff. In July 1967 the *People's Daily* was still trying to persuade the teachers, refuting each of the objections they could make to starting work again: 'We cannot teach properly.' 'We can't be expected to fetch the pupils from their homes.' 'How can we struggle against indiscipline, prevent brawls, and stop the pupils from ruining State property?' This was why soldiers had to be sent into the schools to act as instructors, enlivening sessions of studying the works of Mao Tse-tung and giving physical training. This was how the middle schools of Taiyuan, in Shansi Province, spent their time during May: in the morning there was one hour of political education and three hours revising mathematics, physics, chemistry and foreign languages; in the afternoon the pupils studied the works of Mao Tse-tung or took part in meetings criticizing enemies of the people and 'evil in-

[79] *Pengpu Red Guard*, March 26, 1967.

fluences,' learning to investigate once again the mistakes of the past that had been denounced by the Cultural Revolution.[80]

The reform of higher education was only to be embarked upon much later. It will be discussed below when the Cultural Revolution's balance sheet is drawn up.

The special role of the students

The reopening of the universities was obviously a fundamental question as regards the role of the students in the new political scene. In addition to having helped 'destroy the old,' they had contributed to the overthrow of men in power by arousing the masses against them. Student activity had made it possible to overthrow even T'ao Chu. Then, at the end of December, the workers had joined in the revolution. What role were the students to play in the revolutionary order?

The concept of revolutionary order was of course ambiguous in itself. The Shanghai *Wenhuipao*, which had been calling on students since February 15th to 'return to their classrooms to make revolution,' could not be suspected of conservative tendencies: it had been 'captured' by the revolutionaries at the beginning of January. They might have been following the instructions of the three Shanghai Red Guard groups, who circulated an urgent six-point notice urging the students and teachers who had gone away for the 'exchange of experiences' to come back to their schools to work together for the power seizures.[81] In most schools revolutionary administrations had yet to be installed, and this was a job facing the students. But the revolutionary order also expected the Red Guards, who were beginning to get some political experience, to stay among the masses and bring them into the revolution. Leaders who invoked the idea of revolutionary order may have been influenced as much by a desire to

---

[80] See *Ajia Keizai Jumpo*, no. 735, October 1968, p. 6.
[81] *Wenhuipao*, February 17, 1967.

keep the students active in appropriate ways as to keep a check on the extreme activists.

The students, aware of their separate status as intellectuals, generally disliked being a group apart. As we have seen above, some of them had proposed that the Cultural Revolution teams and production teams should not be formed separately. In their wish to resolve the contradiction between activities aimed at transforming society and the necessity to sustain it through continued production, they wanted to leave the schools, where their ideological movement was too far detached from the revolution, and take it among the workers.

K'uai Ta-fu was preoccupied with a related problem: during the revolution was a student primarily a student or was he, if of proletarian class origin, primarily a proletarian? If class came first, students had no option but to leave the university for the duration of the struggle to establish a new order. His conclusion was that the universities had to be kept as an entity, irrespective of the class differences within it.

> In the previous period there was a discussion over the slogan 'Revolutionaries are heroes; reactionaries are villains,' and other questions. Then a bad tendency began in the universities, with all kinds of 'associations for the children of workers, poor and lower-middle peasants and revolutionary cadres.' This was hard on all those who did not come from labouring families, especially on professors and administrative personnel. . . .[82]

K'uai Ta-fu later took part in the work of the Peking Revolutionary Committee and stayed with it to the end. The Centre showed its interpretation of revolutionary order by urging the students to form alliances and proposing to them that they should co-operate with the representatives of other organizations in revolutionary committees. At first the reaction of the students was to recognise that one period was now over. The Red Guards of Peking's

[82] K'uai Ta-fu, 'Open letter to the Prime Minister,' August 6, 1966, Tsinghua.

Third Headquarters, who had come to Shanghai to make revolution there, left Shanghai for good on March 10, 1967.[83] They concluded an analysis of the situation with these words:

> Chairman Mao has taught us: 'It is up to us to organize the people. It is up to us to organize them and overthrow reaction in China.'[84]

Nieh Yuan-tzu, K'uai Ta-fu, T'an Hou-lan, Han Ai-chin and others entered the Peking Revolutionary Committee to play the game the Centre wanted them to: alliances, revolutionary committees and reform of education, leading to steady careers as political cadres.

What part was played by such organizations as Peita's *Chingkangshan* and by youngsters regarded by their comrades as Chinese Trotskyists, such as T'an Li-fu, Yi Lin and Ti Hsi?

The different social origins of students affected how they formed their groups and remained the criteria by which the more proletarian judged their fellows. On February 17th three organizations met in the Workers' Stadium to debate the proposition that discrimination on grounds of heredity should be eliminated. Outsiders came to the meeting to make trouble, and brawls resulted. The majority did not want differences of class origin to divide the students.

But some poor students were more persistent. Peita's *Chingkangshan* was undoubtedly an organization of the children of real proletarians.[85] It refused to compromise with the system, criticizing Nieh Yuan-tzu because of her relationship with the new Peking local authorities, organizing its own defence on the campus, and remaining to the end a thorn in the side of the regime in Peita.

[83] They took their leave of Shanghai in an article in the *Wenhuipao* of March 8, 1967.

[84] In an article by the editorial group of the paper *Chingkangshan* of the Further Education College in the *Peking Daily*, April 24, 1967.

[85] Probably mainly of peasant origin. This organization welcomed members of poor peasant associations to the university. See *Hsin Peita*, September 22, 1966.

At the other extreme, turning their backs on class problems, T'an, Yi and Ti made the most of the sole common heritage of the students, their freedom of speech, and chose a libertarian course. As we have seen, T'an Li-fu said and wrote a great deal, criticizing everyone, even Chiang Ch'ing, Ch'en Po-ta and Lin Piao. Perhaps he now thought it prudent to withdraw. He left for Canton but was summoned to come back if he did not want trouble with the Public Security. This police intervention made him much talked about.

Yi Lin and Ti Hsi had written an open letter criticizing Lin Piao for saying that Mao Tse-tung was greater than Marx, Engels, Lenin, and Stalin, adding that his conclusions ran contrary to historical evolution.[86] Ignoring the argument that Mao Tse-tung integrated the whole of Marxism when dealing with contemporary problems, they continued to act as 'theoreticians' and tried to win support for their views.

One should also mention the students who permanently left the universities to go among the workers and peasants and win them over for the revolution, insofar as the workers and peasants accepted them. But most of the students became students again. Those who enjoyed independent ideological activity returned to the scene when a swing to the left gave them their chance.

[86] See the *Revolutionary Liaison Journal* of the International Political Section of Peita, January 1967.

5. The Rebellion at the Head of the Party and the Rebel Leadership

From one anniversary of the Party on July 1, 1966, to the next on July 1, 1967, the Thought of Mao Tse-tung ruled supreme, but between the two dates its interpreters changed. In 1966 the official press designated Liu Shao-ch'i, Chou En-lai, Lin Piao and Teng Hsiao-p'ing jointly to celebrate it. In 1967 it was Lin Piao alone.

In the interval the revolutionary leaders had taken a major strategic decision: to throw the workers and peasants into the struggle. The Cultural Revolution was propagated among them, probably going deepest in the cities, but it had gone beyond any plan. The sheer weight of the working masses could have led the movement towards some social changes that were not envisaged in its original political aims. The social demands made by the workers, especially in Shanghai, were no easier to control than the anarchism of the students.

The Party machine continued to function for some time through those of its organs that still obeyed its orders. The Central Committee's Secretariat was thoroughly changed as a result of the Cultural Revolution, but to the revolutionary leaders its strong men were merely the new 'bosses.'

As one power seizure followed the next, the secretariat lost its territories. People in executive positions were perplexed, not knowing whether to obey the instructions coming from what remained of the Party machine or those that

the Red Guards passed on from the Central Committee's
Cultural Revolution Group. The government too underwent its own power seizures, which affected the coherence
of its activities, but the damage was less than that suffered
by the Party as Chou En-lai ensured co-ordination between
the State Council and the revolutionary leadership.

The new permanent organs of the Central Committee
were challenged by the old machine, but within the new
unified leadership they were backed by the Military Commission. It was important that all decisions of the Centre
should be absolutely binding on both the cadres and the
population as a whole. To this end they were all, from a
certain date onwards, jointly signed by the Cultural Revolution Group, the Military Commission, the State Council and the Central Committee. The last of these, despite
the manipulations it had undergone, remained the symbol
of supreme authority.

These four bodies together constituted the leadership
in this time of crisis. It was to some extent insurrectionary
as it broke the Party constitution whenever it saw fit to do
so (regarding it as obsolete and needing to be replaced
by a new one at the end of the Cultural Revolution) and
because it suspended officials without ratification by a new
congress. The composition of the Party's new central organs resulted, in theory at least, from revolutionary initiatives, and was influenced by criticisms from the masses.

Two important conferences were held in the Central
Committee during this period, in October 1966 and March
1967. Liu Shao-ch'i was criticized at both of them, but
within limits. The most extreme of the revolutionaries
would perhaps have liked Liu publicly tried and condemned—as Louis XVI was tried and executed—to open
up the way to a general liquidation of the establishment.
But the policy chosen was only to repudiate Liu Shao-ch'i
and condemn his writings. To have set the masses on the
Party might have been to drag it down into the grave.

It was a hard task to keep the Party in being while
profoundly changing the composition and the policies of
the ruling group. Some of the top leaders would doubtless

have been prepared to sacrifice Liu Shao-ch'i and then an-
nounce the end of the Cultural Revolution. These were
the very people who were supposed to make their own self-
criticism at the same time as Liu Shao-ch'i. The history of
the Cultural Revolution revolves in large part around this
problem: it was the struggle not of individual against individual, but of the individual against the majority.

In response to pressure to accelerate the pace of the
Cultural Revolution, the moderates brought the cadres into
a real participation in it. No durable organization could
be set up without the participation of technicians and people with administrative experience. Campaigns were
launched to encourage cadres alarmed by the revolution
to participate boldly in the new institutions. Some of them
probably made their self-criticisms when told to do so,
and were then given important political jobs. Mao Tse-
tung's policy was to implant the idea that there should be
one big proletarian revolutionary family instead of factions divided among themselves. It was reiterated that the
people to be removed were few in number, a 'small handful,' and that it was against this 'small handful' that everyone should unite.

The advocates of intensified revolution demanded a
tougher line, giving the revolutionary committees and control committees special powers that would have made them
like the Committees of Public Safety in revolutionary
France. They later tried to exploit a number of serious
incidents and to seize power in areas hitherto out of
bounds, such as the army and the Foreign Ministry. The
curb on these attempts marked the limits of the Cultural
Revolution. Up to July 1967 the contradiction revealed
by the extremist wing remained 'within the people,' and
the image of its leaders was that of spokesmen for the
rank and file.

The decline of the Secretariat

July 1, 1966, was the forty-fifth anniversary of the foundation of the Chinese Communist Party. The *People's Daily*
ran the headline, 'Long Live the Thought of Mao Tse-

tung,' associating the Party's top leaders with this declaration of homage. Lin Piao, the Minister of Defence, had equal space in the paper's columns with Liu Shao-ch'i, the Chairman of the People's Republic, Teng Hsiao-p'ing, Secretary-General of the Party, and Premier Chou En-lai. The article had to say something about the purge that had just hit the Peking Municipal Committee and the propaganda machine:

> Every time our Party has undergone a large-scale conflict we have purged a small handful of alien class elements who had infiltrated our ranks.

In these lines can be found the concept of the 'small handful' that was to be so extensively used by Mao Tsetung's supporters. Beside it is another, non-Maoist idea: that certain elements were alien to the Party. Four days later the Party's theoretical journal *Red Flag* replied:

> Comrade Mao Tse-tung has long told us that if there were no contradictions or struggles within the Party it would die. In some conditions contradictions within the Party change, and non-antagonistic ones can become antagonistic.[1]

The Central Committee, meeting in plenary session from August 1st onwards, provided Mao Tse-tung with an enlarged audience, expanded with members from the Party's less senior bodies. A fair number of regular members of the Central Committee were absent; revolutionaries, probably representing student organizations for the most part, made up the group, so that it was possible for a new majority to emerge. Moreover, the entirely fresh enthusiasm of the masses attending the Central Committee for the first time afforded new opportunities to the speakers.

On the fifth day of the meeting Mao Tse-tung set the tone of the meeting by producing a poster in his own handwriting, in the manner inaugurated by Nieh Yuan-tzu at Peita University:

[1] *Red Flag,* July 4, 1966.

Let Us Bombard the Headquarters—
My First *Tatzupao*

How well-written was that first Marxist-Leninist *Tatzupao* to appear in China (at Peita), how excellent the wording of the transcription in the *People's Daily!* Comrades, please read them again. But in the last fifty days some leading comrades in the Centre as well as in the provinces have got it all wrong. Adopting the reactionary stand of the bourgeoisie, they have enforced a bourgeois dictatorship, repressed the surging movement of the great Cultural Revolution of the proletariat, turned it back to front, presented black as white, surrounded and attacked revolutionaries, stifled opinions differing from their own, imposed a white terror, encouraged the bourgeoisie, disheartened the proletariat, and felt very pleased with themselves. What a talent for harm they have yet again shown! Viewed in connection with the right-wing deviation in 1962 and the trend of 1964 which was Left-wing in form but Right in essence, shouldn't this make one wide awake?

Mao Tse-tung, August 5, 1966.[2]

This initiative was followed by the surprise appearance of the Chairman among the crowd on August 9th, when he had the gates of Chungnanhai opened. This had a considerable effect on the population of Peking. The official press had not been warned in advance and was apparently divided in its counsels when the *People's Daily* wanted to give the Chairman's mingling with the people the maximum publicity. Its confusion was such that the August 10th issue was withdrawn almost as soon as it had been put on sale in the morning.[3] Another issue appeared at 5 p.m., hardly different from the first, and still making much of the event, which suggests that the Chairman's keenest supporters finally won the day.

It was in this overcharged atmosphere that the resolution that shaped the whole Cultural Revolution, the *Sixteen-Point Decision,* was passed on August 8th. It has

---

[2] Quoted by Konno, *Peking Kono Ichinen*, p. 222, *op. cit.*
[3] See *Far Eastern Economic Review 1967 Yearbook*, p. 151.

since been reproduced and analyzed throughout the world.

According to this document the minority had to be protected on the grounds that truth was sometimes on its side (Point 6). Arguments should be reasoned and there was to be no constraint or coercion. The masses could only be liberated through their own efforts and no actions should be taken in their name (Point 4). They had to 'educate themselves in the movement.'

The cadres, it was stated, could be put into four categories: 'good; comparatively good; those who had made serious mistakes but were not anti-Party, anti-socialist rightists; and a small number who *were* anti-Party, anti-socialist rightists.' The movement was therefore directed against right-wing elements, but the great majority of the cadres fell into the 'good' or 'comparatively good' categories (Point 8).

This text also envisaged institutions of a new kind—cultural revolutionary groups, committees and congresses, comparable to the institutions that were supposed to develop in the Socialist Education Movement (Point 9): 'It is necessary to institute a system of general elections, like that of the Paris Commune. . . . The lists of candidates should be put forward by the revolutionary masses after full discussion. . . . The masses are entitled at any time to criticize (their representatives). . . . If these members or delegates prove incompetent they can be replaced through election or recalled by the masses after discussion.' (References to the Paris Commune of 1871 were popular during the first part of the Cultural Revolution, perhaps because Mao Tse-tung had called the first *tatzupao* at Peita 'the manifesto of the Peking People's Commune of the 1960s.')[4]

The Central Committee resolution threatened a number of cadres who had committed errors, but apart from those who had already been condemned in May, and those who may have felt threatened by Mao Tse-tung's *tatzupao* because of their role during the fifty days, nobody knew who was going to be attacked. One thing, however, had been

[4] See the editorial in *Red Flag*, no. 3, 1967.

gained: the two separate centres of the Party were combined again at last. The secretariat, now purged, may well have expected to regain the near absolute power it used to exercise between conferences. The secretariat had made big sacrifices: three of its members—P'eng Chen, Lu Ting-yi, and Lo Jui-ch'ing—had been dismissed.[5]

Teng Hsiao-p'ing reckoned perhaps that the organization of which he was the formidable head had thus paid its tribute to the Cultural Revolution, and was now going to be allowed to devote itself to the new politics, its workload increased by the current events. Even in its reorganized form the secretariat could still rely on its oldest members, T'an Chen-lin[6] and Li Hsüeh-feng,[7] as well as T'ao Chu.

T'ao Chu, whose sudden rise to the fourth rank in the hierarchy made him something of a star, seemed to have given sufficient proof of his Maoist spirit. He doubtless owed some of his reputation to having asserted the possibility of a direct transition from capitalism to communism, and maintained that class struggles would continue throughout the period of transition,[8] a position that was to be stated again in the communiqué of the Central Committee's Tenth Plenum. He also attracted attention by organizing large-scale progressive campaigns (such as cadres going to live with the workers, or teach-ins on the Thought of Mao Tse-tung) in his old domain, south China, that were made much of by the propaganda machine.

But T'ao Chu's decisions in his new job at the Centre,[9]

[5] On the composition of the Secretariat, see the article of C.H.: *'L'équipe dirigeante chinoise et la Révolution Culturelle'* in *Notes et Études documentaires*, no. 3448–49, *La Documentation française*, Paris, December 26, 1967.

[6] Vice-premier and Minister of Agriculture.

[7] Li Hsüeh-feng could not have been appointed P'eng Chen's successor without the consent of Mao Tse-tung. He probably helped Teng Hsiao-p'ing to reorganize the Secretariat during May.

[8] Article by T'ao Chu in the *People's Daily*, August 5, 1960.

[9] Head of the Central Committee's Propaganda Department and in charge of the ministries dealing with culture. See Joan Robinson, *The Cultural Revolution in China*, pp. 141–42.

to judge by those that have been revealed, were not revolutionary. There was a festival of 'the criticized film,' which enabled audiences to see old films. Although the sale of writings by P'eng Chen, Lu Ting-yi and Chou Yang was forbidden, the stocks held by the bookshops were allowed on the market.[10] Mao Tse-tung's swim in the Yangtse on July 16th was given the most extravagant publicity. The Great Socialist Cultural Revolution finally became the Great Proletarian Cultural Revolution.

With few exceptions the main Peking papers were run by Maoists who had taken the initiative during the Cultural Revolution, but the provincial press was still under the control of provincial Party committees. The provincial Party committees continued to work with the Central Committee's Secretariat. As long as the Red Guards did not feel that they had the authority to push their investigations as far as the provincial committee level, cadres wishing to raise protests could only make them to the Secretariat.

In September 1966 a dismissed joint secretary of the Ipin Administrative Region in Szechuan came to Peking to lodge documents criticizing Li Ching-ch'üan, the First Secretary of the South-western Bureau of the Central Committee. He was unable to make contact with the leaders of the revolution. As he had been punished, the secretariat followed the usual procedure by sending him on to the Party's Control Commission. He was, however, protected from the emissaries whom his enemies had sent against him in Peking. He turned to the Red Guards of the Second Headquarters and the Peita Red Guards, only to be told that as he was not a student they could not take charge of his documents. It was not until early October that the Third Headquarters was prepared to take his problem in hand.[11] The Central Committee's Secretariat fought a rearguard action, but the students finally outflanked it.

A Central Committee Work Meeting began on October 8th. It was only intended to last three days, but it continued for seventeen, and was virtually a continuation of

[10] See Red Guard paper *Peiching Hungse Hsüanch'uanping*, no. 4, May 10, 1967.

[11] *China News Analysis,* no. 670, July 28, 1967, Hong Kong.

the Eleventh Plenum.[12] After its conclusion the journal *Red Flag*[13] repeated the threats made in July:

> The contradictions between those comrades who committed errors of line on the one hand and the Party and the masses on the other are still contradictions among the people. . . . Nevertheless, these comrades must be sharply told that no matter who they are, and no matter how great their past achievements, if they cling to the erroneous line, the nature of the contradictions between them and the Party and the masses will change . . . and they will slide down the anti-Party and anti-socialist road.[14]

Both Teng Hsiao-p'ing and Liu Shao-ch'i made self-criticisms at the meeting. They both accepted that they were essentially responsible for the deeds criticized by Mao Tse-tung in his *tatzupao:* supporting rightists in 1962, distorting the Socialist Education Movement in 1964, and creating the Work Teams.[15] Mao Tse-tung, however, was not satisfied with the sacrifice of a few scapegoats. He felt that the whole Central Committee should join in the self-criticism. New trials awaited the Secretariat. T'ao Chu was attacked in January 1967 and T'an Chen-lin scarcely two months later.

It is no longer possible to know exactly what T'ao Chu's political line was. One can only observe that his personal power made him almost a state within the state. As was related above, Red Guards had accused him of wanting to create a Cultural Revolution Group under his own orders. Could he possibly have used his connections to support dissident Red Guard groups with the aim of bringing them under the control of the Secretariat, as the Third Headquarters had done?

Red Guards published impressive lists of T'ao Chu's

[12] See *Mōtakutō no Chōsen*, Asahi Shimbun *Chōsa Kenkyūshitsu*, p. 39, and *Lin Piao chuan chi*, Hong Kong, 1970.
[13] No. 14, November 1, 1966.
[14] *Peking Review*, no. 45, November 4, 1966, p. 7.
[15] See Konno's analysis of the self-criticisms in *Pekin Kono Ichinen*, pp. 67–68.

political friends. Speakers and writers underlined his op-
portunism and cynicism. He had even said, 'The sun itself
(with which Mao Tse-tung was so often compared) has
dark spots.'[16]

It was probably the Central Committee's Cultural Revolution Group that asked the Standing Committee to dismiss
him as head of propaganda. His fall also marked the end
of Teng Hsiao-p'ing's power. Mao Tse-tung had this comment to make:

> T'ao Chu was introduced to the Central Committee by
> Teng Hsiao-p'ing. I told Teng that T'ao was not honest,
> but he said T'ao could be trusted. I failed to solve the
> problem of T'ao Chu, and you did too. The Red Guards
> succeeded in it as soon as they rebelled.[17]

The Rebel leadership

January began with the events of Shanghai. The appearance of revolutionary organizations among the workers
was soon followed by an extended strike, and the huge
city was in danger of being paralyzed. Electricity was cut
and the trains stopped running. The revolutionaries'
Headquarters appealed to the people of Shanghai to pull
themselves together and return to work.[18] Mao Tse-tung
decided to have this appeal published in the press immediately. A great deal was now at stake in Shanghai. If
disorder were established in the great industrial metropolis
of the eastern coast, the regime might well be swept away.
The journal *Red Flag*[19] maintained that Mao Tse-tung
took a 'great strategic decision' in ordering the general

[16] *Mōtakutō no Chōsen*, p. 41.

[17] According to a leaflet issued in Peking on January 12th
from the Peking Proletarian Revolutionary Rebel Headquarters.

[18] 'Message to the People of Shanghai' from the Shanghai
Workers' Revolutionary Rebel General Headquarters, January
4, 1967, in *Wenhui Pao,* January 5th. See *Peking Review,* no. 3,
January 13, 1967, p. 5.

[19] *Red Flag,* no. 2, January 15, 1967. 'Proletarian Revolutionaries, Unite!' See *Peking Review,* no. 4, January 20, 1967,
p. 15.

publication of the workers' appeal and the Urgent Notice of January 9.[20]

By his personal support for these appeals to the masses Mao Tse-tung brought a greater influence to bear on the situation. Shanghai gradually went back to work. But it should be noted that the initiatives which the Party theoreticians saw as great revolutionary decisions were not acts of violence. Instead they were appeals or exhortations to follow some example, which were exceptional in that they were distributed without the endorsement of the Central Committee.

Chang Ch'un-ch'iao later related how he prepared to put the running of the city's affairs into the hands of the Shanghai revolutionaries:

> Yao Wen-yuan and I agreed that key departments should be taken over first, so as to ensure the safety of life and property. Next we had to take over the municipal Party Committee and People's Committee, and we already had the control of these two bodies in our hands. At this period we used to hold joint discussions. We would ask the rebels to come to our meetings to discuss each problem. One day forty organizations might be represented and the next day a hundred. Nobody knew anyone else. Although we were very busy and often in a state of chaos, we felt that this sort of thing was liable to happen in a revolution, and this was the way to get problems solved. It would have been wrong to be too hasty.[21]

Power seizures by the masses were not possible everywhere, even when resort was made to violence. In order

[20] The Urgent Notice of the Shanghai Workers' Revolutionary Rebel General Headquarters and thirty-one other bodies announced that bank accounts were frozen, salary levels were to remain at existing levels until the end of the Cultural Revolution, all public buildings and capitalists' houses were to be nationalized, and all revolutionary organizations had to contribute to the restoration of order. See *Peking Review,* no. 4, January 20, 1967, p. 7.

[21] From a speech by Chang Ch'un-ch'iao on October 22, 1967, to revolutionary delegates from Anhwei.

to neutralize the largest number of 'authorities' at once, the revolutionary leadership advocated military control where seizures of power were not practicable. The army, now that it had been committed to the struggle on the side of the revolutionaries, was a trump card in their hands if they wanted to play it. But military control could only be a temporary solution.

In order to give the new workers' power the chance to establish itself firmly, the takeover had to come from the inside. Chou En-lai said:

> The accent must be on one's own unit. It is impossible to coordinate the seizing of power throughout a whole system at one blow. First, power should be taken in the sections, after which the revolutionary rebels will be the main force within the sections. . . . We do not agree to revolutionary organizations on a national scale.[22]

This vital reservation was intended to ensure the survival of the Party.

Despite everything, the leaders of the revolution wanted to move fast. As they were in the minority everywhere they were quite likely to be wiped out. As Mao Tse-tung said,

> Power must be seized straightaway without going into details. Discussions can be held later. . . . The nature of the authorities who were in power will be discussed in a later stage of the movement. . . . Take power, report to the State Council, and obtain its consent.[23]

In other times the Central Committee's Secretariat would have been the ratifying authority. Now it had been completely short-circuited. But why did power seizures have to be ratified by the State Council rather than the Central

[22] 'Leaders at the Centre discuss the question of power seizures,' *Yutien Fenglei*, February 10, 1967.
[23] Speech at an enlarged meeting of the Military Commission on January 27th, according to a *tatzupao* posted on February 3, 1967, by the delegation of the Cultural Revolution Preparatory Delegation of the Sian Military School to Peking.

Committee's Cultural Revolution Group? One explanation is the role played in the revolution by Chou En-lai himself. As Premier he was the head of the State Council, and with his splendid diplomatic abilities he was the best arbitrator between conflicting revolutionary organizations.

On January 10th Chou En-lai told some Red Guards that the Central Committee's Cultural Revolution Group[24] represented the general staff of the movement, the Military Commission its headquarters, and the State Council its executive organ.[25]

As we have seen already,[26] military and political leadership in the revolution had been unified despite the objections of some army chiefs. The people grew accustomed to seeing important orders issued over the signatures of these three bodies together with the Central Committee, listed perhaps more as a symbol of the Party's continued existence than as a real body.

The new composition of the Political Bureau's Standing Committee, which probably resulted from a compromise, did not give it the strength to be a real revolutionary leading body, and it probably remained locked in struggle after Liu Shao-ch'i's self-criticism at the October meeting. The top leadership remained collective, but the few who can be supposed actually to have been involved were not enough to make it an effective body: Mao Tse-tung, Lin Piao, Chou En-lai, Ch'en Po-ta, K'ang Sheng and Chiang Ch'ing. Foreign Minister Ch'en Yi reflected the popular idea of who the leading group were when he made a speech protesting against the Red Guards' loss of political direction:

[24] The composition of the Group in November was as follows: Ch'en Po-ta (head); K'ang Sheng and T'ao Chu (advisers); Chiang Ch'ing (first deputy head); Wang Jen-chung, Liu Shih-chien, and Chang Ch'un-ch'iao (deputy heads); Chang P'ing-hua, Wang Li, Kuan Feng, Ch'i Pen-yü, Lin Chieh, Mu Hsin, Yao Wen-yuan, Hsieh T'ang-chung, Liu Wei-chen, Cheng Chi-ch'iao, and Yang Chih-lin (members).

This list is taken from Konno, *op. cit.*, p. 81.

[25] 'The Diary of the Cultural Revolution,' *Asahi Evening News*, Tokyo, May 1967, p. 32.

[26] See above, Chapter 3.

In our great Party are we only to believe in six people:
Chairman Mao, Vice-chairman Lin Piao, the Premier,
Ch'en Po-ta, K'ang Sheng, and Chiang Ch'ing? Or in
eleven, if we add five deputy premiers?[27] Are there only
eleven honest people? I will not take this course. Take
me away and display me to the crowds.[28]

Power was also seized in the Central Committee's bureaus, whose executive functions were now controlled by
revolutionary organizations. Those in the Party machine
who were resisting the revolution were now deprived of
any channel by which to communicate their instructions
without the knowledge of the leadership. The Party's machine being brought under control in this way made a big
difference as far as orders to the provinces were concerned.

The army was apparently mollified by the compromise
of deferring the Cultural Revolution in frontier regions,
where priority was given to national defence. But when
struggles between revolutionary groups connected with the
army developed in the frontier regions, the military chiefs
who had opposed the reorganization of January 11th and
12th were pitilessly attacked.

There were particularly striking cases in Sinkiang of
soldiers firing on soldiers during the fighting at Shihhotzu
from January 25th to 28th. Revolutionary rebels of the
Agricultural Institute of the Sinkiang Production and Construction Corps, an army organization responsible for economic development in the region, carried out a local power
seizure in a textile factory and arrested some officers. Some
army units then came to the support of a 'reactionary' organization[29] that was fighting against the revolutionaries,
and held prisoner some officers from the Production Corps'
staff who had come to investigate. Loyalist army units had

[27] Li Fu-ch'un, Li Hsien-nien, Nieh Jung-chen, and Hsieh
Fu-chih, with either himself or T'an Chen-lin as the most likely
candidates for the fifth. Of the sixteen vice-premiers, including
Lin Piao, one had died and many had been severely criticized.
[28] Hungwei Chanpao, April 18, 1967.
[29] The 'August 1st Campaign Army of the Production
Corps,' abbreviated to 'August Campaign.' Chou En-lai ordered it dispersed in March 1967.

to be sent in to engage them.[30] The situation was very serious, with the deputy commander of the Production Corps among those who had been captured. According to *tatzupao* reports, the Sinkiang military commander, Wang En-mao, took the side of the reactionaries, and nine of the ten divisions under his orders followed his lead.[31]

Red Guards brought up incidents such as these in criticizing members of the Military Commission whom they knew to be in disagreement with Lin Piao. As had happened with T'ao Chu, the revolutionary leaders allowed several of them to be overthrown by their critics. Ho Lung disappeared. Old Marshal Chu Te had a very difficult time. The composition of the Military Commission's vice-chairmen changed. Lin Piao himself seems to have been mocking Chu Te when he said to him:

Kao Kang[32] tried in a roundabout way to become chairman. Would you have been clever enough to do this? Isn't it true that you were never really commander-in-chief for a single day? After the Nan-ch'ang Uprising you gave up and strayed into anarchy. Before the Tsungyi Conference Chu Te was in command, but after that Mao Tse-tung took it over. During the Anti-Japanese War the front commander was X, and during the Liberation War Mao Tse-tung was in command, not you. But you still regard yourself to this day as a hero.[33]

Legendary heroes were thus consigned to the shadows. Chu Te, Mao Tse-tung's comrade in his darkest hours, was the model of a stalwart old soldier even to those too old to remember the war. Ho Lung was a veteran who had

[30] According to a *tatzupao* of the 'Red Missile Military Corps,' a revolutionary rebel group of the Production Corps' Agricultural Institute quoted in *Asahi Shimbun* (Japanese edition of that date). This group was affiliated to the Second Red Headquarters of Sinkiang.

[31] 'The Diary of the Cultural Revolution,' p. 48.

[32] Dismissed in 1955 on charges of conspiring to seize Party and government leadership.

[33] Cited by Konno, *op. cit.,* p. 94. 'X,' not named in the text, may be P'eng Te-huai.

been brought up with weapons since childhood, a hero of the secret societies until he joined the revolution to fight for the Party.

However, the strategy of vigilant frontier defence was affected neither by the criticisms of the veteran marshals nor by the new army propaganda. 'The international forces of imperialism are hostile to the Chinese Cultural Revolution,' said Yeh Chien-ying,[34] paraphrasing a notice issued by Mao Tse-tung:

> An intense level of activity by Soviet aircraft has been reached in the frontier regions of Sinkiang, and Soviet ground forces have been mobilized. All front-line units must be put on the alert. The Tsinan, Nanking, Foochow, Canton and Kunming military regions must also make preparations. To this end the Cultural Revolution may be somewhat toned down.[35]

In order to win support for power seizures from the men who were least sympathetic to this kind of struggle, the high command sent them practical instructions. In many cases they may have been like this 1968 directive, recommending a bare minimum of action in the service of politics:

> In supporting the left, you must follow the example of unit 7335. You are free not to take part, but you must take actions that help the rebels.[36]

Finding a formula for revolutionary committees

The traditional Centre had lost its branches, and behind the rebels was the shadow of the army; the revolutionary

[34] Vice-chairman of the Central Committee's Military Commission.

[35] According to leaflets of February 11, 1967, issued by the Red Guards of the School of Applied Engineering.

[36] Notice from the General Bureau of Civil Aviation to the Sinkiang Civil Aviation Administration. See Canton *Tahan Tachiao*, no. 8, January 30, 1968, quoted in *South China Morning Post*.

organizations, flushed with their newly-won power, wanted to purge the Party themselves. The revolutionary leadership lost no time in telling them that only Party members had the right to impose punishments on other members of the Party.

But people who did not belong to the Party found themselves holding new powers with revolutionary cadres who had 'rebelled.' They wanted to exclude some regular members of the Party and they did so. The new Centre issued the following notice on February 12th:

> According to the Party Constitution, sanctions against members can only be taken by Party organizations. The masses and their organizations do not have the right to apply the sanctions provided for by the Constitution to members.[37]

This reaction indicates what changes the rebel leadership thought the Cultural Revolution should bring about in the Party. It gave grounds for believing that the Party would be maintained in its old form within the 'provisional organizations of the proletarian dictatorship.'[38] The February 12 Notice is unlikely to have been applied everywhere. A year later there still existed in Canton a body called Hung Ch'i Lienwei, a commission that consisted of specialist groups formed by eleven revolutionary mass organizations to get rid of the leading cadres of the former committees who were still holding power in the province.[39] Initiatives of this sort, which ran counter to the Centre's policies and were aimed at creating all-out class war, put considerable obstacles in the way of winning over provincial cadres. In Peking, however, the Centre was able to carry its policies through. A 'group for verify-

[37] See *Asahi Jyanaru,* vol. 10, no. 18, 'Wakagaetta Tososhiki no Taishitsu,' p. 21.

[38] It also throws light on the concept of 'Revolution under the control of the Dictatorship of the Proletariat,' to which it conforms.

[39] Canton leaflet, February 12, 1968.

ing special cases' was entrusted with 'studying the report on the crimes of Liu Shao-ch'i.'[40] This was, of course, composed of Party members.

The question of how the Party should be represented in the 'provisional organs of power' arose as soon as the first efforts to establish the 'Shanghai Commune' were made.

Chang Ch'un-ch'iao went to great trouble to have the greatest possible number of revolutionary organizations taking part in the commune's committee in fair proportions. Workers' representatives were in the great majority. Chang, influenced perhaps by the long strike that had just occurred, was eager to have as many as possible of the workers' organizations that had helped to overcome it participating in the new leading organ. We shall see below how long these negotiations lasted. In February Tsingtao, Shanghai and Kweichow each established a revolutionary committee or a 'commune.' Mao Tse-tung, however, showed a preference for what was being done in Shansi; as in Shanghai, this took a long time: from the seizure of power on January 12th to the establishment of a revolutionary committee on March 18th. The official press concentrated mainly on the example of Heilungkiang, whose committee emerged fully armed, like Athene, on January 31st.

The Chairman's preference for what had been done in Shansi may have been founded on one or more of the following considerations: this was the province that first produced the 'triple alliance' of people, Army and Party; the leaders of the movement in Shansi spent sufficient time in consultations with representatives of the revolutionary masses, revolutionary cadres and the army to reach a satisfactory balance of forces; and the balance consisted of one half for representatives of the masses, a quarter for soldiers, and a quarter for revolutionary cadres—in other words, Party members who had come over to the revolution.

On the first point one may observe that, as of January

---

[40] See communiqué of the Twelfth Plenum of the Eighth Central Committee. *Peking News*, 1968, no. 44.

25th, when a message was sent to Mao Tse-tung by the 'Shansi Rebel Headquarters,' the elements responsible for the seizure of power fell naturally into three groups:[41] first, workers, peasants and soldiers; second, the revolutionary cadres; third—a group whose support the other two acknowledged—the army. In Shansi members of the Party came forward to represent the Party in the revolutionary body, and the leaders of the seizure of power made a note of it.

On the third point, posters quoted some of the advice given by Mao Tse-tung to Chang Ch'un-ch'iao and Yao Wen-yuan in the middle of February. Among other things he said: The Shanghai Commune should follow the example of Shansi, where 53 per cent of revolutionary masses have allied with 27 per cent of soldiers and 20 per cent of cadres.[42]

The Party's theoretical journal, *Red Flag*, introduced the concept of the triple alliance, though without using the term, in its editorial of January 30th. It recognized that it was necessary 'to establish temporary organs of power which will undertake the responsibility for directing the struggle.'

The model of the Shanghai Commune was not followed. Indeed, the Commune changed itself into a revolutionary committee. Perhaps Shanghai could have established a worker's democracy, but its leaders had embarked on class struggle without making any deep analysis of what forms of proletarian dictatorship were possible in the rest of China. In particular, the Commune involved the principle of grass-roots elections.

At the beginning of March a poster reported Chou En-lai as saying that it would be premature to establish a commune in Peking. A commune after the style of the 1871 Paris Commune would have implied that 95 per cent of workers, peasants and soldiers would have to vote. The time was not yet ripe for this. The poster

41 *Mōtakutō no Chōsen, op. cit.,* p. 54.
42 Tsinghua *Chingkangshan,* February 23, 1967.

added that Mao Tse-tung and Lin Piao agreed with this statement of Chou En-lai.[43]

As the revolutionary committees had been approved of as bodies to direct the struggle, this implied that they would have, at the local level, a power of decision that was normally reserved for the Party.

A system of general elections was normally envisaged only for Cultural Revolution groups and committees. Had the Shanghai Commune formula been applied generally, the Party would have been permanently weakened. The political understanding of the Shanghai masses was higher than that of the rest of China. Here again we find that concern for social revolution was more or less in contradiction with Mao Tse-tung's simple plans to establish rural people's communes in the spirit of hard work and self-sacrifice.

The abandonment of the Shanghai Commune was, as we shall see later, a measure taken to confirm the grip of the Party leadership, despite its temporary loss of standing.

The February counter-current

There was considerable disorder in Peking during January. The power seizures in the public services succeeded one another so quickly that the revolutionaries themselves were unable to tell whether those in power in other branches of the administration had been approved by the Centre. In some offices, uprisings failed; in others, rival revolutionary organizations kept overthrowing each other; and in others still, the old leadership intervened to help the organizations they favoured, with the result that there were 'fake seizures of power.'

To top it all, the official news media were being so badly shaken by their own power seizures that even the advice of the press, hitherto authoritative, was put in doubt. The dismissal of T'ao Chu and his group caused

[43] *Asahi Shimbun*, evening edition of March 3, 1967, reporting a Bulgarian News Agency report monitored by AFP in Sofia. See *China News Analysis*, no. 653, p. 7.

an earthquake in the propaganda services, which were given new leaders.[44] The Peking local paper, the *Peking Daily*, underwent a complete seizure of power on January 19th. Meetings were called by the propaganda chiefs to let revolutionaries know about the reorganized press.

At the Centre, the State Council was trying to co-ordinate the revolution while having to maintain public order, now called 'revolutionary order.' At the same time it had to keep the country's economy going. Chou En-lai, supported by the surviving deputy prime ministers, did his best. This naturally involved some unpopular orders. As he had to validate seizures of power, he also had the job of making inquiries into the various organizations and the role they played.

Some criticisms were levelled at Chou En-lai himself, but this was felt to be going too far. Posters demanding that Chou En-lai should be 'burned alive for conspiring with Li Hsien-nien' were hastily covered up.[45] When Reuter's Peking correspondent wanted to file this story he was surprised to be told that the postal workers' committee would not accept his cable. Many of the malcontents were students who did not want to be sent home before the Cultural Revolution was over.

At this moment deputy premier T'an Chen-lin, the Minister of Agriculture, stepped forward to strengthen authority in the areas under his control. He came to embody a kind of spirit of resistance to disorder that later took the form of resisting the mass line in meetings and led to his fall.

T'an Chen-lin does not seem to have been opposed to the policy changes in the economy and education, nor

[44] According to the morning edition of *Asahi Shimbun,* January 14, 1967, quoting a statement by Ch'en Po-ta, the acting head of the New China News Agency was Hu Chih (chief editor, *PLA Daily*); and the Central Committee's Propaganda Bureau was under Wang Li (joint chief editor of *Red Flag* and member of the Central Committee's Cultural Revolution Group), assisted by Pang P'ing-chu (chief editor, *People's Daily*) and Hu Chih.

[45] *Asahi Shimbun,* morning edition, January 7, 1967, quoting Peking correspondent of the German agency ADN.

was he apparently against the new 'leap forward' that was at the heart of the Cultural Revolution. But he did believe, it would seem, that nothing more could be expected from giving the masses a free hand. He maintained that the past record of such policies was enough.

T'an Chen-lin and a few others with him 'made frantic efforts to run rectification campaigns of the sort launched twenty years ago in Yenan by Chairman Mao, denying that the masses could achieve their own liberation and build Marxism-Leninism for themselves,' K'ang Sheng later said.[46] T'an Chen-lin was against seizures of power, but as it was impossible to avoid them altogether, he organized his own in the sector under his control—agriculture, meteorology and forestry. In his own ministry he helped the more amenable organizations.

On February 11th T'an Chen-lin deceived the Central Committee and Premier Chou. He cleverly arranged that the representatives of five units . . . in which false takeovers had taken place should be received by the Premier.[47]

Such were the accusations made by Red Guards of the Institute of Agriculture and other organizations as they denounced the repression.

The conservatives (they claimed) in various agricultural and forestry departments called mass meetings to denounce revolutionary rebel organizations, in order to carry out the directive given by T'an Chen-lin to 'discredit politically' the revolutionary rebels.

According to incomplete statistics, over twenty organizations, large and small, were suppressed during this adverse trend. . . . Benefiting from this counterrevolutionary current, and thanks to the support of T'an Chen-lin and his lackeys, conservative groups recovered and attempted to come back in strength.[48]

[46] See the special number of *Tungfanghung* of the Peking Institute of Geology, March 29, 1968.
[47] *Peking P'i-T'an Chanpao* (Front-line report on the criticism of Tan Chen-lin), Peking, June 16, 1967.
[48] *Ibid.*

During this affair all the better-known student revolutionary organizations joined forces against T'an Chen-lin. The same sequence of events took place with T'an as it had with T'ao Chu and Ho Lung: criticism grew to enormous proportions, and the Centre abandoned the men under attack.

T'an Chen-lin thus became the culprit in what was called the 'February counter-current,' which the Twelfth Plenum of the Central Committee later denounced as one of the abortive attempts made to distort the Cultural Revolution.[49]

T'an Chen-lin was asked to explain himself at an enlarged meeting of the Political Bureau held in March. It may be that the discussions did not go as planned. The Minister of Agriculture defended himself by expounding his own views, and in doing so he found supporters. The Japanese press spread the news that there was only a majority of one in the voting at the meeting.[50] Although this was denied by an official spokesman, it is quite possible that several of the leaders combined against the Central Committee's Cultural Revolution Group, whose role came into question during the final discussions.

If a CTK news agency story of February 22, 1967, the month of the counter-current, is to be believed, the Central Committee considered setting up a fairly large council to replace the Cultural Revolutionary Group, on which it was expected to include figures who had been criticized. If this is true, this amounted to putting the whole organization of the Centre into question. K'ang Sheng later admitted that an opposition had formed among the ruling group. These people, he said, 'were saying that the Cultural Revolution did not enjoy the support of the Party leadership.'[51] Mao Tse-tung and Lin Piao condemned the

[49] Communiqué of the Enlarged Twelfth Plenary Session of the Eighth Central Committee of the CPC.

[50] See especially Nogami's 'Where is the revolution bound?', Vietnam and China (16), Asahi Evening News.

[51] Speeches by Central leaders quoted in the Peking Geological Institute's Tungfanghung, special edition of March 29, 1968.

line taken by T'an Chen-lin, who then found himself out-
voted and was probably censured.[52]

It can be seen from the case of T'an Chen-lin that the
'February counter-current' was more than a clash between
revolutionary groups: it involved the leading group itself.
It may be that the measures T'an Chen-lin took in his
own sphere threatened to have serious consequences. He
may have sympathized to an alarming extent with conservative tendencies among the peasantry. Conservative
organizations may have found too firm a base in the Ministry of Agriculture. In the last resort, what carried the
day when the Political Bureau voted was the victory of
the revolutionary spirit over a technocrat who wanted to
maintain a flexible line in his ministry while keeping the
organizations within it under tight control. But the extremists in the Cultural Revolution Group who thought
that this victory opened the way for the mob to destroy all
that remained of the Party machine were mistaken.

*Differing views on the intensification of the Cultural
Revolution*

The tide of criticism reached a new level when it brought
down T'an Chen-lin in the Central Committee's Political
Bureau. The revolutionaries poured their forces into the
gap. Behind T'an Chen-lin, they maintained, there was
someone else: the same person who had been behind P'eng
Chen. At an enlarged meeting of the Political Bureau the
left-wing party demanded the condemnation of Liu Shao-
ch'i.

Liu had already made his self-criticism and been de-
moted. Most of the leading members of the Bureau probably now accepted that he could not continue to be head
of state as Chairman of the People's Republic. Many of
them would doubtless have been satisfied with that. But
there were strong pressures to reopen the files on Liu and

[52] T'an Chen-lin was one of Mao Tse-tung's entourage with
members of the Political Bureau on May 1, 1967. His political
elimination must have taken place later.

make a more thorough-going condemnation, pressures coming from the streets and the popular leaders who saw the way forward for the Cultural Revolution in the complete politicization of the masses.

The revolutionary leadership for the most part accepted these pressures, as a deeper criticism of Liu Shao-ch'i could be a rallying-point for the left. Divisions among the students were serious enough, and those among the workers were even worse, as the more conservative of them had vested interests to defend.[53] For the leaders of the Cultural Revolution, putting the criticism of Liu on the agenda would give them the chance to consolidate their ascendancy over organizations threatened by anarchy and revolutionaries who criticized all leaders indiscriminately.

Differences of opinion on how much further to take the criticism of Liu Shao-ch'i were expressions of different views on the intensification of the Cultural Revolution. Those of the new leaders who had close ties with the masses, especially Wang Li, Ch'i Pen-yü, Kuan Feng and Lin Chieh, clearly based their ambitions on the forces they represented. But they also knew that they would have to produce something new if they were to reunite the different tendencies into which the mass movement was splitting. Whether it was to take the form of criticizing T'an Chen-lin or further attacks on Liu Shao-ch'i, the enlarged meeting of the Political Bureau held in March was essentially dealing with the question of whether to intensify the Cultural Revolution. Opinions were divided.

The compromise that seemed to emerge was a decision to criticize Liu Shao-ch'i's writings rather than Liu himself. In the following months the book on 'self-cultivation'[54] was to be the main target of official criticism. Despite this distinction, the leftist leaders brought the criticism of Liu Shao-ch'i himself to the attention of the

[53] The workers had their own special demands.
[54] *On the Self-Cultivation of Communists,* better known in the west under the title of the Peking translation, *How to Be a Good Communist.*

people. As a result, the objectives of the 'great criticism' were ambiguous.

Ch'i Pen-yü opened the attack, and immediately went beyond the issue of Liu's writing by taking as his theme an old film, 'The Secret History of the Ch'ing Court'[55] which Liu Shao-ch'i had admired and recommended, and which had 'still been widely shown in Peking even in 1950.' Ch'i Pen-yü called his article 'Patriotism or Treason?'[56] and used it to show that the criticized leader's earlier career was marked with weakness and compromise. He ended in the style of the posters then covering the walls of the city with eight questions which exposed to full view the 'fifty crimes of Liu Shao-ch'i.' As his parting shot Ch'i made personal attacks on Liu, and did so in an article published in the Party's theoretical journal.[57] He called Liu, for the first time in the official press, 'the chief of the executives who, though Party members, have committed themselves to the capitalist way.'

Ch'i chose in the list of 'fifty crimes' one of the three to which Liu had not already confessed in his self-criticism: first, making the Party his 'personal party' by putting his friends in responsible positions; second, eliminating the Thought of Mao Tse-tung from his report to the Second Plenary Session of the Eighth Party Congress (after the Twentieth CPSU Congress Liu Shao-ch'i and Teng Hsiao-p'ing had taken pains to show that there was no cult of personality in China);[58] and third, having in 1936–37 instructed some Communists who were in prison to recant in order to be released. Liu was accused of having done a deal with the Kuomintang at that time. It was this last 'crime' that Ch'i Pen-yü denounced in his article:

Why did you, on the eve of the Anti-Japanese War, preach the philosophy of survival, surrender and be-

[55] A film made in 1948 in Hong Kong about the Ch'ing emperor's reaction to the Yihot'uan (Boxer) struggle.

[56] Peking Review, 1967, no. 15, April 10, 1967.

[57] Red Flag, 1967, no. 5, March 30, 1967.

[58] For a comparison of the self-criticism with the various 'lists of questions' see Chugoku Kenyū Geppō, no. 231, Tokyo, 1967, pp. 2–6.

trayal? Why did you press others to betray and denounce themselves? Why did you let them betray the Communist Party and defect to the Kuomintang?

The object of exposing events and personal activities of the past which had not been covered in the self-criticism made to the Central Committee, and publishing it in the pages of *Red Flag*, could only be a demand for a new self-criticism. It also amounted to presenting the Political Bureau that had just met with a *fait accompli*.

Did Mao Tse-tung approve this initiative? To find the answer to this question one must look at the next issue of *Red Flag*,[59] which contained a reply to Ch'i Pen-yü's article under the title, 'The essence of the book on "Self-Cultivation" is the betrayal of proletarian dictatorship.'[60] This appears to be a hint that the writings and not the personality were to be criticized. Then Wang Li,[61] the new head of propaganda, gave this piece of advice to the leadership of the New China News Agency:

> *Red Flag* and the *People's Daily* have published an important article. It would appear that Chairman Mao has criticized and corrected it himself. This article is the consequence of discussions at the enlarged meeting of the Political Bureau.[62]

The only conclusion to be drawn from this is that Ch'i Pen-yü, and with him the Central Committee's Cultural Revolution Group, were being brought back into line, and that Mao Tse-tung himself had taken a direct part in doing so. Wang Li was giving the news agency the correct line.

But despite this the ultra-left did not lay down its arms. On June 19th Lin Chieh, another member of the Central Committee's Cultural Revolution Group, brought out a

59 No. 6, May 8, 1967.

60 Translation in *Peking Review*, no. 20, May 15, 1967.

61 Member of the Central Committee's Cultural Revolution Group.

62 Letter quoted in the paper of the Steel Institute's Red Guards, May 17, 1967.

spirited article in the *People's Daily* in which he demanded
considerably more than that revolutionaries should unite in
the service of the Party: he wanted total and absolute
obedience to the revolutionary committees or the groups
that were preparing to set them up. In his piece, 'Down
with slavery—strictly observe proletarian revolutionary discipline,' he demanded that the provisional institutions
should be drastically strengthened. His policy, if adopted,
would doubtless have involved the creation of revolutionary tribunals. This is how Lin Chieh spelled out his idea
of the absolute ideological authority of the Thought of
Mao Tse-tung:

> We must follow the instructions of Chairman Mao
> whether or not we have fully grasped their import.
> A proletarian Party must have its own really supreme
> leader. His absolute revolutionary authority must be es-
> tablished over the whole Party. Failing this the Party
> will lack iron discipline and its victory will not be certain.

This line of thought was getting too far away from the
principle of correcting the Party's errors through criticism
by the people. The next day a warning against the tendencies of the extreme left could be read between the lines
of a *Red Flag* article.[63] It amounted to a statement that
there was no need to turn society completely upside down,
in view of the fact that the bourgeoisie had only usurped
the proletarian dictatorship in certain sectors:

> Certain people are wrong to press for the 'complete
> renewal of the dictatorship of the proletariat.' Some peo-
> ple with ulterior motives want to deny the whole of
> the past and reverse all past events, that is, to overthrow
> the dictatorship of the proletariat and install a bourgeois
> one.

As far as we can tell, Mao Tse-tung at that time
only wanted the revolution speeded up. 'I am not in

[63] No. 10, 1967. 'A Theoretical Weapon for Making Revolution Under the Proletarian Dictatorship.'

favour of the people everywhere overthrowing too rapidly the organizations and associations of the Party,' he is reported to have said on March 29th.[64] He no longer hoped to achieve the immediate regeneration of the Party, which would have involved at least a minimum of reorganization by the revolutionaries. He said on the same day that the reconstitution of the Party would have to wait for a while.[65]

No doubt the line was to encourage the revolutionaries to reunite through combining against such indefensible figures as P'eng Chen and Lo Jui-ch'ing, who had in any case been condemned without any possible reservations.

The anniversary of the May 16th Circular, which was finally made available to the general public a year after its appearance,[66] offered a chance to put this policy into practice. However, the Mao Tse-tung group gave the impression from this time on of having to take leftist pressures into account. Those in the army who were most inclined to take political action were calling criticism meetings in their units even before May 16th. On May 12th Lo Jui-ch'ing was once again brought out and shown to the people by the students of a military academy. On July 1st, the Party's anniversary, the official press demanded an end to pressures on the revolutionary centre to change its decisions,[67] also reminding its readers of the necessity of struggling 'against the various non-proletarian ideas that appear among the people and in the revolutionary ranks.'

[64] Quoted in Ito's article 'Mono iwanu Liu-Teng ha,' *Asahi Jyanaru*, 1967, vol. 9, no. 37, p. 24.

[65] *Chūgoku Bunka Kakumei wo dō miru ka*, op. cit., p. 221.

[66] In a *Red Flag* article called, 'A great historic Document.' This title had a touch of humour to it. Exactly a year earlier the *People's Daily* had entitled a Sino-Albanian communiqué 'A Document of great historical Significance' at the very time the Central Committee was adopting the May 16th Circular. The similarity between the two titles may imply that Liu Shao-ch'i was satisfied with token agreements which he called 'historic' at a time when real history was being made elsewhere.

[67] *PLA Daily*, July 1, 1967. New China News Agency despatch no. 070119 (French language series).

The people, the cadres, and the army

The industrial workers and peasants were not, in general, sufficiently politically conscious to feel concerned over ideological discussions. For them, class struggle was aroused from convictions born of the most straightforward social contacts. Most of them turned up on Cultural Revolution demonstrations without really being involved. The whole business of demonstrating was formalized, as was ingenuously admitted when the time came to settle accounts. In Weishih county, Honan, for example:

In our administrative district and *hsien* everybody had to make a little flag and every village, big or small, a banner. Although many cadres realized that this was not consistent with the spirit of 'making revolution frugally,' anyone who dared say this was at once made to wear a dunce's cap. So we had to make them, even if it meant going into debt in order to do so.[68]

Many other examples of such half-hearted involvement could be cited. Peasants complained of working time lost in visits to town for demonstrations, and flour wasted making paste for posters. One institute won popularity for teaching how a poster stuck up with mud would last long enough to do its job, 'given that it is generally sufficient for *tatzupao* to stay up for three to five days.'[69] Among the artisans and industrial workers of the cities of the hinterland, class consciousness was felt less sharply than the social heritage of the former guilds. Rebels were to complain that attachment to obsolete forms of society emasculated the proletarian class struggle:

It may seem that the present tendency of the revolution in Szechuan is excellent. But there are some abnormalities to which attention must be paid. Some revolution-

---

[68] Cited in *Mōtakutō no chōsen*, p. 191.

[69] The Nanking Institute of Engineering—see *Mōtakutō no chōsen*, p. 192.

ary organizations which have not grasped the overall orientation [to be followed] are concerning themselves with internal struggles rather than involving themselves fully in criticism. Some comrades belonging to revolutionary organizations who are well aware that internal struggles are wrong are moved by a kind of 'gratitude.' 'Those who helped us when we were in trouble,' they say, 'now ask our help. We can't forget our obligations and let them fall.' Such ideas of obligation and gratitude come from the feudal guilds. There is no place for them in the working-class Communist consciousness.[70]

But the peasants' inclination to wait and see could turn to irritation, and the turbulence among the workers to anger, if the Cultural Revolution failed to give birth to a renovated political system. All the sceptics could see for the time being were dunce's caps and people being treated as 'dogs' heads' and forced to confess their sins on their knees. Moreover, the leaders decreed that 'beating, looting, pillage, requisitioning and arrests'[71] were forbidden, in itself not a good sign. The revolutionaries would score some points if they managed to get the revolutionary committees on their feet. If the committees were to be viable they had to include a basic minimum of competent public administrators. These were inevitably cadres, and the cadres had been antagonized.

Cadres were afraid of being made scapegoats, of being 'shown to the masses' for the least initiative they took. Most of them avoided any deep commitment and shouted 'Long live the Revolution' for the sake of peace. The leaders saw that they had to be won over. As we have seen above, it was highly significant that the struggle against Liu Shao-ch'i was directed at his writings, not at the man himself. Revolutionary cadres were 'not in any circumstances to wait passively, stand aside from the struggle, or, following the teachings of the book on the "self-cultivation" of communists, examine their consciences

[70] *Ibid.*, pp. 194–95, quoting the Szechuan Railway Bureau employees.

[71] Important Notice of the Peking Municipal Revolutionary Committee, published in *People's Daily*, May 22, 1967.

behind closed doors while nursing the hope that one day they would suddenly be "liberated" and allowed to join the triple alliance.'[72]

The revolutionary leadership judged it prudent to remind cadres that few of them would really be prosecuted, that 'even if there are some bad people there can only be a few of them,'[73] and that the general direction of the struggle was to lay the blame only on 'the small handful of top leaders taking the capitalist road.'

Once the objective and the tactics had been settled, the Centre could lay down the law on the policy towards the cadres. They were not the stakes in the game between the revolutionaries and the conservatives. Neither were they the symbols of the power to be overthrown. They had to be analyzed as a political force. 'What we need to do is to find the truth by examining the facts and making class analyses, not by giving preference to a "left" over a "right." '[74]

This was a rebuttal of the ultra-left line that all former cadres should be excluded from the movement. The question of winning over the cadres, like that of the revolution's accelerating pace, was the subject of a political quarrel. 'Some people . . . do not believe that the cadres who are now coming forward to make revolution can be sincere. They have no trust at all in these cadres, and regard them as undesirables, even going so far as to call them "speculators." ' So said the *People's Daily*[75] in a discussion on the sincerity of eleventh-hour rebels. The position taken by the intransigents was not necessarily leftist, but the Party press described it as a leftist one.

Leftists may well have had good reason to suspect some

[72] *People's Daily* editorial of April 24, 1967.

[73] Speech by K'ang Sheng to revolutionary delegates from Anhwei visiting Peking to learn from the experience of Shanghai, October 22, 1967.

[74] K'ang Sheng's speech to the revolutionary delegates from Anhwei visiting Peking to learn from Shanghai's experience.

[75] *Jenmin Jihpao*, April 18, 1967, 'Let us encourage the cadres to come forward and make revolution.' The article was signed 'The Commentator.'

of these convenient changes of heart. It sometimes happened that local leaders brought back cadres whose services were needed. Even in Peking Wu Teh, Liu Chienhsün, Kao Yang-wen and Ting Kuo-yü[76] seemed to have come over together in order to hasten the establishment of the municipal revolutionary committee. The top men of the Cultural Revolution needed leaders from among the old cadres to set alongside the Revolutionary Rebels.

There was no lack of soldiers to place alongside the Rebels. The army, which had been asked to represent authority in many sectors of life, slid into this new role without hesitation. The power it had been given in order to fight against reactionary or trouble-making organizations made it somewhat high-handed. The Military Commission had to issue a directive on April 6th to remind the soldiers that they should confine themselves to political work. The people were not to be forced to write confessions, beaten up, subjected to confiscation, or pilloried. The directive also pointed out that the fact that an association of the people had given itself a para-military organization did not indicate whether it was a rightist or leftist body.

Chou En-lai later made a comparison[77] between this and the directive of January 28th, which had been issued at the time the army started to play an active part in the revolution. The aim of the first was to urge the people to love the army; that of the later one was to urge the army

[76] Wu Teh was previously Secretary of the Central Committee's North China Bureau and First Secretary of Kirin Province. These four politicians joined the Peking Municipal Revolutionary Committee. Their collective self-criticism (March 7–11, 1967), and the speed with which it was made in public, both suggest that this was a tactical manoeuvre intended to achieve a specific end. Liu Chien-hsün was later sent on a mission to Honan, becoming Chairman of Honan's Revolutionary Committee.

[77] Speech of September 17, 1967, to delegates of the Congress of Students from Peking University and Institutes of Higher Education. Chiang Ch'ing had made the same comparison on April 20th, when the Peking Municipal Revolutionary Committee was founded. See 'Diary of the Cultural Revolution,' op. cit.

to love the people. The soldiers must have been guilty of
some abuses.

On April 25th the *People's Daily* reprinted an article
from the *PLA Daily* of the previous day telling the military what was expected of them: 'in supporting the struggles of the left, the comrades of the army must be the
friends of the people and not their bosses.' It urged the
soldiers to accept the criticisms of the masses. The prevailing policy seemed to be that the army should only
intervene at the invitation of the revolutionary committee,
if there was one. But this was not always the case.

Public proclamations gave the army increasingly greater
powers of decision. For example, the Peking Revolutionary Committee issued a notice that read:

> The Peking Garrison of the PLA and its military repre-
> sentatives have the right to deal with cases of violent
> conflicts. The disputants must obey them and must not
> refuse to carry out their orders.[78]

A circular from the Centre on June 6th was in similar
vein:

> Local troops, as well as troops stationed in the area, are
> responsible for the carrying out of directives. . . .
> They are empowered to arrest, imprison and try accord-
> ing to the law trouble-makers, those who urge them on,
> and criminals who have wounded or killed people.[79]

In these conditions some military leaders could easily
believe that they were in control. In some districts direct
conflict developed between them and the civilian members of the 'provisional organs of power' to such a degree
that the latter attempted to impose a purge:

> Ideas and actions which imply that the Party committee
> of a military zone has authority over the local revolu-

[78] 'Important Notice,' of the Peking Revolutionary Committee printed in the *People's Daily* of May 22nd (extract).

[79] This circular, also known as the Six-Point Circular, is
included in full in Konno, *op. cit.*, pp. 231–32.

tionary committee must be criticized seriously and corrected.[80]

Circumstances thus gave the soldiers an advantage over the politicians in general and the propagandists of ideology in particular. At the same time the Communist Party organization in the army had retained a cohesion that its civilian counterpart had certainly lost. It would appear that the chances for the latter to take part in the revolutionary committees alongside the cadres who had been won over soon faded into the background, among such other problems of political orientation as those concerning students and revolutionary theorists.

There were no discussions among the military as to who was suitable to join the revolutionary committees and who was not. The Party committees in the army simply appointed the delegates they thought suitable. The Party organization inside the army seems to have passed through the Cultural Revolution undamaged, and it went on to play a major part in the reconstitution of the Party as a whole.

As it had been prepared for the Cultural Revolution before the rest of the country and had the additional advantage of being allowed to sort out its own problems undisturbed, the army gave the impression of being a stable force. This stability brought it the support of conservative elements. Some reactionary organizations announced that they wished to be put under army command.[81] This would have been their passport to the revolution without their having to find their own ideological course.

[80] 'The four main lessons' of members of the Tuyun Military District Party Committee. Radio Kweichow, March 10, 1968. This concerned the autonomous *Chou* of Chiennan.

[81] Especially noteworthy was the demand of the *Lien Tung* (Joint Action Committee), for example, that 'all organizations should be put under the leadership of the Central Military Commission.' This demand brought protests from other revolutionary organizations, who said that this would have set the Cultural Revolution Group and the Military Commission at loggerheads. See *Shoutu Fenglei*, January 27, 1967.

However, the Military Commission and the Cultural Revolution Group seemed to be co-existing at the Centre without friction, until a minor incident revealed that there were difficulties.

On May 1st and October 1st each year a list was normally published showing the ranking of Party and government figures. On May 1st many of these were invited to take part in the celebrations with the top leaders. The papers usually published their names the next day, and the order in which they were listed was significant.

One therefore expected the *People's Daily* of May 2, 1967, to list the members of the Central Committee and the Cultural Revolution Group, the army leaders, and the top men in the Party and the government who had been able to come to Peking and had watched the fireworks with Mao Tse-tung the previous evening.

The paper did not come out on May 2nd. The May 2nd issue was not distributed until the next day, and there was a slight difference between the order of names in the New China News Agency release of the evening of May 2nd and the list in the paper published on May 3rd. The five most junior members of the Cultural Revolution Group, who had been listed after the army representatives in the news agency bulletin, were raised above them in the paper, so that the Group now took precedence over the army.[82] This seems to have been a minor victory, not over the Military Commission (which was not listed as a body, its members being divided between the Central Committee and the group of military leaders), but in principle.

If anyone's ambitions were satisfied that day it was not those of the senior members of the Cultural Revolution Group—Ch'en Po-t'a, K'ang Sheng and Chiang Ch'ing—who were listed in Mao Tse-tung's personal entourage, but those of the men who were later to emerge as the leaders of the ultra-left wing. One may well imagine that there were mixed reactions in the army to the changed listing. The supporters of the Cultural Revolution Group in

[82] The five young propagandists were Wang Li, Kuan Feng, Ch'i Pen-yü, Hsieh T'ang-chung, and Mu Hsin.

the army must have been triumphant, and this may be why the campaign of criticism against Lo Jui-ch'ing was intensified after May 16th. The Military Commission does not appear to have retaliated against the Cultural Revolution Group.

The leaders did their utmost to maintain the cohesion of the army, despite criticisms made by the revolutionaries of the authoritarian attitude of certain local military commanders. But although the army leaders may have yielded precedence, they took their revenge elsewhere by restraining the revolutionaries in their criticisms of officers who had indeed become 'the authorities' in their own regions.

6. The Workers Seize Power and Refuse to Lay Down Their Arms

Could the Cultural Revolution have taken place without the industrial workers? The answer must be 'no', for it had to succeed in Shanghai. The Party machine had most of its strength in the cities, and it favoured urban over rural development, so that it had strong support in the cities. The great industrial metropolis of Shanghai was in particular a stronghold of the trade unions.

December was the month for financial settlements in all enterprises and communes. At this time of year several decisions affecting wage-earners were taken: the awarding of bonus payments, and the allocation of profits which could be either kept as reserves or distributed in part to the workers. The 'authorities' presided over these decisions, but criticisms were being levelled against the Party committees in general, and lively disputes were bound to develop almost everywhere in December 1966. Whether the 'authorities' opted for austerity or distributed public wealth in order to win appreciation, they were bound to be criticized. The result would probably have been the same in the end, in that more was distributed than usual. The revolutionary leadership could not allow them to win an advantage over the Cultural Revolution. They therefore had to try to control the Revolution in the factories and the countryside, and to do that they had to admit that the Revolution had spread there.

On December 9th the Central Committee passed a draft directive on the Cultural Revolution in factories and mines that was posted at the entrances to the enterprises. This directive, still 'under discussion' at the time, was to be carried out in a number of places as an experiment.[1] This came at a tense moment in the development of the conflict between the 'Workers' Revolutionary Rebel Headquarters,' already in existence, and the Shanghai municipal committee which, together with the unions, was supporting another powerful workers' organization. This second organization was using the same methods as the revolutionaries but with even greater boldness. Its determination to win was the cause of the big strikes in Shanghai around the New Year.

The response of the revolutionaries and the creation of proletarian political power was called the January Revolution. It bore some resemblances to a classic proletarian revolution. It was born during an extended crisis involving all ten million of its inhabitants, and on this scale it could almost be regarded as a national crisis. The crisis had been provoked by the Party leadership, which proved incapable of resolving it, either because it was already too weak to take power, or else because it was afraid of losing its privileges. The January Revolution was thus the result of an abortive bourgeois revolution, with the Party playing the role of the bourgeois power. In addition, the workers did not bring it about single-handed: a considerable proportion of the population joined in with them.

Despite their indisputable political achievement in establishing the Shanghai Commune, which though short-lived did not end in tragedy, the revolutionaries did not consolidate the power they had won by and for themselves. They handed over their conquests to the Cultural Revolution. The industrial worker Rebels, who held the key to the whole situation, turned their fire towards those who represented the old trade unions, which generally meant other organizations within their own class.

[1] *Nihon Keizai,* December 29, 1966.

Most of the workers' demands concerned their conditions: hours of work, protests against work-rates, bonus systems, regional differences, and the status of temporary workers. Only a part of their demands were approved by the Centre and written into the orthodox revolutionary line. The Centre only accepted what fitted in with the struggle against 'economism,' by which it meant the whole range of material stimuli that offered differing rewards among workers of the same category. The eagerness of some workers to abolish extra payments for enthusiasm or endurance fitted in with the Cultural Revolution policy of equality in austerity. But when other forms of social equality were brought into question the Centre was very reluctant to co-operate. A case in point was that of the wages of peasants working in factories on collective or individual contracts.

The Centre seemed more than once to be about to allow their wages to be brought up to the level of regular workers, but in the end they did not yield to the most pressing demands on this point, even when they were backed up by the most orthodox of the Revolutionary Rebels. Reducing the gap between urban and rural standards of living was on the programme, but the ways of achieving this needed to be looked into carefully by the leadership of the revolution. According to all the evidence, it was recognized that this should not be done by raising the wages of peasants working as contract labourers.

The ideal solution would have been to abolish the system of temporary workers—peasants working in factories under seasonal or annual contracts—and to establish them as regular workers. But pressure of population meant that there were not enough jobs available to keep some of the rural population permanently in the cities. Peasant-workers still had their homes in the countryside and had to go back there when they had fulfilled their contracts. On their return to the villages they took back useful technical know-how with them.

In the words of a Japanese specialist, 'the active population is growing by seven or eight million people a year,

and only 300,000 of these can be found jobs.'[2] Everybody
wanted to become an industrial worker and get a job in a
factory. The story was told of some Red Guards of fourteen
and fifteen who went to join the workers in a Peking factory and hoped to spend the rest of their lives there.[3]
T'an Chen-lin said:

> Control of the population is now being proposed, but
> the population keeps on growing. It is increasing at
> about the same rate as production. Can this be called
> affluence? Given our methods of production, who would
> choose freely to go to the countryside? Everyone wants
> to go to the cities, where you can earn thirty or forty
> yuan a month just by sweeping the street, whereas you
> can't earn more than 200 or 300 yuan a year in the
> countryside. Will anyone here volunteer to be a
> peasant?[4]

This debate touched on basic policies, and they were
taken to heart by some of the revolutionary workers to
such an extent that they carried the dispute beyond an
exchange of views between supporters and opponents of
trade unions. They gave the working-class revolution
a specifically working-class tendency. But the workers did
not dare to take this kind of demand too far: the regular
workers had too much to lose from a general social
shake-up.

The regime, however, was not afraid of social shake-
ups: indeed, it regarded them as counterparts of its economic policies. One has only to remember the circumstances in which the people's communes were created:
the Party decided that a more communist form of society
would be suitable in view of the rising production of con-
sumer goods, an unexpected growth in the output of capi-

[2] *Asahi Shimbun,* January 22, 1967: round-table discussion
with Professors Ishikawa and Oka of Hitotsubashi University.
[3] Kaizuka, 'Chūgoku to wa nani ka' *Asahi Jyanaru,* February 26, 1967, p. 105.
[4] *Peiching K'ochi Hungch'i* (Science and Technology Red
Flag), March 6, 1967, quoting a speech made by T'an on September 7, 1966.

tal goods, and the backwardness of scientific and technical education.[5]

The regime reacted in a way that would have been unusual in the West: it changed the social structure. The workers did not want to take the risk of this kind of disruption. They were doubtless well aware that it would not be to their own advantage to destroy the balance between workers and peasants. This might lead to different kinds of work, such as long periods of service in underdeveloped regions or reregistration in new industrial centres. For their different reasons the workers and the Centre agreed on maintaining the *status quo:* the workers in order to keep what they had won, and the Centre in order to preserve the chances of reconstituting the Party at a time when it was very vulnerable.

The Shanghai Commune had an executive committee with twelve members, of whom only two were soldiers; and Shanghai often gave the impression of wanting to dispense with the army in making its revolution. The revolutionaries who founded the Commune established it on the basis of the workers' committees, that had already taken charge in factories and other areas of activity, and of the organizations that had joined these committees. The history of Shanghai after the general strike was the history of the workers who ran its essential services. The new power structure was built from the bottom upwards: economic control groups, 'committees to make revolution and hasten production,' the Commune, and later the Revolutionary Committee. The revolution's leadership would have liked the same procedure—taking over the organization of work, then taking charge of finances, politics and security —to have been followed in the power seizures throughout the country.

When the Commune handed over to the Revolutionary Committee, the organizations that had been supporting it lost some of their confidence in the workers' Cultural Revolution. They, like the other organizations that had

[5] See Peter Shran, 'On the rationality of the great leap forward and rural people's communes,' in *Ventures*, Yale Graduate School, vol. 5, no. 1, January 1965.

been against the Commune, objected to putting their political activities blindly under the orders of the Cultural Revolution Group in Peking. They all preferred to concentrate on the reorganization of industry. The Centre was worried by the revived corporate spirit shown by some of these organizations. Some organizations went beyond the structures established by the Party. This was when the Centre called a halt, announcing that if changes were necessary they would be held over until after the end of the movement (which also implied 'after the rebuilding of the Party'—for the time being its reorganization was not to be endangered). Thus organizations that went beyond existing structures and threatened to become pressure groups could not be tolerated. Some associations were dissolved. A limitation on the right of association was the first restriction of the freedoms that had been conceded.

Priority was given to the economic situation. The state's economic plan had already been postponed,[6] and throughout the country seizures of power brought about interruptions of work and strikes. Many cadres who were threatened did not return to their posts, as the directive that only a small number of them (those who were actually guilty of abuses) were to be attacked had been misinterpreted by the extremists.

The whole country had to take the consequences. The Centre also reminded workers of labour discipline: 'Let us stop putting forward demands that will be looked into fairly later on, and let us resume the eight-hour working day.'

The Centre felt that the workers would be able to sort out the questions that especially concerned them within the revolutionary committees, where they were represented among the mass organizations. But in many Units the power seizures had not been thoroughly carried out—revolutionary committees had been poorly established or not set up at all—and struggles against the top figures in the

[6] Chou En-lai said in a speech on February 2, 1968, 'We shall be able to take a decision during February on our 1968 plan. . . . Last year we postponed it, and we must not do so again this year.'

former administration were becoming weak and ineffectual. Sometimes the revolutionaries even found their opponents in the majority.

The extremists in the Central Committee's Cultural Revolution Group, lacking Mao Tse-tung's patience, complained that the disorder might bring about the collapse of the Cultural Revolution. They put pressure on the revolutionaries to complete their seizures of power. A number of workers' organizations in Shanghai decided to treat the revolutionary committees as organs replacing the Party, making the dictatorship of the proletariat as absolute as the Centre would allow.

There was trouble during the summer. The new power seizures provoked another wave of strikes. Conservative groups of workers threatened the revolutionaries and beat them up in Wuhan, Shanghai and Shantung. In retaliation worker rebels in Shanghai set up revolutionary tribunals.

East China, the middle Yangtse, and the Canton region were particularly badly hit by clashes among workers. Mao Tse-tung himself made a journey of investigation through Eastern and Central China, and gave a new editorial line to the *Wenhui Pao*, which became once more the paper of the revolution. At the height of the crisis articles were published on the regulations for the work force. Mao Tse-tung felt that workers who were fighting among themselves had not made a class analysis of the situation. His ruling was widely published: there was nothing to divide the working class.

From that moment onwards there could be no possible privileges for workers who were more leftist or revolutionary than the others. The Centre told the army to act as catalyst between the different factions. Soldiers sent into the factories were given the job of bringing about alliances among the workers. The incidents that were still frequent and serious showed that there were more contradictions between the protesting workers and the state than there were between rival workers' groupings. The further wave of strikes that ensued were in protest against the reorganization of work in forms that had yet to be accepted by everyone.

The Centre's policy of 'alliances' (i.e. regrouping), threatened those of the workers' organizations that had always been the most revolutionary with the loss of their individual identities. They struggled to keep their independence and political power, demanding arms and making renewed critical assaults on the old trade unions. This revealed that what they were afraid of was a return to the old order, and they made it clear that in their view workers' rights would no longer be defended if the old trade unions, which had always been primarily concerned with production, were revived. But as the reconstruction of the Party took priority over everything else, the leadership of the revolution decided to neutralize step by step the forces of the liberated workers.

The January Revolution

There were similarities between the first few months of the Cultural Revolution in Shanghai's factories and Peking's universities. First, the Party sent work teams into certain factories. Later on Red Guards who had been sent out as scouts by the organizations in the capital established 'liaison posts' in them. To Factory No. 31, for example, came members of the Institute of Aviation's Red Flag. They urged the workers to join in that movement.

A few of the workers sympathised with the revolutionary students. The secretary of the factory's Party committee made enquiries about them, probably because he was suspicious of students from Peking. The Party committee favoured another organization that was created on the model of students groupings and went on later to link up with other similar bodies under the name of *Ch'ih-wei-tui,* or 'Red Defence Teams.' These were often referred to as the 'Scarlet Guards.'

The workers whose sympathies lay with the revolutionary students formed their own confederation on November 9th; they decided to form 'Revolutionary Rebel' groups in the factories and a Shanghai Workers' Rebel

Revolutionary Headquarters. They were now about 4,000 strong.

The Revolutionary Rebels adopted a series of resolutions condemning the Scarlet Guard organizations, and sent a group of their members to Peking. This delegation had a quarrel with industrial workers of the other side as it set out, and the train crew that was taking them north refused to continue the journey. They were left at Anting, eighteen kilometres from Shanghai, without food or money. The Centre sent Chang Ch'un-ch'iao to find out the true situation in the revolution there when it heard of this.

Chang, the secretary of the Shanghai Municipal Party Committee, had gone to Peking for the Eleventh Plenary Session of the Central Committee, and stayed on there as vice-chairman of the Cultural Revolution Group. On his return to Shanghai he recognized the Shanghai Workers' Rebel Revolutionary Headquarters. When the rebels held a new rally on November 13th, Chang Ch'un-ch'iao pressed the municipal committee of the Party to approve their demands. The top man in the committee, Ts'ao Ti-ch'iu, finally agreed to sign them after he had telephoned the Cultural Revolution Group in Peking.

When the municipal committee met again on November 24th it disavowed Ts'ao Ti-ch'iu's assent to the demands. The Scarlet Guards, they said, represented the majority, and Ts'ao Ti-ch'iu had been wrong to sign.[7] The Scarlet Guards had apparently been formed at the instigation of the top figures in the trade unions. Chang Ch'un-ch'iao left for Peking again the day after the municipal committee's meeting.

During his absence there was fighting at the offices of the *Liberation Daily*.[8] The Scarlet Guards wanted to pre-

[7] See the account of these incidents in *Chūgoku Kenkyū Geppō*, 230, April 1967, pp. 6–9.

[8] Publication of the *Liberation Daily* (*Chiehfang Jihpao*) was suspended and there were fights. The editors of the Rebel sheet, *Hungwei Chanpao*, barricaded themselves inside the premises. The municipal committee came under heavy pressure from the Scarlet Guards, but its desire to see this important paper published again moved the committee to allow the rebels to circulate their sheet as they wished.

vent a Rebel sheet being distributed with the newspaper, but after initial hesitations the municipal committee gave in to the Rebels. Its indecision put both sides against it.

The Scarlet Guards held their inauguration on December 6. Soon afterwards they brought discredit on themselves by a serious attack on the Rebels. There was an armed clash at Cotton Mill 24 at Sechih.[9]

It was just then that the Centre decided to extend the Cultural Revolution to the workers. The scene now shifted briefly to Peking. The directive that was adopted was quite moderate in character, but it was the result of a much more vigorous intervention by the Central Committee's Cultural Revolution Group. This had two objectives: the overthrow of the trade unions whose forces were using Red Guard methods to fight against the Red Guards, and a solution of the question of temporary labourers, a problem that most of the workers regarded as a very serious one.

The directive of December 9th[10] reflected the idea that workers should be allowed the right of criticism just when the Party committees in industrial enterprises were trying to buy popularity with generous hand-outs. The old 'authorities' still held the purse-strings everywhere, and December was the month in which accounts were drawn up and decisions on profit-sharing and bonuses were made, decisions that affected all the employees. According to Radio Peking, those in authority had been advocating 'the free discussion of financial problems and the raising of salaries; more recently they have even been distributing state funds.'[11]

Seventeen days later the Cultural Revolution Group took things one step further when Ch'en Po-ta and Chiang Ch'ing allowed the workers' rebel organizations to take

[9] *Wenhui Pao*, December 24, 1967.
[10] Adopted in draft form to be applied experimentally in a limited number of establishments only. See *Asahi Shimbun*, December 20, 1967 (Japanese morning edition).
[11] January 16, 1967.

over the trade union federation.[12] The next day, December 27th, it was the scene of one of the first major seizures of power.

As soon as it was installed, the new trade union federation announced that the system of temporary and contract workers was irrational.[13] The revolutionary leadership thus seemed to be approving one of the main social demands of the workers. The *People's Daily* also announced that revolutionary workers should be compensated for all lost pay. This was open to the interpretation that the Centre agreed to the readjustments being made at the end of that year.

It thus appears that when the workers became necessary to the revolution, the revolution's leaders were induced to promise them certain material benefits. This weakness may have caused embarrassment later on, when the distribution of benefits by the men in power was condemned as 'economism'[14]—the corruptor of the working class. The policy was soon changed: fifteen days later Chou En-lai overruled the condemnation of the system of temporary workers, declaring that the pay rises for contract and temporary workers were unacceptable as they might arouse resistance from the peasants.[15] The prime minister quoted a letter to Lin Piao from Mao Tse-tung himself.

To return to Shanghai, the Scarlet Guards were trying to get themselves recognized as the principal and most representative working class organization, despite the hesitation of the municipal Party committee, which was well aware that the Cultural Revolution Group of the Central Committee preferred the Revolutionary Rebels. At a big rally on December 23rd the Scarlet Guards adopted a list

[12] See P. Bridgham, 'Mao's Cultural Revolution in 1967,' *China Quarterly*, 34, 1968, p. 8. See also *Asahi Shimbun*, Japanese morning edition, January 10, 1967.

[13] *Ibid. Wenhui Pao* reported on January 6, 1967, that 100,000 temporary and contract labourers held a rally in Shanghai to demand the replacement of the system by a new one that conformed to the Thought of Mao Tse-tung.

[14] An adaptation of the term used by Lenin in *What Is to Be Done?*.

[15] According to Japanese press sources quoted in *Current Scene*, vol. 6, no. 5, March 15, 1968, p. 11.

of eight demands that they wanted the municipal committee to adopt, demands that if accepted would have made them the armed guards of the Party, the State and the Cultural Revolution. Ts'ao Ti-ch'iu refused to endorse them and they laid seige to his home. The Scarlet Guards started to send representatives to Peking to present their demands. Their factories and offices gave them their travelling expenses and their pay arrears.

The Revolutionary Rebels tried to resist the departure of the other workers for Peking. Brawls continued till December 30th, and the posters listed some dead and many wounded.

Thus it was that the strike began. The Scarlet Guards regarded it as their unanswerable weapon to bring the municipal committee to its knees. According to statements made by some other members after the event, the committee reckoned that even with the mills and postal services on strike, the city's life could continue, and that if the committee held firm only a transport strike would follow.[16] At 5 a.m. on December 30th the trains came to a halt on the two principal lines serving Shanghai.

The transport strike ended by depriving the city of fuel and power. The Rebels decided to take over the main papers and call upon the masses to go back to work. The *Wenhui Pao* was seized on January 3rd with the cooperation of the Red Guards of the Third Headquarters. The next day Chang Ch'un-ch'iao went back to Peking and the 'Appeal to the People of Shanghai'[17] was published, a document that had great repercussions.

The appeals published in the press denounced the crimes of 'the authorities who have tried to obstruct production' even more vehemently than they attacked the Scarlet Guards. Some of the people, whether from exhaustion or

[16] *Wenhui Pao,* December 24, 1967.

[17] The appeal was signed by eleven organizations, including four Shanghai Red Guard organizations, three 'liaison posts' of Red Guards from elsewhere, some workers' organizations, including the powerful Revolutionary Rebel Headquarters, and the Revolutionary Rebels of the newspapers. See the translation in *Peking Review*, 1967, no. 3, January 13, 1967.

anger, were ready to go back to work, but they had to be offered a change of management. This was the job of the 'Shanghai Front Line for Revolution and Production,' which started work at 6 p.m. on January 9th by taking over the traffic control room of the Shanghai Railway Bureau. 'People's Train No. 1' left on January 10th for Urumchi in Sinkiang.[18]

'Production committees' were established by the personnel of the Yangshup'u power station and the shipyards. The first of these committees appeared on December 27th at the Shanghai glass factory, and it was a favourite topic of revolutionary propaganda for some time. It had ten members elected by secret ballot and liable to recall at any time. Propaganda insisted less on this observance of the precedent of the Paris Commune than on the fact that the bureaucracy disappeared from the factory.

The confrontation between two big organizations, the Scarlet Guards, a league of bodies defending the interests of the workers that the rebels regarded as reactionary, and the Workers' Revolutionary Rebel Headquarters, followed the general pattern of the Shanghai crisis. These two workers' groupings were so strong in numbers that they eclipsed all the other protagonists. According to the *Asahi*'s sources there were 800,000 Scarlet Guards and a little over 600,000 Revolutionary Rebels. The students' role was marginal but sometimes conspicuous. The T'ungchi[19] students, who recaptured the main railway station, reported Chairman Mao as saying, 'Excellent: union between students and workers has been achieved at last.'[20]

The Shanghai Municipal Party Committee had been holding aloof for some time, although it had the responsibility for ending the strike. The *People's Daily* held it

[18] *Wenhui Pao*, January 12, 1967. The paper added: 'Traffic between Shanghai and Nanking, and Shanghai and Hangchow, returned to normal on January 11th with 135 passenger and goods trains, although the number was reduced to half of that during the crisis.'

[19] A college of architecture and engineering in Shanghai.

[20] A leaflet from the Peking Automobile Factory, no. 2, March 6, 1967.

responsible for the system of extra payments intended to corrupt the industrial workers. The Rebels accused them, not perhaps without justification, of having shown partiality towards the Scarlet Guards, who had their headquarters on the top storey of the municipal offices and were led by a 'work hero.'

Nevertheless, the municipal committee held on for a little longer, trying to use what power was left to it and hoping, perhaps, that the pendulum would swing back its way. It refused to dissolve itself because it had not been dismissed by the Party, because Ts'ao Ti-ch'iu had never openly flouted the Centre, and because Chang Ch'unch'iao, the leader of the rebels, wished to preserve the good name of the Party. The attitude of the Shanghai committee explains why the confrontation with the authorities lasted so long in most of the provinces. Unlike the masses, who confined themselves to facts, the cadres regarded themselves as obliged to obey the 'Party leadership,' which for them had not changed. To this the Rebels replied:

This is to confuse black with white. As far as proletarian revolutionaries are concerned, Party leadership means the leadership of the Central Committee headed by Chairman Mao, the leadership of the Thought of Mao Tse-tung, and the leadership of the proletarian revolutionary line embodied in Chairman Mao.[21]

This quarrel over definitions would not have mattered had not some surviving members of the machine called on their rural cadres to mobilize the peasants of the district against the workers. They called meetings of delegates from Rebel organizations that had been set up among the peasants, and, according to the official press, told them, 'The workers want to rebel against you, so you had better take your turn to revolt against them.' At their instigation:

Commune members who were both peasants and industrial workers, and workers sent by their communes

21 *People's Daily*, January 19, 1967.

on contract work, have spread contradictions and aggravated differences . . . hindered the normal distribution of revenue at the end of the year . . . We must
oppose those who refuse to build up reserves, who do
not want to keep their reserves, or who reduce the allocation for collective accumulation.[22]

Briefly, this was an explicit charge that the temporary
workers had been incited to take at once all the benefits
they were demanding in the year-end share-out in the
communes. This was the second time that the revolutionary leadership had spoken against 'economism,' that is,
attempts to corrupt the insurgent masses.

The Revolution and Production Front reacted vigorously,
asking all organizations of workers, students and revolutionary cadres to try to persuade the peasants to look after their collective capital and not share out their reserves.
It decreed that the responsible members of the municipal
committee would be handed over to the masses for criticism in Shanghai's ten rural *hsien*.

The journal *Red Flag* lost no time in drawing up a
balance sheet for these struggles. It praised the Shanghai
revolutionaries and declared that 'their policy, their organizational forms and the means they have adopted in the
contest'[23] should be taken as examples to others.

The Shanghai Commune

There was a very considerable number of revolutionary
organizations in Shanghai: Red Guards in the schools
and universities; groups of Revolutionary Rebels or activists of varying persuasions in the units; and associations
for people of the same origin or sharing a common background, such as the 'Red Defence Army' of army veterans
and demobilized soldiers, or the 'Second Corps of North-
erners Back in Shanghai,' a body of workers who had been
sent off to other industrial centres but who were able to

[22] Message of January 16. *Wenhui Pao* and *Liberation*, January 20, 1967; *People's Daily*, January 21, 1967.
[23] *Red Flag*, no. 2, January 15, 1967.

return to the city thanks to the Cultural Revolution. A member of the Revolutionary Committee announced in November 1967 that there had been seven hundred organizations of every kind in the total number.[24]

To bring the January Revolution to its conclusion, a 'Preparatory Committee for the Shanghai People's Commune' was convened. It was led by Chang Ch'un-ch'iao and Yao Wen-yuan, who tried to draw in the greatest possible number of sympathetic organizations representing most of Shanghai's urban districts and suburban rural counties. The meeting of the Preparatory Committee was the result of three weeks' work. Considerable difficulties had arisen as a result of disagreements between the Workers' Revolutionary Rebel Headquarters and the various cells in the districts and *hsien*.[25] Behind the difficulties there evidently lay the antagonism that the revolutionary organizations felt for each other. 'After contradictions of every kind had been fundamentally resolved,' thirty-eight organizations joined the Preparatory Committee, which met at 1 a.m. on February 5th.

At two that afternoon a proclamation founding the Shanghai People's Commune was passed, and it was agreed that the Commune would be run by a Provisional Committee invested with 'supreme power.' Under the Committee there were commissions, each of which assigned a member to the Provisional Committee, which also included eleven permanent members.

The long period of work needed to set up the Commune consisted mainly in negotiations with the various organizations. Some of them insisted on being represented on the committee, while others coveted a commission. The Commune was set up as a result of democratic discussions, though it is unlikely that all the street organizations were satisfied with it.

[24] Joan Robinson, *The Cultural Revolution in China, op. cit.*
[25] The story of the formation of the Shanghai Commune and the composition of the committee were explained by a poster put up in Peking by the '*Tungfanghung* Commune of Chinese Scientific and Technical Universities' on the afternoon of February 5th.

Two student organizations were put in charge of the liaison and 'external relations' commissions. Control of the commission of investigation went to the revolutionary cadres employed by the municipal committee, and the organization commission was put in the hands of the Workers' Revolutionary Rebel Headquarters. There was also an operations commission entrusted to the Revolution and Production Front that had been formed to cope with the strike. The Provisional Committee thus consisted of seven workers, three students, two peasants, two cadres and two soldiers, giving the workers a strong relative majority.

On the day of its creation the Commune published a manifesto and the Provisional Committee issued its 'Order No. 1.' The manifesto proclaimed that a 'new type of local organization of the proletarian dictatorship, born on the Yangtse Delta, has arisen in the East.' It announced that the members of the Commune had been elected according to the principles of the Paris Commune, and urged a general closing of ranks and a seizure of power everywhere. Order No. 1 proclaimed the dissolution of the Shanghai Municipal People's Committee and Party Committee, and declared that all their decisions after May 16, 1966, were invalid. The Public Security Forces were mobilized against the opponents of the Central Committee's Cultural Revolution Group, and declared unconditional war against 'the authorities following the capitalist way' towards whom an attitude of 'beating the dog in the water' was recommended.[26]

Realizing that it would have to extend its base, the Provisional Committee announced that affiliation was open to all revolutionary organizations that wanted to join. But when it came to arranging for newcomers to join, the

[26] A reference to Lu Hsun's essay, 'When to stop playing fair.' In answer to Lin Yutang's deprecation of the habit of 'beating the dog in the water' Lu Hsun said that there was no reason why dogs which one had oneself thrown into the water should be treated differently from any other kind. 'It is a mistake to place on the same footing all those who have lost their power, without distinguishing between the good and the bad' (*Selected Works of Lu Hsun*, vol. 2, p. 213).

committee ran up against strong prejudices. Problems arose within the committee, while outside its militancy was not enough to overcome scepticism everywhere. Its opponents questioned the ability of the Cultural Revolution Group's officers to cope with a city the size of Shanghai.[27] The Centre was afraid that the Commune lacked competent members, and reckoned that they had not made enough use of former cadres. The workers, however, were full of self-confidence. 'The world is ours,' was their reply.

The Commune was short-lived. The name disappeared, and it underwent obscure transformations to re-emerge discreetly as the Shanghai Revolutionary Committee, based on a 'triple alliance' which included representatives of the army. 'The army is necessary in order to consolidate the new power and prevent reaction from killing the new leaders,' explained Chang Ch'un-ch'iao at the mass rally called on February 24th to involve the people in the changes. Chang also said that it was up to the people of Shanghai to decide if they preferred keeping the name 'Commune' to creating a revolutionary committee.

Do we still need the Party, now that the Commune has been created? I believe that we do, as we need a hard core,[28] whether we call it a communist or a social-democratic party. . . . In short, we do need a Party.[29]

The reference to another party beside the Communist one is astonishing, and it brings home to us the range of democratic currents finding expression among the workers of Shanghai. Chang Ch'un-ch'iao was casting doubt on whether the Commune was entitled to seize power from the Municipal Party Committee, although the Party commit-

[27] A remark by Ch'en P'i-hsien, secretary of the Shanghai Municipal Party Committee, on January 12, 1967, according to *Wenhui Pao*, March 21, 1968.

[28] An allusion to the first quotation in The Little Red Book: 'The force at the core leading our cause forward is the Chinese Communist Party.'

[29] Extracts from the speech of Chang Ch'un-ch'iao at an oath-taking rally on February 24th on the 'Cultural Revolution Square,' Shanghai.

tee had ceased to function long before the foundation of
the Commune, which had filled the gap. It must be significant that at this level a power seizure had to be confirmed by the establishment of a revolutionary committee,
guaranteeing the continuity of the Party. We shall also see
below how the Centre protected some of the Party's positions against the Shanghai workers: the Secretariat of
the Party's East China Bureau was not to be seized as it
was an organ of the Central Committee. 'To take over
the buildings alone would be meaningless.'

Thus Shanghai had to abandon her Commune, and all
that was left of the power the workers had once held were
the revolution and production committees that had appeared during the strike.

The power seizures

Throughout the country students and revolutionary cadres
heard the leaders they recognized give the order to seize
power. There was no time to be lost, the leaders proclaimed, 'as the time is now ripe. If you do not seize power
now you may be swept away by the conservatives. . . .
We do not have time to create new systems: all we can
do is act in accordance with circumstances and draw from
them what advantage we can.' As Chou En-lai reminded
them:

> Generally speaking, seizing power means in the first
> place seizing the control of the Cultural Revolution and
> then taking economic control.[30]

This distinction indicated that first of all the Work Teams
which had been assigned the job of applying the Cultural
Revolution in the units were to be supplanted, and then
the management of production was to be taken over. This
was what the workers had done in Shanghai.

The leaders gave tactical advice on how the second aim
was to be achieved. There was a distinction between win-

[30] *Yutien Fenglei*, February 10, 1967, 'Centre Leaders discuss the question of power seizures.'

ning control and being effectively in charge of the running of a unit. The new men in charge should start with an examination of the production units.

> If productivity increases under Revolutionary Rebel control, they may take over management of the work . . . If for the time being one cannot be sure of winning control, one should economize one's efforts. One may allow the Work Teams to go on operating for a while, providing they are not too bad, until the masses mobilize themselves and take control.[31]

Depending on how the people in power had behaved and were then behaving, they would be treated in different ways:

1. The dismissal of corrupt leaders . . .
2. Dismissal while being kept on the books: facing an inquiry after a set period of time; being given the opportunity to redeem their faults; discharge after examination (re-engagement after six months, or a further extension of discharge notice).
3. Suspension from duty while being kept on the books: here again, facing an inquiry after a set interval; discharge after examination (for a period of, say, six months. Another job may be given while the case is being examined.)
4. Kept in employment while under surveillance.
5. No change in duties.[32]

Even if power seizures were regulated to some extent, they were not orderly. The main cause was the rivalry between different organizations all wanting to cover themselves with glory.

Chou En-lai also spoke about successive power seizures:

> In some cases the seizure of power is incomplete; in others it is false. One takeover may then be followed by another. When a second one occurs, the first cannot be regarded as complete; nor can one be considered com-

31 *Yutien Fenglei,* February 10, 1967.
32 *Ibid.* Speech by Chou En-lai.

plete when it starts over again and struggles continue
. . . The problems that arise within the left can be resolved through discussion. One makes progress by as-
similating imperfect alliances. False takeovers must be
carried out again.

He concluded by reprimanding the Rebels:

It is wrong for people on the left to say to each other
'You are the February Revolution and we are the October Revolution,' or 'We are Yenan, you are Sian.'[33]

Ch'en Po-ta quoted some actual cases in order to con-
vince the little revolutionary groups that they had to form
alliances:

There are many national offices in Peking. If a small
group that was not even able to represent a majority in
a single school took over a national office, who would
recognize it?[34]

In some places the leaders allowed power to be taken by
the organizations they favoured rather than by others they
did not. What happened in the Ministry of Agriculture has
been discussed above. Elsewhere, when a power seizure
had been superficial a stronger group carried out a new
one. Power was seized four times[35] in the offices of the
Shanghai Municipal Committee before the Commune was
established; and there were four successive seizures in some
of the colliery offices. Each seizure involved fights in which
people were injured. Sometimes it was felt necessary to
postpone the installation of proletarian power and ask for
an army take-over instead of the seizure of power by the
masses.

Revolutionaries who had just imposed their own control resented army intervention. An example of this may
be seen in the offices of the Civil Aviation Bureau, which
controlled the Chinese airlines. Although the Military Com-

[33] *Ibid.*
[34] *Ibid.* Speech by Ch'en Po-ta.
[35] On January 14, 22, and 24, and February 5, 1967.

mission and the State Council decided on January 26th that it was to be put under military control, the Revolutionary Rebels within the Civil Aviation Bureau protested and increased their attacks on the records of leaders who were being kept in power under army control. Ignoring the protests, the army posted sentries and dispersed the crowd.[36]

Military control was seen by the revolutionaries as a temporary setback, and it was not a formula that the revolution's theoreticians could accept for long. The only people it suited were the administrators and, presumably, the Military Commission, which tended to opt for it too often.

The compromise solution was the 'triple alliance,' in which the army did not take the revolutionaries' place. This was how Chang Ch'un-ch'iao justified it to the workers of Shanghai. But in incomplete seizures of power the army had another role beside throwing its weight onto the scales. As mediator between revolutionary organizations that were implacably opposed to each other, it encouraged the forces of the left to form alliances, and helped them to keep in control despite their weakness. In this mission it was guided by only a minority of the Party leaders. As in the heroic days of the revolutionary wars, the army was needed for 'unity of control.'

By participating in the provisional institutions that were set up after power seizures, the army prevented what could be kept of the Party structure from being swept away. It set the example of submission to the Thought of Mao Tsetung, the essential feature of which was the maintenance of the principle of Party leadership and respect for its image. The army had to bring about alliances between isolated revolutionary organizations in order to ensure that there would not be more than a single left-wing 'clan' to be incorporated into a renovated Communist Party. In his instructions to the Rebels Chou En-lai said:

There are three principles: Hold high the banner of the Thought of Mao Tse-tung and acknowledge the leader-

[36] Konno, *op. cit.,* p. 134.

ship of the Party; follow the socialist road; and obey
the Sixteen Points and the two Ten-Point Directives.[37]
These are the principles of the struggle, the first pre-
conditions. Anyone who breaks them is guilty of the
'three Antis'.[38] A 'grand alliance' should be an agreement on fundamentals; there may be differences on
lesser points. Above all, it is a grand alliance of the left.
If some tiny organizations do not wish to conform to it
they will be utterly isolated.[39]

In the face of these great principles the leftists had erred
in appealing to other motivations among the revolutionaries. After Chou En-lai and Ch'en Po-ta had spoken, it
was Wang Li's turn:

If we, the best of the proletarian revolutionaries, do not
hold power the others may find us guilty in future . . .
But when we are in power it will be for us to deal out
all the black and the white papers.[40] If we do not grasp
this power or if we hold it too weakly, there may be
another reversal, in their favour this time, and it will be
they who will be in a position to deal out black material to us. It must therefore be tit for tat, an eye for
an eye, a tooth for a tooth.[41]

This language was stirring up the spirit of revenge, which
had often found expression during the power seizures, and
which led to excesses. The leaders of the federation of
trade unions, for example, were put on public display on
January 23rd, and on January 26th the Railways Ministers and a deputy foreign minister were exhibited at T'ienanmen on the back of a lorry.[42] The Minister of Coal

[37] Probably the December Directives on the extension of the
Cultural Revolution to factories, mines, and the countryside.
[38] 'Anti-socialist, anti-Party, anti the Thought of Mao Tse-
tung.' This was a most serious condemnation, amounting to
excommunication.
[39] *Yutien Fenglai*, February 10, 1967.
[40] Referring to documents used in drawing up charges, and
dismissal notices.
[41] *Yutien Fenglei*, February 10, 1967.
[42] Konno, *op. cit.*, p. 89.

probably died as a result of mistreatment. The Railways Minister disappeared completely when the railway network was in utter chaos and Chou En-lai was looking for him. Rebels had taken him to a locomotive repair factory outside Peking where he was 'criticized' for four or five days.[43]

At the same time the revolutionaries were interrupting the work of the universities, wasting resources, and destroying the records needed for administration. A reminder was needed that not even seizures of power should endanger revolutionary order:

> All unnecessary expenditure must be halted and means of transport must be used economically. . . . Vehicles used for transport or production may not be turned into propaganda trucks. . . . Capital saved for agricultural production may not be put to other uses . . . nor may agricultural machinery be wrecked . . . The protection and conservation of books and all written documents must be emphasized. They may not be disposed of arbitrarily or destroyed.[44]

The Central Committee, the State Council and the Military Commission were trying to bring those who had seized power to see a little sense. Since the middle of January they had become intoxicated with their own emancipation.

Emancipation

After the first power seizures the industrial workers in the big cities gradually got the impression that the Revolution was ending all kinds of constraints. The feeling that all sorts of new things were possible because everyone was expressing his ideas plunged the people into a kind of intoxication.

Politics came before everything. According to this prin-

[43] *Ibid.*, p. 135.
[44] Notice from the Centre of March 16, 1967, quoted by the Japanese press on March 18th.

ciple everyone had to concern himself with public affairs in his neighbourhood and in his factory, and this took priority over all everyday matters. The people had the right to criticize and then to help build a new order in conformity with the Thought of Mao Tse-tung, which brought the principle of open democracy to the people. It spread confidence in the future and encouraged the humblest to believe that their qualities of spirit opened up greater opportunities for heroism than higher talents would have done. It gave everyone a desire to have ideas. From now on, it was necessary to know what was going on, to find out and understand what had gone wrong and what needed to be changed once power had been seized. It was necessary to find out what others were thinking, what changes were being proposed, and what revolutionary events were taking place. For the present all this was more important than work.

People went hunting for news, and the crowds never ebbed in the city festooned with posters. Those who sold the 'little newspapers' did good business. Everyone wanted to know what was happening in Shanghai, Chungking, or Sinkiang. With all the critical materials they were carrying, the papers were teaching much more about the history of the previous years than people had known about before. Even those who took no interest in political developments wanted to read everything now.

Most of the workers took an interest in politics. Those who did not know much about what went on in the provincial committees were familiar enough with how their own factories were run. The people were invited to express themselves, and they wrote down what they knew. Many posters dealt only with a single workshop or Party cell. In ordinary times many of the workers would never have dared to write in public. It took courage for someone with little schooling to put his penmanship on view, particularly in China, where writing is so skillful, notices dissolve rapidly, and written work is so highly respected.

Rebel organizations had skilled copyists whose work bore comparison with the calligraphy of the students, but small groups and even individuals also expressed their grievances, conveying some injustice they had suffered or faults they had found with an organization. Veteran workers who had lived under several regimes and who may themselves have struggled for workers' rights in the old days would place their paper and ink on the ground, and the crowd would make room for them. After contemplating the blank sheet with much gravity, as if they had long been waiting for this moment, they would begin to write a clumsy script.

The circulation of news of all kinds and the freedom to say new things put people in a relaxed mood. With the bosses suspended and under investigation, all their informers had disappeared. There were no more concealed struggles and secret denunciations. A new period was beginning, one of destruction rather than construction no doubt, but at least the struggles were now in the open. No sooner had almost any poster been put up than it was torn down by a rival organization. Small groups of workers, which other organizations tried to get suppressed, distributed on bicycles barely legible duplicated appeals for help. Movements that had no paper painted their appeals on the roadway in the small hours.

These conflicts contained an element of optimism, and a breath of liberty was in the air during the 'Peking winter.' The press reflected this: 'Try reading the revolutionary papers *Liberation Daily* and *Wenhui Pao*,' wrote the *People's Daily*. 'Now that they are freed from the control of the bourgeois line they have become dynamic and their stifling and dead atmosphere has completely disappeared.'[45]

'There is no reason to believe that we will be unable to get by and make a living without these bourgeois "lords" . . .'[46] 'We, the revolutionary workers, are the masters of the country and of our own concerns.'[47]

Thus, all the hopes for changes in the way of life were expressed as demands. Young workers wanted the period

[45] *People's Daily*, January 19, 1967.
[46] *Ibid.*
[47] *Workers' Daily*, January 14, 1967, editorial.

of apprenticeship reduced;[48] workers in commerce wanted their working hours to be the same as in factories, and they also wanted a guaranteed day off each week;[49] printing workers wanted the rhythm of work eased;[50] and the employees of medium-sized and small enterprises wanted no discrimination between their pay and that of larger enterprises.[51] The Peking bus and trolleybus workers bluntly demanded pay rises too.[52]

The question of bonuses and piece-rates or a fixed hourly wage divided the working class. Maoism was utterly opposed to the first two, but many workers were aware of how they improved their living standards. The eight-hour working day was not openly opposed, though it is significant that it was thought necessary to defend it;[53] and a year later such demands were still being made.[54] With too many workers taking time off for meetings, labour discipline suffered: politics was in command.

The peasants who were working seasonally in factories, and others who had been engaged for several years with the prospect of going back to their villages at the end of the period,[55] demanded the same rights as regular workers. They wanted to be registered in the cities by the

[48] *Current Scene,* vol. 6, no. 5, March 15, 1968, pp. 12 and 21.

[49] *Far Eastern Economic Review,* February 23, 1967.

[50] This demand was made by the personnel in charge of the paper supply at the Hsinhua Printing Works. See the Red Guard *Chen-pao* of February 15, 1967. See also, on the application of the 'Seventy Points' at the Shihchingshan Steel Works, K. Samejima 'Peking plans basic reform of industrial administration,' *Japan Economic Journal,* April 30, 1968.

[51] Konno, *op. cit.,* p. 135.

[52] *Ibid.*

[53] See especially the letters of January 12, 1967, from the workers of No. 1 Machine-tool Factory, Peking, in the *People's Daily* of January 16th.

[54] See the Peking papers of February 28, 1968.

[55] These were often peasants who came in groups from the same rural communes under contracts made directly between communes and companies. Radio Moscow discussed this system in a broadcast on China and the Cultural Revolution on December 11, 1966.

government instead of merely living there on sufferance, and to be paid the same as the regular workers. Maoists sympathised with their demands. Hofei, speaking for the province of Anhwei, said that temporary workers now had the same political rights as regulars, but was silent on economic rights.[56]

The revolutionary leadership could go no further than to grant them the right of urban residence. Despite the advice of the new trade union federation that 'the system of contract workers, temporary workers and seconded workers is not entirely reasonable,' the State Council judged it 'moderately reasonable.'[57] The Maoist programme of eliminating the differences between town and countryside did not rule out compromise solutions, to the disappointment of the worker-peasants.

It appears on reflexion that the distinction between acceptable and unacceptable demands from the workers was decided on the criteria of the arguments against 'economism.' Of the demands mentioned above, only the shortening of apprenticeships[58] and the regularization of shopworkers' hours were accepted immediately. Bonuses were gradually abolished in some concerns despite the attachment to them of some of the personnel.[59] Demands for a shorter working day and pay rises were quickly rejected by the very people who had confirmed workers' power.

After the ferment in which workers expressed their personal feelings, criticisms of the running of enterprises began to follow a set political formula, which became a key part of the Cultural Revolution's programme. The revolutionary leadership held up the Anshan Steelworks Constitution—a group of recommendations to which Mao Tsetung had given some attention in 1960 but were then ignored by the Party—in opposition to the 'Seventy Points'

[56] *Current Scene*, vol. 6, no. 5, March 15, 1968, pp. 23–24.

[57] *Ajia Keizai Jumpo*, no. 683, May 1967.

[58] Urgent instructions of Chou En-lai and Liu Ning-yi on wages and the organization of work—see *Current Scene*, vol. 6, no. 5, p. 12.

[59] The Shihchingshan Steel Works abolished bonuses in the autumn of 1967. See *Japan Economic Journal*, April 30, 1968.

for industry,[60] that Liu Shao-ch'i had recommended to industrial managements and were, according to the revolutionaries, based on the Magnitogorsk Steelworks Constitution.

The Seventy Points, the revolutionaries charged, had been put together by the Party machine in contravention of the spirit of the Ashan Constitution; they centralized managerial control, played down the authority of the Party in the factory, and forced Communist cells and groups in the company to be inactive.[61] In other words, they involved the same error as the one committed by the army leadership when it allowed Party committees in the units to atrophy. In material terms, the Seventy Points gave the management considerable discretion in finance and accounting, with the aim of maximizing returns.

The State Council had other worries besides sorting out the demands of revolutionaries, not least the restoration of normal working in factories. To this end it issued instructions on February 17th that were backed up by the Central Committee's 'Letter to Revolutionary Workers and Cadres' later published in the press:

> You should in accordance with the regulations laid down by the Party's Central Committee, firmly adhere to the eight-hour working day and carry on the Cultural Revolution during the time outside the eight hours of work. During working hours it is impermissible to absent oneself without good cause from one's production or work post. We must fight against any unhealthy tendency towards absenteeism. . . .[62]

The workers were apparently divided into two schools: one supported the politicization of their movement along the approved line of the 'Grand Alliance,' the single 'clan' of the Maoists, with the sacrifice of workers' demands that

[60] The 'Draft regulations on the work of industrial enterprises' of September 1960.

[61] *Yutien Chanpao*, published by the Tungfanghung group of the Postal Ministry, Peking, June 28, 1967.

[62] 'Letter from the Central Committee' in *Peking Review*, no. 13, March 24, 1967.

this involved; and the other reverted to corporate activities, withdrawing their organizations from political involvement. In March 1967 workers spontaneously formed 'friendly societies,' such as those of mechanics, drivers, and 1965 graduates of universities and colleges. The Shanghai papers published an article condemning these associations that was reprinted in the *People's Daily*.[63]

The Centre had acknowledged, however, that such associations were natural, by allowing the revolution and production committees that had helped end the Shanghai strikes to continue for a long time; and it even supported the 'economic control groups' that helped the revolutionary committees. But it was alarmed by the indiscriminate violence indulged in by the rebels and agitators. The leaders of the revolution decided that it would be necessary to restrict freedom of association by suppressing some organizations.

Was there division within the working class?

The revolution in the big cities was complicated by some special problems, one of which was the large number of workers moving back from the countryside.

The Party's policy had been to use the surplus population of the cities to develop underpopulated and climatically inhospitable regions. Workers from Shanghai or Tientsin, who were technically more proficient than peasants, had been sent to work on state farms, in oil search, or in forestry. They had been sent off for long spells. Many of them wanted to return home, and regarded their jobs as temporary missions to distant parts, though it was intended that most of them should stay on to populate the empty spaces. They were not generally willing pioneers. Many went out unwillingly, bitter at the cadres who had picked them out from among their fellows.

Workers from the Shanghai region were generally sent to reinforce the production and construction corps in Sin-

[63] *People's Daily*, March 15, 1967. See *China News Analysis*, no. 654, April 7, 1967, p. 6.

kiang or to the forests of Anhwei. From Tientsin and Peking they went to Inner Mongolia and the northern wastes of Manchuria; some went to the oilwells of Tach'ing, which became an industrial centre. Youngsters in Canton were recruited by the local Party Committees to develop regions in South China, generally in Kwangsi or Kweichow.

When the Cultural Revolution was extended to workers of all categories in late 1966 and early 1967, the most discontented of the pioneers became virulent in their criticisms of the Party. As they were not wanted in the places where they were working, and they demanded in the name of Chairman Mao to be allowed to carry out the Cultural Revolution at home, the local authorities let them go.

> Some of them wanted to come back to Shanghai. If they did not succeed they fought against the local cadres and the development cadres. . . . In Sinkiang production was badly hit by the departure of many youngsters going back home.

This was Chang Ch'un-ch'iao's explanation of the situation to the Revolutionary Rebels. The aggrieved colonists had boarded trains like the students and the city workers, and came back to rejoin the population of the cities, where they formed their own organizations.

These organizations generally took as their targets the cadres of the neighbourhood. This was contrary to the Cultural Revolution line, as these cadres were not really responsible for the errors of the past. Instead of seeking out the 'small handful,' these revolutionaries, whose grievances were personal, attacked the main bulk of the cadres, terrorizing them, and thus paralyzing the basic-level administration and bringing insecurity to the alleys.

There were thus three problems to be solved: the loss of personnel by production units in the development areas;[64] the alienation of the cadres; and insecurity in the cities.

[64] Speaking to railwaymen on January 10th, Chou En-lai said that over 10,000 youngsters had left Tach'ing (according to posters).

The mistake of striking at all the cadres, instead of searching out those who had really been responsible for abuses, was not confined to the returnees among the Shanghai workers. In Canton the secretaries of the lowest-level Party committees were 'driven out' and 'put on public display,' to be blamed for having sent hundreds of people to labour camps.[65] In some power seizures in Peking all the cadres, good and bad, were attacked indiscriminately on the principle that bosses were bad and would not be needed in future.

The Centre must have regarded this as a serious deviation, for the Party press reprinted a text Mao Tse-tung had written in 1929 in criticism of extreme egalitarianism. On January 28th the *People's Daily* carried Mao's 'On correcting mistaken ideas in the Party,'[66] which maintained that absolute equality was impossible, and said that leaders who worked for others should be allowed to set themselves somewhat apart.

To reestablish order in the cities the Centre relied on the Public Security, now under army control, in order to eliminate pressure groups organized as revolutionary bodies. In the middle of February the Central Committee passed a resolution insisting that the Rebels should allow the police to function.[67] Various facts quoted in the Red Guard press indicate that the local military control committees were entrusted with neutralizing organizations without reference to the Centre. The Public Security in the provinces seems to have taken considerable initiative in late February and early March.

After a period of comparative calm in Peking and Shanghai, where mass criticism was directed against the works of Liu Shao-ch'i, there was a new wave of power seizures in early June. This was when some of the extremists in the Central Committee's Cultural Revolution Group decided to accelerate the Revolution. The slogan 'Beat the

[65] According to posters in Canton around March 1st.

[66] See Kaizuka, 'Bunka Kakumei no shōkon,' *Asahi Jyanaru*, March 19, 1967, pp. 102–3.

[67] 'Rules on the help that must be given to the Public Security in the Great Proletarian Cultural Revolution.'

dog in the water,' was raised again with greater ferocity.

Some revolutionary organizations in Shanghai published a resolution demanding that the Revolution should move forward again and that the Public Security forces should be used to strengthen the proletarian dictatorship. The policy was to involve the revolutionary committees in the application of full powers for the Revolution. All opposition and even contradiction was to be ruthlessly punished.[68]

The fresh assault by the Rebels provoked a new series of work stoppages. Management and cadres in the Anshan steelworks and in most mines, where they had continued to function despite agitation by the workers, were finally overthrown. Workers' committees then led the workers to achieve record output, enthusiasm for which only lasted for a while. As some key technicians, particularly in the mines, had absented themselves, maintenance of the mines and breakdown of machinery was causing difficulties. Workers began to quarrel over who was to blame, and the moderates criticized the rebels.

It was at about this time that the reactionary workers' organizations in Wuhan moved over to the offensive. We shall deal later with the bloody violence of July and August in the cities. Under provocation from the Lien Ssu, a reactionary organization, the Rebels in Shanghai called for revenge, but a fresh outbreak of strikes cut off the city's electricity supplies on August 11th. Every day seemed to bring news of workers rioting somewhere in China. At this critical moment different initiatives began to develop in the two main urban centres.

In Peking, the reaction of the workers took the form of silent protest. On August 19th the Workers' Congress[69] led a procession through the streets of all who were against the 'great leap forward in violence.' The solemnity of the demonstration, which consisted simply of a column of

[68] Compare with the contemporary article by Lin Chieh: see above, Chapter 5.

[69] An organization belonging to the Workers' Alliance, which represented them on the Peking Revolutionary Committee.

people holding placards, without slogans or chanting, was in sharp contrast with the usual exuberance of revolutionary demonstrations.

In Shanghai, however, the workers invoked their right to 'use violence in self-defence'[70] thus demonstrating their fear of the reactionaries and their individualistic concept of proletarian dictatorship. Some organizations had long been trying to get arms for their own defence. The papers mentioned the creation of the 'Red Guards of the Military Region of Huangp'u'[71] and praised organized and militant bodies of fighting men.[72] Chang Ch'un-ch'iao nevertheless persuaded the Workers Revolutionary Rebel Headquarters to put its weight behind a solemn appeal to renounce the use of force. He put seven demands to the rebels, among which were these:

> Mass organizations are not authorized, even on the pretext of force in self-defence, to make, transport or use without permission any lethal weapon. The use of chemical poisons is strictly forbidden.[73]

These efforts were in vain, for extremist elements were leading the revolutionaries to adopt methods that should only have been used in exceptional circumstances. Revolutionary tribunals appeared in Shanghai at the end of August, dealing at first with ordinary criminal cases: the owner of a clandestine factory or workshop, an illicit deal in a hundred thousand pounds of grain and ration tickets. A little later it was learned that a people's court had condemned two people to be shot and six others to prison sentences for counter-revolutionary conspiracy. It seemed as if a regime of 'committees of public safety' was about

[70] After the Wuhan incidents Chiang Ch'ing, probably speaking on behalf of the Cultural Revolution Group, said that henceforward revolutionaries would no longer be obliged to respond with argument alone but could now defend themselves with arms. Speech of July 20th, in wall posters of July 22, 1967, in Peking.

[71] A district of Shanghai and the name of its river.

[72] *Wenhui Pao*, August 23, 1967.

[73] *Wenhui Pao*, August 11, 1967.

to be installed in the manner of the French Revolution.

At this point Mao Tse-tung made a tour of inspection in north, central-south and east China.[74] This was guessed at when the Shanghai papers began to speak with unaccustomed authority on fundamental questions.[75] On August 25th they wrote that reform of working conditions was 'the task of the Party.'[76]

All the signs are that when the Chairman analyzed the struggles taking place within the working class he decided that it was more urgent to discuss its problems than to inflame its passions. The quarrels that were disturbing the Centre could have been avoided had the revolution been considered solely from the point of view of class. Verbal violence, which tended to push the proletarian dictatorship to extremes 'for ulterior motives,' made internal disputes too heated.

At the end of his journey[77] Mao Tse-tung issued these brief instructions:

> There is no fundamental clash of interests within the working class. In the conditions of a proletarian dictatorship, there is no reason for the working class to be divided into two irreconcilable organizations.

In the days that followed, peaceful seizures of power took place under the eyes of the army. The small groups of soldiers who had been sent to factories since the summer[78] to 'aid the left' and teach the Thought of Mao Tse-tung were heavily outnumbered: there were five or ten soldiers to several thousand workers. They could bring no

[74] It was not announced by the New China News Agency until September 24th.

[75] The Peking press was inflamed at the time by the anti-British campaign and the polemics against Liu Shao-ch'i.

[76] *Wenhui Pao, Liberation Daily,* and *Cell Life* published jointly a series of important editorials.

[77] Probably around September 12. See *Peking Review,* no. 40, September 29, 1967. According to the *Ajia Keizai Jumpo,* no. 741, p. 16, it was September 14th.

[78] In some places since May. In July 1967 there were about 200 military missions in Shanghai factories and nearly as many in Peking.

pressure to bear through force. The Chairman's oracular words, repeated in the stern tones of the soldiers, came just when most people were longing for an end to the tension, and acted as a precipitant.

At the Peking Hosiery Factory opposing groups joined forces when they learned of Mao Tse-tung's latest instructions, and six days later they quietly took over the financial administration of the factory. In the Sixth Ministry of the mechanical industry, where there were twelve different rival organizations, a small group of soldiers brought the revolutionaries together by making them go together by departments to study classes in the Thought of Mao Tse-tung.

In the city of Ch'angsha two organizations were fighting each other: the 'Ch'angsha Workers' Alliance' and the 'storm on the River Hsiang.' In the eyes of the Centre they were both acceptable. Through the good offices of the army they united after an exchange of self-criticism.[79] These conclusions appear banal in comparison with the excitement of the preceding period, but a change of policy went some way towards explaining them.

The excessive violence of August led the Centre to condemn the extreme left and issue some authoritarian decrees, notably a decision that threatened the suspension of pay for anyone guilty of violence.[80] This was perhaps the first time that such a sanction had been introduced in the course of the Cultural Revolution. Doubtless some of the workers appreciated this appeal to wisdom.

Another way of explaining why an easy solution should so suddenly have been found for such deep-rooted

[79] With the help of the 'preparatory group for the revolutionary committee' and the responsible comrades of PLA Unit 6900, a discussion was held between the two groups, who recognized their errors and admitted that the split between them was unreasonable. This took place in November 1967, according to Ch'angsha Radio. See also *China News Analysis,* no. 694, p. 6.

[80] Decision of September 1, 1967, by the Peking Revolutionary Committee, which had met in an enlarged session with several national leaders taking part. This decision, although only a local one, was publicized throughout the whole country.

conflicts was that the alliances within the revolutionary committees and the preparatory groups designated by the Centre to form revolutionary committees had been strengthened. The committees, for cities or administrative departments, realized that once the extreme left was disowned they could win themselves a little stability by ending the unwanted fighting. Their most committed members then had no choice between taking exception or keeping their factions quiet.

Many conflicts continued, but for some time less was seen of the extremist rebels. They closed in on themselves and restrained, not without bitterness, their demands for an armed proletariat, waiting for the day when new social demands from the industrial workers would divide society again.

Wages and ideology

The Centre had to make the workers understand that, in the interests of the nationwide revolutionary movement, they should give up the advantages the revolution was bringing them. Many workers, encouraged by the ferment of ideas in Shanghai, felt that the revolution could not end without leaving behind it a minimum of workers' democracy—later they were to demand simply unsupervised trade-unionism.

As the long-term intention of the revolution's creators was to reconstitute the Party, the themes and objectives proposed for the workers' movement had to take account both of the leading role of the workers among the people, and of the Party among the workers' organizations. The worker revolutionaries would have preferred to see an acknowledged leading role for working-class organizations in the Party. There was thus a certain ambiguity in the slogans they jointly adopted. The most useful were those repudiating the old trade unions, for people of varying beliefs could all subscribe to them while keeping their own interpretation.

'We don't want the old trade unions,' proclaimed the posters in Shanghai in December 1967. In fact this could mean several things. The leaders of the Workers Revolutionary Rebel Headquarters, who had previously declared that the organizations affiliated to the Headquarters were the class organizations of the working class,[81] were counting on the new unions being run by Rebel workers.

On their side, the workers who were not Rebels rejected the old unions because they detested their political control. They felt that the revolution should give them the right to defend their social interests in society without having to act through the Party. As for the Centre, it could strictly speaking claim that all the workers who were combining under this same slogan agreed on repudiating the policies of the old Party machine and the revisionist methods of the old unions.

In December 1967 the revolution's leaders avoided making too clear what they meant by their joint slogans. They kept things vague, saying that no workers' group had the right to speak on behalf of the people or of the Party. Some regrouping of organizations, such as the one that had just taken place in Shanghai, was the result of long and arduous political work, and it was not to be compromised.

The Shanghai Congress of Revolutionary Rebel Workers was inaugurated on December 3rd.[82] Among the speeches made was one in which Wang Hung-wen, one of the leaders of the Congress, dealt with working-class activity and its possibilities:

> Comrades, we are all ordinary workers, the flood-tide of the Great Proletarian Cultural Revolution, a rampart protecting those responsible for leading us. . . . Our political and ideological standards are still fairly low, and we are still inexperienced in this work. . . . We must have the courage to turn towards the old and the young cadres in order to learn from them.

[81] Speech by Wang Hung-wen at the inaugural ceremony for the Shanghai Congress of Revolutionary Rebel Workers, December 3, 1967. (*Liberation Daily*, no. 6739, December 4, 1967.)

[82] The formation of the Workers' Congress followed shortly after one for the Shanghai students.

But in other passages he echoed those who were demanding a toughening of the dictatorship of the proletariat:

> The bourgeoisie laughs at our low standard. Don't worry! We can learn to fight in the fight itself, and learn the job on the job. . . . We must actively create the preconditions and all necessary preparations for arming the workers.[83]

Was he referring literally to the arming of the workers, or to arming them with the Thought of Mao Tse-tung? In this otherwise moderate speech there were elements such as this in which the most extreme workers' groups could find justification for their fight.

As far as the Centre was concerned, the creation of the Workers' Congress was above all a stage in the reconstruction of the Party. This was the line taken by the Shanghai press at the time.[84] The revolutionary leaders had thus succeeded in incorporating one part of the worker rebels, a process through which the workers' organizations that had always been loyal to Chang Ch'un-ch'iao saw their chance of participating in the restored Communist Party.

In some sectors a part of the profits was distributed at the end of that year, and the temporary workers were promised equality of status with the regular ones. This was an attempt to calm them down by letting them know what had, then at least, been guaranteed. Twenty days later another decision[85] ruled that reforms in the status of temporary workers could be considered after investigation and

[83] *Liberation Daily,* December 4, 1967. The old cadres were former cadres who had come over to the revolution; the young cadres were revolutionaries carrying out the functions of the cadres.

[84] See *Liberation Daily,* December 2, 1967, 'The cadres and the people join in angry criticism of the revisionist line on reconstruction of the Party.' On December 5th *Wenhui Pao* published four pages of quotations from Cultural Revolution texts on the reconstruction of the Party.

[85] Central Committee resolutions of December 28, 1967, and January 18, 1968, quoted in the organ of the Rebels in the Canton railways. *Kuangt'ieh Tsungssu,* no. 28, February 1968.

detailed inquiries into the local situation. But then the Centre condemned concessions made in contempt of the Cultural Revolution; it revoked pay advances already made, disowned the cadres who had allowed them, and ordered them to make their self-criticisms.

The Centre was then putting the finishing touches to the national economic plan for 1968, and it found itself faced with realities that allowed it no room for compromise. The hardening of its policies provoked a new wave of strikes that were nothing to do with power seizures.

While other sections of the economy were doubtless affected by the strikes, it is mainly through Chinese news reports on the mines that we know of their extent and gravity.[86] Since the power seizures in June, industrial management had taken a very weak line with the masses in all the units that had yet to achieve their 'alliances.' The cadres were ignored, technicians did not co-operate with the new managements with any enthusiasm, and the managements themselves, representing some faction or other rather than the workers as a class, resorted to demagogy in order to survive.

Some revolutionaries were saying that the eight-hour day had been imposed by the detested old regime, and that the aim of their rebellion had been to overthrow the old system. The official press insisted that these arguments should be answered, and printed the following conversation on the front page of the *People's Daily* (February 29, 1968) in the guise of a fable.[87] An old miner is talking with a young one:

> Old miner: 'The eight-hour working day is a victory won by the working class at the cost of long struggles. You

[86] In May the New China News Agency reports from the provinces referred more than once to production delays in previous months, and noted the 'record' production increases of that month.

[87] The New China News Agency reported (from Hofei on February 6th) another conversation in which old miners said to young workmates: 'You never knew the Kuomintang. You don't know how lucky you are. Even being able to form your groups is something you owe to Mao Tse-tung.'

claim that leaving the pit early is rebelling against the old system: but why don't you leave the pit late instead? The more hours you put in, the more coal you mine for the country. I can see that your mind has been warped by anarchist ideas. . . .'

Young miner: 'Yes, I'm in the wrong. I haven't been working the eight-hour day that Chairman Mao established for us. . . .'

Something had to be done to deal with the threat that faced the economy. There were important talks in Peking during February among the top leaders of the Party, the State Council, and the army.[88] It is probable that in their meetings they agreed that the Party spirit, 'which was the collective spirit,' would have to prevail, and that old cadres and new would have to work together, drawing their inspiration primarily through correct ideas, no matter where they came from.[89]

One propaganda theme was the duty of the leaders of revolutionary committees to go among the people. If setbacks had occurred, they were to be attributed to the managers' lack of interest in their employees' work. The New China News Agency gave as an example a mine in the North-East,[90] apparently in order to show what managers could do to get the dismissed cadres back in their jobs. The cadres in question were those involved in production, foremen, and gangers, who could not or would not return to work for fear of being beaten up.

Mining output had been poor in February, with a deficit

[88] Li Fu-ch'un, a leading planning executive but not one of the Cultural Revolution's ideological leaders, played a part in receptions of delegates after this that was disproportionate to his importance in the Cultural Revolution (e.g. The reception by Mao Tse-tung, Lin Piao, and six national leaders for army units seconded to 'support the left, support industry and support agriculture' on February 19th. See New China News Agency report of that date.

[89] *Wenhui Pao*, February 19, 1968, 'What road should a revolutionary committee take?'

[90] New China News Agency report from Harbin, April 4, 1968 (in Chinese), 'Ssufangt'ai Mine.'

of nearly 2,000 tons on February 20th. But people were saying that it did not matter as they could make it up the next month. 'The revolutionary committee of the mining district sent two members of its leading group, who brought with them over thirty cadres belonging to the mine's management.' Thus the cadres, who were eventually reinstated by the district's 'provisional administration,' and the revolutionary committee which had not wanted them back, both began to study together the Thought of Mao Tse-tung. Revolutionaries and cadres were reconciled at a seminar on the Chairman's works: neither side could refuse to attend. This was the formula for reconciliation recommended by the revolution's leaders.

The rehabilitation of the cadres was complemented by the punishment of those who had been keeping them out for so long. The Shanghai Revolutionary Committee was purged at the end of February.[91] It met in an enlarged session on the 26th, and on the 27th there was a rally of revolutionary workers to call for 'thrift and economy in the revolution,' a theme aimed at the longest established revolutionaries, the Red Guards, some of whom were almost making a career of the Cultural Revolution. Writing about those days, a Shanghai paper noted, 'some elements sought to abuse their power in a spirit of self-aggrandisement.'[92]

Soon afterwards there were some revelations about the armed organizations of the proletariat. The *Wenhui Pao*[93] spoke of a unit formed in Shanghai under the name of 'Attack with words and defend with weapons,' a 'mailed fist of the proletarian dictatorship' to 'educate and win over the oppressed masses.' This unit, according to its commander writing in that paper, 'struck' (rather than

[91] Some militant workers who had made a name for themselves in Peking were also removed from political life. On April 14, 1968, Wang Ching-jui, a member of the standing committee of the Peking Municipal Revolutionary Committee, and also a leader of the dissident Peking Workers' Congress, was arrested.

[92] *Wenhui Pao*, February 19, 1968.

[93] March 28, 1967, and April 7, 1968.

'dragged out') the 'small handful' wherever it was to be found. As the unit was operational at the time, the press coverage it was given was not without significance. Was it still competing with the army for power in the revolutionary committees? Whatever the facts were, the *Wenhui Pao* was purged[94] soon after opening its columns to the commander of this unit and shortly before the usual May Day truce.

The advocates of social revolution were finally incorporated within the revolutionary committees of the second period, with the help of the army, which played a dominant role. Meanwhile the demands of production were making themselves inexorably felt. The industrial workers understood that their work followed a cycle as inflexible as that which nature imposed on the peasants. They had to see themselves as being like peasants, being superior only in the technical know-how that they put at the service of the people. The norms of the new 1968 plan were applied in March and April. On the eve of May Day the reformed *Wenhui Pao* told the workers:

> Production must be taken in hand; whatever is inappropriate to the superstructure of a socialist economy must be reformed; a movement for progressive management must be launched; and there must be a revolutionary transformation of the leading groups.

The leaders now being required to reform themselves and be 'progressive' were not the old cadres. They were already those who had seized power the previous year.

[94] *Wenhui Pao* was purged at mass staff meetings on April 28th, 29th, and 30th. This paper provided a very varied news service and published many readers' letters, including some which said that a second revolution and a new power takeover were needed, as the first had failed and had not led to democracy.

7. The First Revolutionary Committees

When the mission assigned to the revolutionary students had been extended to overthrowing some of the members of Party committees, it had been impossible to confine them to a critical role. Once committed to the struggle, in roles that were modified first by the bold counter-measures of the Party committees and then by the crisis brought about by the strikes, they followed a course that ended with their taking a part in the revolutionary command. The reasons for not dispersing the industrial workers were even stronger. Once they had joined in the revolution and many of them had become Revolutionary Rebels, it would have been impossible to deny their political abilities in the organs whose cadres they had replaced in order to run local affairs.

Nevertheless, the recognition of the political role of students and workers in some institutions created problems concerning the aim of the Cultural Revolution. The latter was to bring about a change of policy with the participation of the people and the transformation of the Party, both to be done without affecting the dictatorship of the proletariat. It was necessary that the Party should be rectified through general criticism, but not that everyone should take part in the institutions of government. The Centre, however, decided that revolutionary committees should be set up everywhere, and this decision was presumably taken on tactical rather than ideological grounds.

There was, however, an ideological connection between seizures of power and propaganda for a new policy for China that would be consistent with the Thought of Mao Tse-tung. The preparation for the former was done through rectifying the policies of the old committees, as Chiang Ch'ing explained in her speech at the inauguration of the Peking revolutionary committee:

The struggle, criticism and repudiation and transformation in the various departments can serve to bring about a fuller exposure and a more profound criticism and repudiation of the poisons spread on various fronts by the top Party persons: in authority taking the capitalist road.[1]

Once the seizures of power had been decided on and approved, all that remained for the Centre to do was to organize them, or at least to register and co-ordinate them.

The movement in Shanghai had come from below. The revolutionary proletariat had reacted to the strike by taking over the city's essential services and only then set up some sort of leadership. Afterwards, however, as a result of the calls to seize power and the publicity given to the first examples, revolutionary power was generally established in other provincial capitals from above. First there would be a power seizure in the provincial Party headquarters, after which a local revolutionary Centre gave its sanction to other seizures. This was the pattern followed by revolutionary committees, with the exception of the Peking one, until the middle of 1968.

There was one difference between the first six committees and those that followed. In the first ones the masses were represented by people more deeply politicized than was later to be the case. The revolutionary organizations that had been ready to take part in the committees from the beginning were enthusiasts for the revolution. Their

[1] *Peking Review*, no. 18, April 28, 1967. This is one of several passages that explain why this speech has been regarded as a programmatic document for the Cultural Revolution.

confidence—at times arrogance—led them to despise any alliance with other mass organizations. When the triple alliance was first put into practice there was no difficulty in finding enthusiastic representatives of the people among the Red Guards and the Revolutionary Rebels of the various Headquarters to serve on the new provincial committees. But a year later purges seemed necessary: their insistence on their own points of view, and their intolerance of other organizations, created too many difficulties for the committees.

The principle that the people should have a third of the representation on the committees was sufficient justification for all the organizations to claim right of entry to the committees. In the speech to Anhwei revolutionaries quoted above, Chang Ch'un-ch'iao told how he had been obliged to manoeuvre between the organizations in Shanghai that had founded the Commune and others that had not been there to take part.

When the thirty-eight founding organizations held a meeting to draw up a document establishing the 'Shanghai People's Commune,' it turned out that twenty-five other organizations had held another meeting to found the 'New Commune of the people of Shanghai.' The latter maintained that 'as you did not invite us to take part in your organization, we are calling ours the New Commune, and it will be new in relation to yours.' This caused a problem, as the thirty-eight organizations represented the majority, and moreover were unquestionably Rebels. The twenty-five others formed a minority, and the two groups quarrelled, with accusations and counter-accusations of conservative tendencies.

'We worked in opposite directions,' Chang Ch'un-ch'iao said when he explained how he pleaded with the founding organizations to extend the base of their committee. He also pleaded with the Central Committee in Peking for the Propaganda services to make no distinction between the original organizations and those that came over later. When the twenty-five negotiated one by one the terms on which they might come over, demanding equal privileges with the founder members under threat of founding a new commune, Chang had replied that being a founder brought no advantages; he and Yao Wen-yüan had been entrusted by the Centre with taking part in an organ of political power in the form of a commune, and there could only be one such organ in Shanghai, and those organizations had better realize this.

In general, all organizations regarded themselves as good, capable and devoted to the Thought of Mao Tse-tung. They did however exclude each other, making accusations concerning resistance to, and collaboration with, the Party authorities. Underlying these charges there were sometimes social prejudices. For example, many students rejected a general alliance with the workers as the latter were not willing to make unlimited sacrifices.

The students at Sian were divided between an intransigent majority and a group from Chiao Ta university that had formed a tentative alliance with the worker Rebels. The majority group started a quarrel with the workers by preaching to the miners that they should win glory by attaining new output records.[2]

While it was difficult for the Centre to say that one organization was worse than another in Cultural Revolution terms, and less deserving of a place in its institutions, it was also necessary to ensure that no really reactionary organizations slipped into the federations and committees. Mao Tse-tung himself confirmed that what had to be done now was more difficult than it had been during the revolutionary wars, as in those days the enemy had been visible, whereas 'now cases of ideological mistakes were being confused with ones involving antagonistic contradictions,' and 'this took some time to be sorted out.'[3]

The suddenness with which the Centre ordered the setting up of revolutionary committees by generalizing from the experience of two or three provincial capitals without an overall pre-arranged plan meant that the people who had to carry the policy out had their own ideas of what

[2] Andrew Watson, 'Armageddon Averted,' *Far Eastern Economic Review,* May 25, 1967, p. 451.

[3] As quoted by Lin Piao in his report to the Ninth Party Congress, April 28, 1969.

the committees should be like. Some of these ideas harmed the committees instead of winning wider acceptance for them. Many groups felt that only truly proletarian revolutionaries, poor and lower-middle peasants, and cadres of genuinely proletarian origin deserved places on them. This was an attempt to interpret these new and unexpected institutions in fundamentalist Maoist terms; while to the Cultural Revolution's leaders the new committees were functional institutions rather than the outcome of ideological principle.

Ideally, cadres in top positions in all the provinces would have seen the light and spontaneously taken the lead in seizing power, which would have avoided having revolutionary committees made to order. But the Shanghai experience could not be repeated everywhere. There was a number of reasons, including the level of political awareness of the people of the province in question, and the demoralization of the victorious revolutionaries when faced with their own incompetence. Good guides for the people would have been 'the Party's treasures.'[4]

But too few cadres were able to bring over their provinces to allegiance under Peking. The Centre therefore designated 'preparatory groups' to lead the alliance between the cadres and the people and to make preparations for revolutionary committees. While this may not have been making revolutionary committees to order, it still left the men designated by the Centre with too much authority. That such a course was taken indicates yet again that there was a wholesale dismissal of cadres.

'A quick survey of the situation today shows that most departments need military control,' said Chou En-lai on April 30, 1967,[5] a conclusion indicated by the fact that the administrative departments were no longer functioning, although their staffs—still overwhelmed by events—continued to work. In the spring of 1967 the cadres were under the impression that the Cultural Revolution was

[4] New China News Agency, 1967, no. 021017 (in French).
[5] Speech by Chou En-lai to representatives of ministries and other delegates in the hall of the State Council at 11 p.m. on April 30, 1967 (reproduced in a revolutionary pamphlet).

something outside their sphere, or even being waged against them, a student upheaval that had grown to formidable proportions which they did not really understand.

As soon as it realized that too few local cadres were taking command, the Centre must have considered using the Party's organization in the army, which had generally been sheltered from criticism and was thus in a good position to work for the reestablishment of the Party.

The story of the failure to achieve revolutionary committees was also, ironically, the story of the army. This may have been because the army only came in after the failure of the revolutionary forces, when the situation had already deteriorated so badly that nobody could have set up a revolutionary committee quickly. This was the case with Nanking. It may also have been because the army misunderstood the policies it was meant to carry out, believing that its temporary responsibilities gave it the right to silence all ideological quarrels. The fact that the army had been entrusted with establishing power from above became awkward when it used its powerful resources to crush revolutionary pressures from below. Fearing disorders, the military men gave the people no outlet for their feelings, and the positions of both sides hardened instead of becoming flexible enough to make alliances possible. Among the results were the serious incidents at Wuhan.

The principles

The northern province of Heilungkiang, whose capital is Harbin, and which makes up the northernmost part of Manchuria, provided the first example of a 'triple alliance.' P'an Fu-sheng, the first secretary of the provincial Party committee, made his self-criticism after the Eleventh Plenum of the Central Committee and supported the revolutionary cause.[6] The 'Red Rebels of Heilungkiang' gave

[6] A leaflet entitled *Basic Experience of the Heilungkiang Red Rebels in the Struggle to Seize Power*, written collectively by the 'leading comrades of the Rebels in Heilungkiang Province' and published by the People's Publishing House in February 1967

this account of what happened one day at the beginning of January:

> Comrade P'an Fu-sheng and leading members of the Provincial Military Area took the initiative and went to the Harbin Red Rebels United Headquarters to discuss how to seize power, and the latter took the initiative in proposing that Comrade P'an Fu-sheng and Comrade Wang Chia-tao, the Provincial Area Military Commander, join the Heilungkiang Red Rebel Military Committee, when the founding of this committee was being considered.[7]

On January 12th the Rebels seized the newspapers, the radio station and the Public Security Bureau, where they met with a vigorous resistance, though 'all their contrivances were thwarted by the left within the bureau.' Rightwing organizations counterattacked in order to retake the papers, after which the army brought out its weapons and disbanded these organizations on January 26th.[8] One of these, the *Jung Fu Chün*, which had taken defensive positions in the Harbin Palace of Friendship, was forced to surrender. The army then confirmed the rebels' seizure of the papers and 'imprisoned the ringleaders of the counter-revolutionary organizations.' On January 30th P'an Fu-sheng, the commanding officers of the military sector, and the leaders of the Red Rebels—'the three parties' —'joined together and drafted the first proclamation.' The revolutionary committee, which was officially established January 31st, was held up as a model by the national press. The *People's Daily* wrote:

> Acting in the light of the concrete conditions of the local struggle, the revolutionary rebels carried out the Party's policy in a clear-cut way: they united with the senior leading members of the Provincial Party Com-

gives an account of the events of January 1967 in Harbin. [A translation can be found in *Peking Review*, no. 8, February 17, 1967, pp. 15–17—translator]

[7] *Ibid.*, p. 15.

[8] See *Mōtakutō no chōsen*, Tokyo, 1967, p. 57.

mittee who followed Chairman Mao's correct line and with senior leading members of the People's Liberation Army to form a 'three-in-one' force to seize power.[9]

The revolutionary leadership was thus urging the Rebels to look for support actually inside the main targets of power seizures: municipal and provincial Party committees. The Heilungkiang case was also a model in that the local leaders went to see the Rebels. An emphatic reference to the Party's line was a reminder to the Rebels that they were working for the benefit of the Party: the revolution was not for opportunists.

This constituted a theory on the relative roles of Rebels and revolutionary cadres. This theory may have been somewhat idealistic, and the example of Heilungkiang may have been a little too good. All the same, the Centre seemed to have reckoned that in many places the leading cadres would declare themselves ready to lead the people in the style of P'an Fu-sheng.

> The role of the revolutionary cadres in participating in the 'three-in-one' provisional organ of power must be given full consideration. They should and can play the role of nucleus and backbone of the provisional organ,

wrote *Red Flag* on March 10, 1967,[10] showing how much hope was still being placed in them. The Heilungkiang Rebels were proud of having been more accommodating towards the cadres than their Shanghai colleagues: as they wrote of themselves, 'they did not automatically and in a doctrinaire fashion imitate the experiments undertaken

[9] *People's Daily* editorial, February 10, 1967, 'A good example in the struggle by proletarian revolutionaries to seize power,' translated in *Peking Review*, no. 8, February 17, 1967, pp. 17–19. This editorial includes a detailed study of how to deal with various categories of cadres, divided according to their political attitudes.

[10] 'On the Revolutionary "Three-in-one" Combination,' *Red Flag*, no. 5, 1967; see *Peking Review*, no. 12, March 17, 1967, p. 15.

in other parts of China.'[11] Perhaps they did not realize just how lucky they were in having the co-operation of the provincial Party first secretary. Shanghai's chaos had developed under a Party committee as unwilling to carry reaction to the extremes as to support the rebels. In most other provinces the 'hawks' in the Party machine had used the police as a means in their struggle against organizations loyal to the Central Committee's Cultural Revolution Group. After this the Rebels and Red Guards put those they were able to capture under house arrest.[12]

The Centre tried from then on to make people accept that many cadres had been wrongly dismissed or mistreated. The word came from Peking that it was bad tactics to put guilty men on public display at meetings.[13] Criticism rallies gradually tended to be held for other reasons, and for the time being were aimed at Liu Shao-ch'i.

The cadre problem, therefore, whatever form it may have taken, was that fault was being found with the cadres; and the army's cadres were substitutes for them. Where did the soldiers come from to participate in the revolutionary committees? The military command sent them wherever they were needed:

> At various levels, in those departments where power must be seized, representatives of the armed forces or of the militia should take part in forming the 'three-in-one' combination . . . Representatives of the armed forces should be sent to the county level or higher, and representatives of the militia should be sent to the commune level or lower.[14]

The new organs of power varied widely, containing all

[11] *Basic Experience*—see *Peking Review*, no. 8, p. 15.

[12] Andrew Watson tells how the senior Party cadres in Sian were kept in the provincial committee's offices, where they were forced to write their self-criticisms and do manual labour. On some days they were put on public display at mass meetings or driven through the city in open lorries. *Far Eastern Economic Review*, May 18, 1967, p. 405.

[13] *Ibid.*

[14] 'On the Revolutionary "Three-in-one" Combination,' *Peking Review*, no. 12, 1967, p. 16.

kinds of *ad hoc* teams working to unite the left and organize committees. Many of the cadres from the army's
Party organization were assigned to these tasks. At the
lowest level there were regroupings of revolutionary organizations being formed into 'alliances,' which were generally called 'congresses' when at provincial or municipal
level. Cadres from outside did not take part in them, preferring to work for their establishment by means of preparatory groups.

The 'preparatory groups for revolutionary committees,'
whether in a Unit, a university, or a province, were teams
designated by the Centre or by an existing revolutionary
committee to do what P'an Fu-sheng, the Red Rebels, and
the local army command had done in Harbin: amalgamate
the revolutionary forces and give a popular mandate to
a committee. When a preparatory group created a favourable climate of opinion, it formed an enlarged preparatory
group, containing only those elements that accepted the
idea of 'alliance.' This was a step towards a revolutionary
committee because the preparatory group had thus
acquired a definite following. Then, when a revolutionary
committee was formed, recognition had to be won from
the Centre.

The Centre's Cultural Revolution Group and the State
Council granted the recognition without which a committee's position was still liable to be disputed. Once recognized, however, it became a provisional organ of the
proletarian dictatorship, and anyone who opposed its decisions would be declared a counter-revolutionary.

This lengthy procedure often had to be undertaken.
While in some provinces the elements of a revolutionary
committee quickly joined forces, in others rival organizations continued to struggle with each other, while some
figures, though accepted by the Centre, continued to be
interminably criticized. In other cases military control prevented the development of political debate.

The necessity of keeping order gave the provisional
organs even more power. Even preparatory groups were
given the authority to maintain 'revolutionary order.' This
was a very delicate stage in the process, for the provi-

sional groups and the military administrators had no popular bases; and it became even more complicated when there were delays in forming revolutionary committees.

The first six revolutionary committees

The first six provincial revolutionary committees were those formed in Heilungkiang, Shantung, Kweichow, Shansi and the great cities of Shanghai and Peking. Events in Shantung and Kweichow were similar to those in Heilungkiang, though less straightforward and exemplary.

In Shantung the revolutionary organizations first followed the example of Shanghai by uniting and proclaiming the revolution in one city, Tsingtao, where twenty-three organizations joined together on January 22nd. They announced that power had to be seized from the municipal authorities, because they had repressed the Cultural Revolution and set up a 'Tsingtao Revolutionary Rebel Committee.' However, immediately afterwards the chief position was filled by a local public figure in the province, the vice-mayor of Tsingtao, Wang Hsiao-yü.

The committee defied the provincial authorities, proclaimed several cadres unsatisfactory and ordered them to surrender themselves within three days, and acquitted the rest on condition that they returned to work. In other words, enough of the workers' and students' organizations recognized a leader who was able to make the administrative personnel stay on under the new authorities. This force overthrew the provincial Party committee on February 3rd and replaced it with a revolutionary committee which several army units supported with enthusiasm.

In Kweichow power was seized on January 25th. Eight days later, and probably also under Shanghai influence, the First Rebel Headquarters decided that it wanted elections held rapidly in which revolutionary rebels could democratically elect a provisional revolutionary committee with full powers.[15] But, from January 25th, a senior army

15 New China News Agency, no. 020507, 1967 (in French). Unlike Tsingtao, Kweiyang is not a great industrial city. Kweichow is a backward province, and observers were surprised by

cadre had been offering the revolutionaries his services as leader: Li Tsai-han, the deputy political commissar of the Kweichow Military District. He became chairman of the revolutionary committee on February 13th, with the Kweichow military commander as one of his vice-chairmen.

There was a somewhat different story in Shansi. There was a trial of strength with the provincial Party committee, which put up resistance. Liu Ko-p'ing,[16] the political cadre who put himself in charge of the masses, was on bad terms with the heads of the old bureaucracy, and thus probably also with his colleagues in the provincial Party secretariat in Taiyuan. He had a long-standing personal quarrel with Liu Shao-ch'i.[17] Was he unpopular with the cadres because he had been involved in the 'revolutionary revolt?' Whatever the reason, the provincial committee put forward a rival Headquarters in opposition to the rebel one.

On January 12th over 20,000 rebels surrounded the provincial committee's offices, captured several cadres, and carried out searches.[18] Then, according to revolutionary sources, the authorities laid in wait. Operating from a 'clandestine headquarters' they incited the workers' organizations to attack the rebels. Strikes followed. Taiyuan is an industrial and mining city, and it may well be that events followed the same course as at Shanghai. Chang Jih-ch'ing, the second political commissar of the Shansi Military District, played an important part in the workers' alliance[19] some time before the army as a whole was

---

the turn taken by the revolution there. Later on, in April 1968, the Kweichow revolutionaries maintained that the working class controlled the revolution, although events in Shanghai gave no grounds for believing this. The power seizure in Kweichow was doubtless the work of a small and dynamic minority of workers in the city of Kweiyang directed by cadres newly appointed to the province after the 1965 purge.

[16] Deputy governor of Shansi.

[17] Liu Ko-p'ing had opposed Liu Shao-ch'i's advice to Communists imprisoned by the Kuomintang to recant, according to the story of the quarrel given in many posters.

[18] See *Ajia Keizai Jumpo*, no. 694, Tokyo, September 1967.

[19] *People's Daily*, January 25, 1967.

drawn into the revolution. There were lengthy consultations between the army, the cadres and the revolutionaries. The revolutionary committee was finally appointed on March 18th, with 245 members, of whom slightly less than half were representatives of the people and rather more were from the cadres and the army.[20]

In Peking the Red Guards and the Rebels first wanted to found a commune like Shanghai's. Two federations, to which fifty-eight organizations belonged, joined together to form a 'Preparatory Committee for the Peking People's Commune.' In its pride it put up posters in red characters, as if they were orders from the Central Committee. The Central Committee's Cultural Revolution Group, however, keeping direct control over the capital, pressed for congresses in which different social groups were segregated. There were to be four of these congresses, for workers, peasants, university and college students, and middle-school students.

The Central Cultural Revolution Group, obediently followed by the various student headquarters, took charge of the setting up of a student congress, the 'red congress' that was formed in February. But other organizations were harder to combine, and around March 10th Hsieh Fu-chih, Minister of Public Security and a deputy premier, was put in charge of bringing the other congresses into being.

Hsieh Fu-chih was a soldier with experience of Party work in government.[21] He had a soldier's toughness, but was flexible when it came to winning support and justifying ways of applying pressure. When criticized in the streets because of the harshness of the police at Shih-chingshan, he made his self-criticism immediately. In August and September, when Wang Li was falling victim to

[20] *People's Daily*, March 23, 1967.
[21] He had been chosen by Teng Hsiao-p'ing as first secretary of the Yunnan Provincial Party Committee in 1953, but he no longer felt himself bound to his protector. 'Hsieh used to be under the protection of Teng Hsiao-p'ing, but he has since made honourable amends,' said Chou En-lai in a speech on January 11, 1967. (*Shoutu Hungweiping*, January 21, 1967.)

the Wuhan affair, Hsieh seemed to be in no trouble although he too was directly involved. He was a clever politician, and was said to enjoy the confidence of Chou En-lai.[22]

The congress of poor and lower-middle peasants from the rural districts of Peking was set up on March 19th, and a similar body for revolutionary workers on March 22nd. It was the congress of Red Guards from middle schools that caused him the most trouble. In order to organize the turbulent and sharply divided middle-school students, whose passions threatened to wreck the alliance that had already been achieved in principle among the students, Hsieh Fu-chih used the army. He used the meetings called at the beginning of the new school year to win recognition from the school delegates for their new military instructors. Then he told them that these new teachers would be responsible for building a federation of secondary-school students under the control of the military committee.[23] The secondary-school Red Guards congress finally met on March 25th.

Next, approval had to be won from the committees of the various congresses on the composition of the revolutionary committee that was to represent all of them. Rivalries between big and small as well as moderate and militant organizations were reappearing. The birth of the committee was delayed until April 20th. Of its ninety-seven members only seventeen were soldiers and thirteen cadres. There was a careful balance between workers' and students' representatives: twenty-four workers and twenty students (fourteen university-level students and six from middle-school students). There were also thirteen peas-

[22] See 'Kokusai Tenkizu. Hito no Kadai (4)' in *Asahi Shimbun*, December 22, 1967. Hsieh was put in charge of the revolutionary committee in order to set an example to China. His success, and the strength of the Public Security, gave him an exceptional political position, independent of alliances with other top leaders.

[23] See the Red Guard organ, *Chünt'uan Chanpao*, March 20, 1967. The military affairs committee for the Peking region was established on February 11th, with the special mission of eliminating the associations that had been disbanded.

ants, six members of cultural and social associations, and four urban residents.[24] And the balance between different tendencies within each group was even more skillfully administered. The Peking committee was weak because it had been formed before the alliances were achieved. A congress was a good formula for a system of representation through elections, but not for an organ of the dictatorship of the proletariat. The participants were agreed on the composition of the committee but not on its policies.

On May 14th, some months after the first revolutionary committees had been established, Hsieh Fu-chih made this point at a meeting of the Peking committee. Enthusiasm for self-expression and participation had grown everywhere as a result of the new freedoms that had been won by the January revolution, and political passions were on the boil. Brawls and work stoppages were a plague in the big cities. The most extreme radicals wanted the revolutionary committees to fight violence with violence.

Hsieh Fu-chih commented on an 'urgent notice' to the people that was issued in the name of the revolutionary committee.[25] He said that all the revolutionaries were giving priority to revolutionary efforts, but it was of first importance to continue working and producing. The Central Committee and Chairman Mao were worried about the drop in output caused by absenteeism, conflicts, and even sabotage. 'Many workers from the Shihchingshan Steel Works have undertaken protest strikes and sit-ins in front of the four gates of Chungnanhai. This is not the way to get work done.'[26] He said that there had been 313 brawls between April 30th and May 10th, counting only those in which over fifty people were involved. He also urged organizations outside the revolutionary committees to follow the important notice of May 14th without

[24] Figures from Konno, *op. cit.,* p. 184.

[25] See the Peking Aviation Institute Red Flag's journal *Hungch'i,* no. 14, June 6, 1967.

[26] Speech at the third session of the Peking Revolutionary Committee on May 14, 1967, according to a *tatzupao* of the 'Propaganda Team of Revolutionary Rebel Corps of the Central Committee's United Front Department.'

delay. He begged them to make propaganda themselves against disorder and violence.

The revolutionary committee was there to give its approval to a decision on public order, but was it governing Peking? Would Hsieh Fu-chih have appealed from the committee to other organizations if it had really been in control? The notice of May 14th stipulated that the armed forces of the garrison, and soldiers everywhere, were permitted to use force, whereas the committee itself was nowhere authorized to do so. This was what the members of the Central Committee's Cultural Revolution Group who were furthest to the left were criticizing when they demanded that the organs of the proletarian dictatorship be strengthened.

The use of force continued to be left to the discretion of the army and the public security, and was a matter to be decided by the Party committees in the army. When founder organizations of the revolutionary committee ignored the appeals for order, work and unity, the army put pressure on them as well as on the committee's opponents. In June the Centre permitted the right to put up posters to certain organizations only.[27] The right of publication, like that of association, was now restricted.

Unsuccessful revolutionary committees

There had been many seizures of power between the end of January and February 11th. They are known to have taken place at the head of at least fourteen provinces, in addition to Shanghai. In every case the course of events was similar.

Rebels seized the local papers, radio stations and public security offices. But then conservative organizations claimed the right to seize power themselves, which was said by some to be the counter-attack of the Party committees. Battles for the control of the papers and strikes then followed. In only six of the fourteen provinces where

[27] It was also in June that the propaganda section of the 'Red Congress' was dissolved and its committee reorganized. (See *Shoutu Hungweiping*, June 11, 1967.)

this series of events took place did revolutionary committees emerge. In all the other cases the situation deteriorated, and the army played a dominant role.

Everything depended on how the army interpreted its mission. It had been ordered to 'support the left.' If it understood that it was meant to let the Maoist current bring new men into politics it let organizations act and express their views, even when they criticized the army, and no disasters ensued. But if it failed to make a distinction between the Cultural Revolution and the government during the period of hiatus which it was supposed to superintend, there was a danger of the situation getting out of hand. And if the army tried to run the revolution itself by silencing the boldest voices it was preparing the way for upheavals.

The soldiers rarely understood this at once; after all, they only intervened when the situation was already chaotic. In Honan, for example, the army made some mistakes, persisted in them for some time, was subjected to an inquiry from the Centre, and only then allowed the appointed cadres to act.

This, in brief, is what happened. The 'Revolutionary Rebel Command' took over the *Honan Daily* on February 7th and held it till the 18th. One of its first actions was to demand the dismissal of Chan Shu-chih, the commander of the Honan Military District, but Peking did not agree. The Rebels joined with Red Guards of the Third Headquarters to found the 'Commune of February 7th.' Hostile organizations[28] tried to take the *Honan Daily* back from them. Chou En-lai turned to the army, which had apparently been held in reserve. He decided that the paper should come under military control, and that representatives of the rival groups should be sent to Peking by the army.[29]

Next, the public security services made their own 're-

[28] Associated with the 'Chengchow University United Committee' (capital of Honan), which may itself have been against Red Guards from outside the province.

[29] On February 17, 1967. Chou En-lai's directive on the *Honan Daily* incident.

bellion,' which resulted in a very strong new group, the
'Honan Security Commune,' which seemed to be favoured
by the army. The Security Commune fought against the
strikes,[30] arrested rebels and even held them in a deten-
tion camp, claiming that it was imposing proletarian dictatorship. The Centre ordered an inquiry on the two communes, but its results were not made available until July
10th.[31] Then it condemned some of the Party officials in
the army, who had made 'mistakes in the support of the
left.'

The Centre appointed a 'Preparatory Group for the Revolutionary Committee' for the province under Liu Chien-
hsün, a Honan cadre who had made his self-criticism and
become one of the deputy chairmen of the Peking revolutionary committee. The army accepted his authority and
proved loyal, even during the very serious incidents in
the neighbouring province of Hupei.

In the latter province the army's rule left no room for
any other political authority. At the end of February it
had established in Wuhan an office of the military sector
in charge of Revolution and Production, with departments
for agriculture, irrigation, industry, commerce and finance.
The whole was under army control. On March 6th Ch'en
Tsai-tao, the commander of the Wuhan Military Region,
announced on behalf of the Bureau that the organization had taken over the army's and the Party's powers in
the province.[32] Schools were ordered to reopen on March
20th with very strong discipline.[33] Fifty thousand teachers,
students and workers met on March 13th to be told that
disputes, anarchy and abuses of democracy in schools
would be dealt with.

The workers had hardly any more freedom to express
their ideas than did the students. The Second Headquarters of the Wuhan workers could not demonstrate without

[30] Chengchow is an industrial town with large cotton mills.
[31] See *Chingkangshan*, organ of the Peking Further Education College, no. 57 (July 26, 1967).
[32] According to Hupei Radio on March 6th. See *China
News Analysis*, no. 655, April 14, 1967, p. 6.
[33] Order no. 3 from the military command (*Ibid.*).

repercussions. The Cultural Revolution was kept under restraint in Hupei, unlike the other provinces where it was so tumultuous.

There were of course some provinces where defence and security had a high enough priority to leave the army no room for doubts about its role. This applied particularly to provinces with sensitive frontiers, such as those next to Vietnam, the USSR and India. Most of them were also autonomous regions with national minorities. The revolution here was later in time or slower in tempo. And then there were other provinces where the army was on active service: Fukien,[34] where it faced Chiang Kai-shek across the sea, or Kwangtung, the province of Canton. That great working-class city had not, despite its long revolutionary history, played a full part in the Cultural Revolution. The revolutionary organizations were unable to develop the workers' institutions they would have liked. Although the Cultural Revolution got under way, it was almost crushed by the military control that the Centre wanted and kept, even after the revolutionary committee was established much later. Chou En-lai reasoned with the Rebels there:

> Military control is very important, especially in Kwangtung, which is a frontier region at the gates of Hongkong and Macao. The army must be helped in carrying out its task of control.[35]

A seizure of power in Canton at the end of January was the work of Red Guard organizations, reinforced by outsiders from Shanghai, Peking, Wuhan and Harbin, but not allied to the majority in Canton.[36] These organizations formed a Kwangtung Cultural Revolution Federation and

[34] The army had been controlling the Cultural Revolution in Fukien since January 26th. At the end of March representatives of the Rebels went to Peking to demand that the army restore their liberties.

[35] Speech by Chou En-lai in Canton on April 14, 1967, according to posters of April 17th.

[36] On the Cultural Revolution in Canton see *Ajia Keizai Jumpo,* no. 741, December 1968, p. 13 ff.

decided to leave the existing committees in being. On January 22nd they called a meeting of the Party committee, made it hand over its seals of office, then set it to work again, claiming that they controlled it. Other organizations fought against them. On February 28th the army drove out the Cultural Revolution Federation and took control itself.

A strong movement of protest against the army concentrated its attacks on the *Canton Daily*'s[37] 'control team.' Passions rose, and with disorder growing on the eve of the international spring trade fair, at which many foreigners were expected, Chou En-lai arrived in Canton to arbitrate. He presented himself as an advocate of revolutionary unity, and insisted that the rebels should tolerate rival organizations. These latter he rehabilitated in return for their repudiation of some of their leaders. He reiterated his support for the military control groups and introduced Huang Yung-sheng, the general sent by the Centre's Cultural Revolution Group, to take charge of the revolution in Canton.

There was much bitterness against the army. It was in Canton that such slogans as, 'Military control is the new [bourgeois] authority; power must be seized from it,' were first seen. Under army control two main factions were opposed to each other and to military control as well. There were very serious incidents throughout the summer of 1967. It took a long time to form congresses, which only emerged in October and November. A 'preparatory group for the revolutionary committee' was only appointed on November 12th.

Arbitration on the spot was the exception. In most cases, as we have seen with Honan, the rival groups had to send their spokesmen to Peking.[38] Peking was not just an arbitration tribunal; it was also neutral ground where asylum

[37] Formerly the *Yangch'eng Wanpao*.

[38] On February 6, 1967, for example, the State Council and the Military Commission sent two aircraft to Huhehot in Inner Mongolia to bring representatives of quarrelling organizations to take part in a conciliation meeting in Peking in which the Centre would arbitrate.

could be sought. 'It is not possible to make arrests in Peking,' said Wang Li.[39] All factions went there to seek justice and distribute their journals in the hope of interesting public opinion in their own particular dramas. Some asked for help against the 'fascism' of counter-revolutionary authorities, while others appealed against the 'fascism' of the Rebels.

Chou En-lai only judged these organizations on their performance. Mao Tse-tung had said more than once that there was a place for the right as well as for the left. The Centre's arbitration was heeded. Watson has described how, when the instructions came from Peking to Sian, students obeyed with surprising speed and began to criticize themselves for the error of line they had committed during the previous seventy days.[40]

But as for the army, we must emphasize that, despite misinterpretations and, at times, abuses of power, it was always acquitted of its deeds,[41] apart from the condemnation of a few of its leaders. This became even more noticeable after the Wuhan affair.

In Shantung, when a conflict broke out between students and soldiers, despite the revolutionary committee, the high command made a self-criticism[42] and re-established the organizations that the army wanted to suppress. There were serious incidents in Szechuan at the beginning of May, with troops firing on a crowd in Wanhsien.[43] What happened was certainly a serious reverse for the military leaders. There was a meeting in Peking at which the Military Commission proposed that the political commissars of the Chengtu Military Region and some of their subordinates should be relieved of their duties. Hsiao Hua urged

[39] Speech to the *People's Daily* staff on March 16, 1967. See *Hung Erh-ch'i*, June 6, 1967.

[40] *Far Eastern Economic Review*, May 25, 1967, p. 451.

[41] There was an exception in Chinghai in February. This was the only case in which the leaders, especially Su Yü, recognized that a counter-revolutionary insurrection had taken place. See *Hung Erh-ch'i*, no. 4, June 6, 1967.

[42] On May 28, 1967. The self-criticism was published by the paper *Hungse Tsaofant'uan*, June 22, 1967.

[43] *Asahi Shimbun*, Japanese morning edition of May 7, 1967.

this solution, asking that those put in their place to run
the army be shown confidence, and the Centre's Cultural
Revolution Group agreed.[44] There was no purge in the
army.

Once again, Hsiao Hua's policy prevailed. But the military regime that had established itself at Wuhan was preparing for the day when the army would use its weapons.

[44] Speech by the leaders, evening May 7, 1967, announcing
the decision of the Central Committee for Szechuan—wall
posters. Reported in *Peking Kono Ichinen,* Tokyo, 1968, pp.
155–56, op. cit.

8. The Peasants: A Moderate Cultural Revolution

The Maoist policy towards the peasants was to put into practice the principles that the Party had been putting forward since 1963,[1] not to condemn them. There was no change of policy. This meant that the social climate could be kept under control, as long as the revolutionaries did not go among the peasantry seeking support, and as long as the propagandists remained uncertain about the extent of the sacrifices which policy imposed on the peasants. Once these two conditions ceased to apply, agitation increased in the countryside. The villages on the fringes of the big cities were gradually infected by the spirit of partisan quarrels.

When it became clear that the revolutionary committees, established in the people's communes some time after those in the cities, would have a programme that envisaged the eventual abolition of individual advantages, some of the peasants turned their discontent on the poor peasants, on whom the programme relied for the implementation of the policies of the future.

The revolutionary committees themselves, however, continued to advocate moderation. The Centre made it plain that the rural collective system would be maintained. No retreat was possible now, and the concessions that had permitted certain capitalist practices to revive were condemned.

[1] See Chapter 2.

The only additions that the Cultural Revolution made to the principles that the Party had hitherto been somewhat remiss in supporting were decentralization, and a new stress on the political role of the poor and lower-middle peasants as the people entitled to wield the proletarian dictatorship.

One of the problems on which most ink had been spilt was the equalizing of incomes, whether it should be between different groups working in collective production, or between the individual members of these groups. In the people's communes the groups in question were the production brigades and production teams. The team, consisting of about a score of families, was the lowest-level decision-making unit, and the system was not to be changed for thirty years.[2]

The Communist Party had gone to great trouble to reduce inevitable differences in income, trying especially to balance the land and equipment that was entrusted to production brigades. It also tried to compensate for the inequalities in property between different brigades by encouraging the worse off to engage in subsidiary production, for which the collective provided investment. Regional differences could evidently not be put right, particularly as nothing could modify the natural conditions that made some territories poor or arid, but inequalities between neighbours could be rectified to a certain extent.

The champions of the Cultural Revolution attacked, not these attempts at equalization, but the unprogressive solutions to the problem of individual incomes: quotas for production and rations allocated to each family together with a parcel of land; the right of rural handicraft workers to engage in private enterprise; the private ownership of privately cleared land; and the organization of free rural markets.

In speaking of the 'struggle between the two lines'[3] in

[2] Second revised draft set of working rules for rural people's communes, September 1962.

[3] The ideological campaign to spread the idea of collectivism among the peasants, generally referred to as the 'struggle between the two lines in the countryside,' was the outcome of the Cultural Revolution in the countryside.

the Ch'it'ien production brigade, the peasant Ma Cheng said that after the difficult years around 1961 the Party cadres who were acting on Liu Shao-ch'i's instructions had encouraged the peasants to clear new land that would be their private property. His brigade had ten teams, of which eight had raised their output from collective land, while in the other two output from collective fields had fallen considerably after much private land clearance. In the spring of 1962 a Work Team sent in by the Party committee of their special administrative region had urged the brigade to adopt a system of allocating rations by families and by 'work points.' Ma Cheng had opposed this, saying:

> If we adopt this method, those families which have more labour power . . . will get more grain than they can consume. But those with less labour power will receive fewer work points and therefore will get insufficient grain. So therefore surely differences will once again reappear.[4]

It was true that from most of the policies advocated —land clearance, small-scale private enterprise, and family allowances—the rich peasants stood to gain the most. The plans of the group at the top of the Party had been a 'vain attempt to drag the people's communes back to the stage of the small peasant economy,' a group of proletarian revolutionaries wrote later in a theoretical article.[5] The ensuing state of affairs permitted some to play a privileged political role. T'ao Chu himself said that the control of community life by the better-off peasants involved an element of conflict: 'The principal contradiction in the villages at present is the one between the poor and lower-

4 Ma Cheng, 'Struggle Between the Two Lines in an Agricultural Production Brigade,' *Peking Review*, no. 52, December 27, 1968, pp. 8–10.

5 Article by proletarian revolutionaries in the National Defence Scientific and Technical Commission in the *People's Daily*, from the New China News Agency, February 10, 1968 (no. 021206 in the French Series).

middle peasants on the one hand and the privileged stratum on the other.'[6]

The course the Cultural Revolution was meant to follow in the Units (government offices, factories, people's communes) was summarized in three words: struggle—criticism—transformation. There was hardly any significant transformation in the countryside, except that the poor and lower-middle peasants were given more power within the rural assemblies to prevent the return to power of a privileged class.

This was not the great leap forward towards communism that was sometimes prematurely proclaimed outside China. The Cultural Revolution had a hard job to do among the peasants when it tried to struggle against the non-socialist concessions that it accused Liu Shao-ch'i of having made. The lesser Party cadres had made propaganda for the Liu Shao-ch'i line in the countryside. Some precautions had to be taken before he could be attacked. This explains why the number of people actually censured was so small.

The Cultural Revolution in the countryside was aimed, not at the cadres, but at a few 'landlords, rich peasants, counter-revolutionaries, and rightists.' And the cadres themselves were required to correct their faults of bureaucratism and authoritarian attitudes. But the cadres concerned were mainly minor officials who carried little weight in making the Party's policies; their job was only to carry the policies out by uniting, leading and instructing the people. When the Party collapsed many of them were so confused that they wanted no further involvement. Later on, when the recovery of the Party led to preparations for a congress—an occasion at which the countryside was normally strongly represented—the cadres had to meet to choose their representatives. Militiamen, peasants educated by the army, were generally selected as substitutes for those cadres who had given up and were no longer suitable.

The Cultural Revolution was extended to the countryside in December 1966 by a directive of the Centre. It

[6] Speech by T'ao Chu at the Kwangtung Provincial Committee in February 1965, quoted in *Ajia Keizai Jumpo*, no. 692, August 1967, p. 3.

condemned old customs and put the accent on production, but it steered clear of fundamental problems. Such problems were only put on the agenda later on by peasant revolutionaries in Shansi, the province of the model production brigade of Tachai. The December directive said nothing about seizing power in the spheres of production and finance. The directive outlined a Cultural Revolution in a stricter sense—in ideology—and called upon the poor and lower-middle peasants to direct it. It allowed for those responsible for production to be replaced by substitutes chosen or approved by the masses, but it did not entrust the Cultural Revolution Committees of poor and lower-middle peasants with managing production.

This directive might have been rapidly made obsolete by more radical documents, but this was not to be the case. Another directive on the same subject a year later made no substantial changes on the earlier one. There had, however, been agitation among the peasants in the meantime. Activist organizations had sought recruits among them and tried to draw them into the urban conflicts. In some sensitive areas the army was sent in to 'aid agriculture.' The situation appeared so troubled in places that some soldiers went so far as to arm the militia and use them in local conflicts. When this policy was condemned by the Centre this led to a clash inside the army. But such military interventions in the Cultural Revolution in the countryside seem to have been few in number.

With the roles of the cadres and the army in the countryside reduced, there was a relaxation in centralized control over production, in the planning of collective work, in the control of markets, and even in morals. The revolutionary committees that were eventually set up in the countryside had to deal with all of this. The militia helped the army to educate the peasants in 'Thought of Mao Tsetung' study classes. The soldiers sent to remote areas to do this found to their astonishment that their audiences had scarcely heard of the Cultural Revolution. Their task was not an easy one: this was the first time for years that the peasants had been asked to make sacrifices.

The movement ended by putting cadres on their guard

against acting arbitrarily and confirmed the position of the poor and lower-middle peasants' associations, institutions outside the Party intended to bring about progress in political life but not affecting collectivization. Yao Wen-yuan wrote an article in the summer of 1968 in which he said that the Cultural Revolution would succeed in the countryside when it had consolidated the position of socialism.[7] This was a confirmation that its programme remained a moderate one even when its success was beginning to come into view. It put a check on the privileges and powers of the formerly wealthier peasants, and although it did not give the poor peasants' associations decision-making powers, it confirmed their role in the running of retail co-operatives and rural schools.

The later documents of the Cultural Revolution only refer to agriculture in relation to production, and say nothing about new political victories for socialism in the countryside.

A moderated Cultural Revolution in the countryside

At the beginning of 1967 some Red Guard papers were reporting, in the style of the Rebels, what had happened in the countryside around Peking during the first months of the revolution. The Red Guards, eager to spread their revolt throughout society, had come closest to doing so among the peasants who lived around the big cities. They had, however, soon been forbidden to cause agitation among them.[8]

This did not stop them from expressing their views. Allowing for their sense of urgency and a tendency to exaggerate struggles when describing them, their papers are useful sources of information. Of course, this example would not have been typical of the whole of China. The peasants who lived far from the big cities would not have

---

[7] *Red Flag*, no. 2, 1968, in *Peking News*, no. 35, 1968.

[8] See above, Chapter 4, Mao Tse-tung's instructions of September 7, 1966, and *People's Daily*, September 11, 1966, editorial.

seen Red Guards coming and going. All the same, the story of the people's communes that were used as testing grounds where radicals and conservatives took it in turns to put their theories into practice deserves some attention.

One of these papers[9] said that when the news of the reorganization of the Peking municipal Party committee reached them, the Work Teams responsible for the 'four clean-ups' movement withdrew in disorder. The revolutionaries grew bolder, and were disappointed when Li Hsüeh-feng[10] ruled, on June 25, 1966, that any opposition to the Work Teams would be taken as opposition to Party control. After the final communiqué of the Eleventh Plenum on August 12th, the houses of rich peasants and reactionaries were searched; arms and money were discovered. Women's hair was cut short. But the reactionaries did not lose their self-confidence, for they said, 'Do not make the struggle worse but work hard, otherwise it will be impossible to have our 400 *chin* (200 kilograms) of food grain per head.'[11]

After September 11th and the Centre's decision that the communes should be allowed to make their revolutions for themselves there was a lull. The Rebels in the countryside used this interlude to establish revolutionary contacts. Some of them 'left the country bumpkins to go back to the cities.'

The December directive on the Cultural Revolution in the villages caused new upheavals. At the time the paper came out, February 18th, the peasant movement was still meeting with much resistance in the Peking region, and the amount of progress made differed in the various *hsien*. Where the old authorities were still in control, they were saying to the peasants, 'If you want work points, go to work and don't make revolution. If you don't work we won't pay you.'

[9] *Nungts'un Chanpao*, February 18, 1967.
[10] The new head of the municipal Party committee after the dismissal of P'eng Chen.
[11] Party secretaries and brigade heads were telling them either to fulfil their norms or else accept less rations than had previously been allowed for.

It is clear from this document that even in the Peking region the rural cadres were encouraged by the Centre's moderate decisions and managed to keep the situation under control. This impression is confirmed by the fact that the peasants who wanted to make revolution had to leave their villages. Their arrival in Shanghai has already been mentioned (see Chapter 6 above). In January the *Wenhui Pao*[12] protested against peasants who left their production posts and poured into the cities to present unreasonable demands.

The Centre was well aware that all kinds of personal grudges could add venom to the criticisms of the cadres which the peasants were making. It apparently decided not to allow revolutionary carnivals in the villages, stating that even when accused of criminal offences, Party cadres of below the *hsien* level could not be tried on the spot. If commune officials were charged, their files were to be handed to the *hsien* Party committee, which could dismiss them; and the accused might continue to hold office until found guilty.[13] This resolution must have been intended to prevent the Red Guards who were moving into the countryside from teaching the peasants to hold criticism meetings and public trials.

When the decision was made to involve the workers in the Cultural Revolution it became necessary to specify how the peasants might take part. The Central Committee brought out a ten-point directive to be displayed in the communes. It was similar, even to the extent of being provisional, to the one that applied to factories.[14] Unlike the industrial directive, however, it was not just an experimental one to be tried out in a few trial units, but was of general application; and it was applied unchanged through-

[12] January 20, 1967.

[13] Central Committee resolution of September 14, 1966, quoted in Chapter 4 above.

[14] Published in the *Asahi Shimbun,* December 29, 1966, as 'the Directive of the Central Committee of the Chinese Communist Party and the State Council on the Proletarian Cultural Revolution in the Countryside,' December 15, 1966.

out the Cultural Revolution. In the movement among the peasantry the bids were hardly raised at all.

According to this directive, the Cultural Revolution was to be run by the poor and lower-middle peasants acting through their committees.[15] This same policy could be seen in other clauses: the children of the property-owning classes were not entitled to become Red Guards; their path lay in a return back to the land.[16] On the other hand, the directive made no connection between the Cultural Revolution and the social organization of the country-side. The subject was not even touched on.

Economic considerations were apparently to be taken into account, for peasants were advised to use periods of inactivity in order to 'exchange experiences.'[17] Lastly, in order to keep the communes isolated while the poor peasants were learning to speak for themselves and the administrators stayed in their jobs, student access to the villages was strictly controlled.[18]

All the other measures introduced after this confirmed the Centre's concern with stability and order in the agricultural collectives which had to feed China during the Cultural Revolution, and which, during that year, were working outside the framework of an overall economic plan. According to the Japanese Kyodo News Agency, there was even a Central Committee notice urging the peasants to show restraint in criticizing the Work Teams that had been sent in to lead the 'Four Clean-ups' movement in order to defend the movement's achievements.[19] This defence of the hated Work Teams must have caused discontent among Red Guards. But by then the peasants were preoccupied with the spring ploughing and fertilizing.

From now on there was a strong motive to bring back the peasants who had gone to the cities and were becoming involved in the power seizures. The Kweichow revolution-

[15] Point 5.
[16] Point 6.
[17] Point 7.
[18] Point 7.
[19] Kyodo News Agency, January 31, 1967, reporting posters in Peking.

ary committee and provincial military command ordered all the peasants in the province to go back to their villages.[20] As the contagion of the 'rebellion' had already spread throughout some districts, the Central Committee issued instructions that there should be no seizures of power in the production brigades during the spring agricultural work.[21] The *People's Daily* ran an editorial on the subject on March 13th.

The Centre wanted to use the renewed enthusiasm of the masses for discussions and meetings. The Central Committee sent the peasants an open letter[22] inviting them to hold conferences immediately to discuss the work of spring cultivation. It also recommended that the army should help in this. Three days later the army was ordered to move to 'the help of agriculture.'[23] One may assume that it had a dual role, as in the euphoria of the Cultural Revolution peasants were taking advantage of the relaxation of Party control to share out the agricultural surplus for the Spring Festival (as the New Year by the old calendar has been renamed). There was an appeal from the Ministry of Agriculture to communes not to distribute the seed grain to individuals and to keep the communes' capital (savings and production funds) intact.[24]

The army had to look after the heritage and the reserves of the collective economy, and prevent class struggles from interfering with farm work. On March 16th all mass demonstrations that had no connection with agricultural production were forbidden in the countryside.[25]

[20] Asahi Shimbun Chōsa Kenkyūshitsu, *Mōtakutō no chōsen*, p. 60.

[21] *Ibid.*, p. 60. Central Committee notice of March 7, 1967.

[22] Letter to the villages, February 20, 1967, published in all the papers.

[23] On February 23rd some army units were ordered to move without delay to help the peasants. (*Mōtakutō no chōsen*, p. 60.)

[24] 'Appeal for spring work from the Ministry of Agriculture and the Revolutionary Rebels of the Peking suburbs.' (The Kweichow notice mentioned above recommended that the militia should guard the granaries.)

[25] *Mōtakutō no chōsen*, p. 60.

Ferment

The lack of discipline of the revolutionaries in the cities, who were eager to draw the peasants into their ranks, ended the isolation of the communes nearest the big cities. Thus it was that a coalition of revolutionary organizations conceived the idea of preventing the peasants from celebrating the Chinese New Year. As a struggle against ancient practices and customs this came well within the duties of the Red Guards, but it infringed the principle of the segregation of different sectors. Each branch of the government wanted to play a part: the Rebels in the public security services in guarding the entrances to fairs; those of the rationing departments in confiscating food bought at the peasant market; and those of the purchase cooperatives in 'counter-attacking speculation movements' by 'abolishing the black market and peasant private trading.'

The Spring Festival was a traditional occasion for fairs, where many private pedlars sold food or handicrafts. The 'United committee of Revolutionary Rebels in the financial and commercial departments of the entire country and the Revolutionary Rebel Organization' urged its affiliated organs to try to penetrate deeper: 'Every revolutionary organization without exception must send out a propaganda team and develop a movement that goes deep and has a mass nature.'[26]

Although there was no lack of enthusiastic efforts, as steps had been taken to ensure that everything the peasants were not allowed to put on sale themselves was at least available in state shops, such measures threatened to unleash pointless conflicts.

The most fanatical Rebels did not abandon the idea of seeking reinforcements among the rural proletariat. 'Some mass organizations,' wrote the *Wenhui Pao,* . . . 'have

[26] 'Urgent notice on the strengthening of management of Spring markets in 1967,' reprinted from New China News Agency release, Peking, February 5, 1967, in *Fanghsiu Wenpao,* February 7, 1967.

adopted the anarchistic method of expanding their numbers in the countryside by inciting poor and lower-middle peasants belonging to other organizations to join forces with them.'[27] The people's communes to which peasants battle-hardened in urban power seizures returned, and which were the points of contact between these mass organizations and the countryside, became focal points of agitation.

When, at the beginning of the summer of 1967, both the ultra-leftist movement for the strengthening of the proletarian dictatorship and the reaction of the conservatives to the new wave of power seizures alternately stirred up local conflicts, the peasants were urged by both sides to join in the struggle. In Szechuan the 'Industrial Army' recruited peasants in the countryside to crush the Rebels in the towns. In Wuhan the 'Million Heroes' offered them three yuan[28] a day to demonstrate in town on the side of the conservative organizations. That the Rebels used the same methods was shown in a resolution passed by the Peking Municipal Revolutionary Committee on September 1st, which stated:

> Red Guards, badly led by their leaders, have caused work stoppages in the factories and the countryside by persuading workers and peasants that it was more important to intervene elsewhere than to work and make revolution where they were.[29]

The peasants were a reserve of manpower that all parties coveted. Those who wanted to enlist them were undoubtedly also inspired by the strategic use that Mao Tsetung had made of peasant forces during the revolutionary wars to encircle the towns from the countryside. On July 20th the *Peking Daily* denounced those who were misapplying Chairman Mao's ideas on the encirclement of the

[27] Quoted by Harald Munthe-Kaas, 'Mao's Pinkish Peasants,' *Far Eastern Economic Review*, December 14, 1967, p. 481.

[28] UK 50p.; US $1.20.

[29] Resolution of the Enlarged Session of the Peking Revolutionary Committee, September 1, 1967.

towns. Something was happening at that moment which might well have been very serious. 'To mobilize the peasants to pour into the cities is a crime: a crime against the proletariat, against the people, and from the point of view of the peasants, a crime against themselves,'[30] cried Ch'en Po-ta in a speech on the Wuhan events.

But the peasants who had been drawn into the urban struggles made up only a tiny proportion of the whole. There was no serious crisis, no chain of misfortunes, and the conjunction of circumstances necessary for a peasant revolt did not occur. What the Cultural Revolution did in fact do was to relax control over the cadres after several years of moderate policies. Some peasants were saying that ideological changes were making life progressively easier.

The organizers of the movement to encircle the cities from the countryside probably failed to muster significant forces. But the most serious consequence of their operation was that it set peasants fighting against peasants, for the two sides used the same method. This was made even more serious when both sides tried to use the armed peasants of the militia. The militia had very few arms to distribute. These were kept by the people's armed forces departments of the *hsien,* and they had been instructed that the Cultural Revolution should on no account be used as an excuse for the weapons to be taken from the armouries. Sometimes, however, reactionary organizations looted arsenals, so that the local military chiefs, who had been ordered to help the left and may also have been short of men, decided to arm the militia under their command.

'In general,' said Ch'en Po-ta, 'the mobilization of the peasants towards the cities always started from the military districts and were organized by the people's armed forces departments.'

The army, badly shaken by the Wuhan affair,[31] hesitated during August over what tactics to adopt, and its

[30] Extract from speech by Comrade Ch'en Po-ta on July 21, 1967, in the Peking *Chingkangshan,* June 26, 1967.

[31] See next chapter.

doubts were reflected in the army press. The August 1st (Army Day) issue of the *PLA Daily* had an editorial for the militia that pleaded with the army and Party chiefs 'who were opposed to democratic spirit or political education among the militia.'[32] This article apparently regretted that the militia could not always be relied upon, but it did not condemn their use in the revolution. It was rather a warning against their misuse. The peasant militia was a delicate instrument susceptible to counter-revolutionary propaganda.

On August 18th a similar editorial suddenly sanctioned the use of the militia.[33] It stated that the command of town and *hsien* armed forces should support the left just as the PLA did, adding that the militia was to obey without question. This was perhaps intended to offset the political immaturity mentioned above. It was essential to take Chairman Mao's course and obey, the editorial insisted.

New weapons now came out of the stores. Rival factions did not dare oppose rebels who were now armed. In Canton, Anhwei, and perhaps in many other places too, revolutionary struggles threatened to turn into pitched battles, and the Centre had to cancel its last orders to the army.[34] The army was now divided between those who wanted the militia armed and those who agreed with the Centre that the Cultural Revolution did not justify taking such a risk.

The quarrel that arose on this issue continued until the dismissal of Yang Ch'eng-wu as Acting Chief of Staff. The original order was, however, countermanded in time to prevent further fatal clashes from developing.

At the very time when struggles were at their most violent, the theoreticians of collectivization were quietly laying down the policy that would emerge at the end of the Cultural Revolution. On August 22nd, the same day that

[32] Reprinted in *People's Daily*, August 6, 1967.

[33] Militia editorial of *PLA Daily*, August 18th, reprinted in *People's Daily*, August 20, 1967.

[34] See especially Chiang Ch'ing's speech of September 5, 1967, on the Anhwei problem (quoted in Chapter 9 below).

the British Legation in Peking was burned down, the *People's Daily* published a major article on the organization of the communes,[35] according to which it would have been absurd to wait for mechanization before achieving full collectivization as the peasants could not have used machines when production was organized on a household basis. This was the beginning of a campaign to strengthen the position of socialism in the countryside, a campaign for which the soldiers were to be the first propagandists.

We have seen above how there had been soldiers in the villages since the middle of February. 'We arrived in Hsipu on February 11th at the request of several commune members,' explained one political instructor who had been sent with two of his men to 'support the left' in a production brigade.[36] 'Where I went,' said another soldier in another story carried by the New China News Agency, 'nobody could read, there was only one person in the whole village who had finished school, there was no radio, and the peasants had never heard of the Cultural Revolution.' In places such as this, of which there may have been many, there was no point in starting agitation.

In Lank'ao,[37] a county which had established its revolutionary committee very early, on October 30th, the achievements of the Cultural Revolution for a whole *hsien* of some 400,000 peasants amounted to no more than the criticism of a landlord, an exhibition, some meetings at which old people told stories of the miseries of the past, and the distribution of the works of Mao Tse-tung. Every

[35] 'The Struggle Between the Two Lines on the Question of Agricultural Collectivization,' *People's Daily*, August 22, 1967, New China News Agency, no. 82202, English language series.

[36] 'How the men of the PLA supported the proletarian revolutionaries in a North Chinese village,' New China News Agency, no. 121310, December 13, 1967, French language series.

[37] Lank'ao was the territory of the hero Yu-lu, who alone at that time had been a secretary of the Party committee. It provided the province of Honan with its first *Hsien*-level revolutionary committee. New China, no. 012204, 1968, French language series.

peasant was given the 'three old favourites'[38] and 62,000 sets of the Selected Works were distributed. In short, disturbance in this district was kept to a minimum, while the interest of the peasants in new ideas was directed towards the Thought of Mao Tse-tung.[39]

The Cultural Revolution ended there with the realization of an agronomist's dream: a 'unified command' was established by the *hsien* revolutionary committee to 'guide the transformation of alkaline land into rice paddy and cotton fields.'[40]

Revolution and peace in the countryside

The decision specifying where and how power was to be taken in the countryside was only reached on December 4, 1967. It took the form of a directive that the urban public only saw in a few Red Guard papers. It only concerned the rural zones, and the Centre may well have wanted to keep the announcement little known. It was strikingly similar to the draft directive of the previous year, a fact that by itself shows that the Cultural Revolution in the countryside was straightforward.

The seven-point directive of December 4th[41] did, however, contain two additions: some guarantees and a programme. On the one hand it assured the peasants that there would be no social changes in the countryside:

> There is no need to make general modifications in the system of three classes[42] now current in the people's communes, with production teams as the basic level, or

[38] Three short homilies of Mao's: 'Serve the People,' 'In Memory of Dr Norman Bethune,' and 'The Foolish Old Man Who Moved Mountains.'

[39] New China News Agency, French series, no. 012204, 1968.

[40] New China News Agency, no. 107004, 1968, French series.

[41] Central Committee directive on the Cultural Revolution in the Villages, this Winter and next Spring, December 4, 1967.

[42] Former poor, middle, and rich peasants.

in the system of private plots. There is no need to alter them.[43]

On the other hand, it regulated what kind of power seizures should take place at the various levels of districts and production groups:

> Districts controlled by those who have taken the capitalist road must, through power seizures, come back into the hands of proletarian revolutionaries, the main force of which are the poor and lower-middle peasants.[44]

This limited the inevitable overthrow of committees to the level of *hsien* and upward. Violent seizures of power in production brigades and teams were ruled out, and any changes in the control of production teams condemned.

> It is not necessary to seize power in production teams. In brigades where a power seizure is necessary, the poor and lower-middle peasants must be relied upon in achieving a great triple alliance, and the question must be resolved by choosing a new leading group.[45]

The explanation for this policy was that the overwhelming majority of peasant cadres were good or relatively good. Political activity thus seems to have been encouraged at *hsien* levels and above, while at lower levels all energies were to be devoted to production. Taken together, the guarantees given should have ensured that the winter and the following year would be free of disorder. Although nothing was said about the rebuilding of the Party, this would also have created favourable conditions for an operation needing old cadres who had been won over, and Leadership Groups strengthened with newcomers who had the confidence of the people. Article 5 of the directive specified that once an alliance had been achieved, Leadership Groups should be set up in the *hsien* and com-

[43] Article 4.
[44] Article 6.
[45] Article 5.

munes to direct the Cultural Revolution in production brigades and teams. As many cadres as possible would be
taken back since not many power seizures would in fact
take place. Finally, the poor peasants' associations were
called upon to make their influence felt, particularly in the
districts where political awareness was stirring.

The Centre and the 'provisional institutions' of the
provinces worked together in December to bring about the
creation of revolutionary committees in all the people's
communes. The Peking papers stressed that the revolutionary committees of the *hsien* and other districts (or, in their
absence, the preparatory groups for these committees)
were responsible for achieving this.[46] In the countryside,
more than anywhere else, the higher revolutionary authorities had to encourage their formation from above.

Be that as it may, in order to give the revolutionary committees in the communes some meaning it was necessary
to explain the Cultural Revolution's policy towards the
peasants. On November 23rd the *People's Daily* had laid
down policy in a fundamental article[47] on which commentaries were to be based.

This article may well have reproduced the report that
Ch'en Po-ta gave at the work meeting held by the Central
Committee from October 21 to 27, 1967. The article was
militant in tone, as became an attack on the evil policies
of the past intended to inspire the new men who had to
make the revolution. It condemned revisionism in agrarian
policies in China and the usurpation of the Socialist Education Movement by 'China's Khrushchev.' It urged the
proletariat and the former poor and lower-middle peasants
to 'rely on the powerful strength of the people's dictatorship to consolidate and develop the socialist system of collective ownership, and to take the road of common pros-
perity.' In short, peasant revolutionary committees were to

[46] *Peking Daily*, editorial, December 15, 1968.
[47] 'Struggle between the two lines in China's countryside' by
the editorial departments of the *People's Daily*, *Red Flag*, and
PLA Daily. (English translation in *Peking Review*, no. 49, December 1, 1967, pp. 11–19; also published as a pamphlet by
Foreign Languages Press under the same title.)

emerge on the impetus of criticism of the favours Liu
Shao-ch'i had shown the peasants.

The caustic effect of this doctrine was somewhat offset
by the guarantees contained in the more discreet directive
of December 4th, and these guarantees were to be cor-
roborated. The press was even to suggest that the credit
of the policy of readjustment in 1960 should go to Mao
Tse-tung.[48] This was a pledge that the regime would be
reasonable as regards the three categories of peasants,
the teams, and the private plots, since this was the policy
of Chairman Mao.

Nevertheless, some groups of peasants were fighting on
the side of reaction, which they had not previously been
doing on their own account, it would appear. Were some
of them against the inclusion of the poor peasants in the
management of affairs? Or were the poor peasants making
the mistake of trying to establish themselves by means of
power seizures? Whatever the reason, incidents occurred,
and there was even one in the suburbs of Peking. The
'Red Flag Commune' of the Takou Production Brigade
had the doubtful honour of being mentioned in an official
bulletin when it was ordered to hand over to the army
within three days the murderers of three poor peasants.[49]

The soldiers sent on the 'support agriculture' assignment
were few in number, and although some had been in the
countryside since the Chinese New Year of 1967, most of
them only arrived in the summer. During the year the
confused cadres had been doing little to assert their authority, and their failure to act had affected public order,
the control of production and markets, and the state's attempt to revive economic planning. Planning needed up-to-
date information on the amount of land sown, and statistics on the goods put on sale in collective markets. 'For
the last two years the Ministry of Agriculture has not been

[48] See Anna Louise Strong's *Letter from China*, January
15, 1968.
[49] Notice of the Peking Revolutionary Committee and the
Peking Garrison of January 27, 1968. *Peking Daily*, January
27, 1967 (evening edition).

able to do this;' said Chou En-lai on February 2nd, 'it has been unable to give its co-operation.'[50]

In regions where authority had been in abeyance for some time, the absence of contact was even affecting public morality:

> Feudal superstitions have returned to the villages. There are speculators to be found there; gambling goes on in public; land has been divided up; there are murders, theft and sabotage.[51]

The climate was not right for the establishment of revolutionary committees through assemblies, unless determined men were appointed by the authorities. The Centre thought that such men might be found among those who had positions in the militia. They had to take the place of the army in the triple alliance on revolutionary committees in places where soldiers could not be sent. Thus the militia members were supplied with the simple ideological weapons of slogans like, 'Fight selfishness and criticize revisionism,'[52]—in other words, reproaching the peasants with their loss of a collective spirit and spreading the campaign to repudiate Liu Shao-ch'i in the countryside. The press encouraged them and provided examples, drawing analogies between military problems and those arising in revolutionary struggles.

While the county revolutionary committees were exerting themselves with the militia to show the peasants that Liu Shao-ch'i's methods would only have benefited the rich, as a restoration of private interest would have reduced the poor peasants to serfdom, Peking was continu-

[50] Speech of Chou En-lai on February 2nd to representatives of revolutionary committees of the principle government ministries and departments.

[51] Speech by Li Te-sheng, commander of the troops stationed in Anhwei and chairman of the Anhwei Provincial Revolutionary Committee, quoted from Anhwei Radio by *China News Analysis*, no. 710, pp. 6–7.

[52] Slogan of Mao Tse-tung's put forward by Lin Piao in his National Day speech, October 1, 1967 (*Peking Review*, no. 41, October 6, 1967, p. 10).

ing its theoretical investigation of the problems of collectivization. The revolutionaries in the National Defence Scientific and Technological Commission were entrusted with producing a report to refute the 'theory of productive forces.' The report stated that, judging from past revolutions, 'major developments of productive forces are generally only achieved after changes in the relations of production.'[53]

The strengthening of socialist positions

The argument that a hurried collectivization could not succeed until the communes had been provided with agricultural machinery had to be refuted. All the doctrine of this period stressed that the necessary resources for the construction of socialism could only be achieved after collectivization. The rebels did not try to show that new relations of production were needed, but that the system established in an earlier stage of the revolution, which was being threatened, had to be strengthened. 'Only when the socialist position in the countryside has been firmly established has it been possible for the great proletarian cultural revolution to win victory after victory in the cities,' wrote Yao Wenyuan six months later,[54] acknowledging that the poor and lower-middle peasants were resolute allies of the working class. He reckoned then, in August 1968, that the poor peasants had succeeded in guiding the revolutionary committees and the production brigades. He also confirmed by implication that the Cultural Revolution was content with strengthening the old system of teams, brigades and communes. He also showed that it seemed important at a certain moment to achieve revolutionary committees in the countryside and to stabilize the organization of the villages before any more progress could be achieved in the Cultural Revolution among students and workers.

[53] New China News Agency, French language series, no. 021206, 1968.

[54] 'The working class must exercise leadership in everything,' *Red Flag*, no. 2, 1968; see *Peking Review*, no. 35, August 30, 1968, pp. 3–6.

One might believe that this solution was somewhat easy on peasants who had achieved no revolutionary conquests and wanted to win no trophies. This hypothesis is strengthened by the way that at just this moment official documents suddenly started to speak of the leading role of the working class. But if we realize that the socialist revolution had taken place in the countryside over eight years earlier, and that it was vital not to sacrifice its gains, it is understandable that Yao Wen-yuan should have spoken of nothing more ambitious than consolidation.

The method chosen to make the institutions of the people's communes stronger and more revolutionary was not by overthrowing and replacing the existing authorities, but by reducing their numbers. Some posts were eliminated, and the poor peasants were probably more strongly represented than they had been before. This method was in accordance with the instructions of December 4, 1967, which sought to avoid unnecessary seizures of power. One example held up to the nation was that of Hsi-yang county in Shansi where, after the reform, the leading group of the revolutionary committee was only a third the size of the former Party committee; and the revolutionary committee had less than two-thirds the number of the members of the former *hsien* people's committee. This approach made it possible to achieve a Maoist majority in local revolutionary committees by eliminating conservatives, which was a step towards achieving a Maoist majority for the Party conference.[55]

It must be assumed that the poor and lower-middle peasants thus had an increased right to speak. Their associations were not given a set political role, except that they were given ultimate control over the schools where peasant children were educated. This fitted in with the Cultural Revolution's task of reforming the 'superstructure.' When Mao Tse-tung gave instructions that the working class would in future take over the running of education he

---

[55] A different method was adopted in the army, which was not purged. Party committees in the army were not reduced in size but were swollen with an influx of new cadres.

added, 'In the countryside the schools should be managed by the poor and lower-middle peasants.'[56]

The peasants learned in the classic manner how to organize themselves: they read about the recommended models in the press. Shuiyuan commune in Yingk'ou county, Liaoning, had organized twenty schools, 'basically achieving the target of one school for each brigade.' Each school had 'a committee for the educational revolution, consisting of representatives both of the poor and lower-middle peasants, and of the revolutionary teachers and students.'[57] The press gave many other examples of schools run by poor peasants. The *People's Daily* carried at least one a day between October 18 and November 2, 1968.

Teaching was simplified and the length of the courses reduced. Some courses were based on Chairman Mao's Eight-Point Charter for Agriculture that dated from the time of the Great Leap Forward, and summarized the most useful lessons for the peasants: deep ploughing, soil improvement, heavy fertilization, water conservancy, seed selection, close planting, plant protection, field management, and reform of tools.

Rural schools found a method of practical teaching without ignoring the Thought of Mao Tse-tung and, in order that as many children as possible should have confidence that instruction led to progress, poor and lower-middle peasants became the guardians of knowledge.

[56] Mao's instructions reported by Yao Wen-yuan in the article quoted above. See *Peking Review*, no. 35, August 30, 1968, p. 4.

[57] 'Report of an investigation into the experience gained by Shuiyuan Commune, Yingk'ou district, in carrying out the revolution in education' by *People's Daily* and *Red Flag* reporters. *Red Flag*, no. 3, 1968, and *Peking Review*, no. 39, September 27, 1968, pp. 19–22.

9. The Extreme Left

All the political forces and social groups in the whole country had now joined in the Cultural Revolution. But each of them included certain elements which did not respect 'revolutionary discipline' and encouraged agitation and extremism. In places the revolutionaries themselves turned against the leadership, and tension led to crisis, as when the revolution was too drastically suppressed at Wuhan or Canton. In Peking and Shanghai too the masses could be worked up very rapidly. There were movements devoted to increasing tension, and some groups went to great lengths to get round the restrictions laid down by the Centre in order to keep activity under control.

We know that there was an anarchistic tendency among the students, and that there were forces even inside the Central Committee's Cultural Revolution Group pressing for the revolution to be intensified. The Centre issued warnings against the 'ulterior motives' of these elements.[1] The army also had its own problems of extremism, due to the desire of some soldiers, whose duties had brought them into close contact wtih the revolutionaries, to fight alongside them. Everywhere there were unstable elements who thought they must seize their opportunity, that the revolution was in danger of trampling them underfoot, or that they would have to sacrifice themselves in order to save it.

The movement that had given birth to the first provincial

[1] See Chapter 5, quotation from *Red Flag*, June 20, 1967.

revolutionary committees appeared to have bogged down. Here and there the Centre was bringing in army surveillance. Some Rebels accused the Centre of weakness. They conceded that this was due to the indecision of the masses, but resolved that if the people had not been converted to Maoism through reason, the force of the people's dictatorship must now be clearly demonstrated. The most militant of the Rebels wanted a violent revolution, a witch-hunt against the former 'authorities.' They held up the banner of the struggle against Liu Shao-ch'i, and demanded that it be handed on to the masses.

Tempers began to rise in July. The street mobs were now at flash point, and an incident occurred in Wuhan, where three leaders from the Centre who had been sent to give their approval to the real 'left' were captured and mistreated by some revolutionaries they had refused to recognize. They had come to Wuhan not to condemn these revolutionaries but to restore freedom of action to the Rebels, who had not dared show their faces in public until then: the Wuhan regime had stifled them. Now they began to demonstrate. The army became involved, helping conservative organizations to crush them. Peking's emissaries were saved by the skin of their teeth. Order was restored by uninvolved army units brought in from outside. The local army command was suspended by the Centre and repudiated by the masses.

For the Rebels in the rest of China, who had seen their comrades smashed, the incident was an occasion for a settling of scores and, first, they wanted arms with which to defend themselves. Chiang Ch'ing told them that while they would have to continue thenceforward to attack with words only, they would be allowed to use arms in self-defence. This was printed in the press. Student volunteers enlisted for a crusade to the provinces.

The movement to demand that Liu Shao-ch'i be handed over grew into a month-long siege of Chungnanhai. Many ordinary people were involved without realizing that this was in fact a confrontation with the Centre. Some of the leaders left the Centre in order to take sides with the people in the street. The champions of the extreme left believed that a new revolutionary situation had developed, and formed links between groups that shared the same feverish enthusiasm. They had not a single headquarters, such as the Centre's Cultural Revolution Group, but several: in the editorial department of the journal *Red Flag*, in the Institute of Philosophy of the Chinese Academy of Sciences, and, perhaps, in the army's general staff.

Not content with the ideology that would lead to the reconstruction of the Party, they spoke of overthrowing those in power, a general purge, and absolute obedience. There was a Stalinist current among them. They were preparing for a new series of power seizures that appeared to be aimed at the centre itself. Angry with the government's foreign policy, which they found too moderate towards Great Britain's treatment of the Hong Kong disturbances, they moved to direct action and instigated the burning down of the British Legation in Peking.

The Centre, handicapped by the extremist sympathies of a whole section of the Central Cultural Revolution Group, who were now taking a leading part, used the municipal revolutionary committee to bring the situation back under control. Some of the Centre's leaders went to the meeting of the municipal committee that took decisions essential to the re-establishment of order in the whole of China. Chiang Ch'ing denied the right to armed defence that she had previously advocated herself. Formal instructions were issued that no more weapons were to be distributed and no more seizures of weapons allowed to occur. Once again the restoration of order depended on the discipline of the army.

The Wuhan affair was probably useful to the Cultural Revolution in that, by precipitating a crisis, it hastened the day when those who were deluded in their aims had to admit that they were in an impasse.

Their schemes were supported neither by the Centre nor by the great majority of the people. Their isolated forces consisted on the one hand of students, intellectuals and revolutionary cadres whose extremist demands could never be satisfied, who wanted all or nothing, but rarely had a practical political programme. On the other hand they included military men who saw the army as a force for renewal that needed purging first. Since they were responsible for dividing the army, they were the architects of their own weakness. Finally, there were the supporters of Liu Shao-ch'i, who had a national network, but whose ideas did not attract the mass of the people. The Cultural Revolution was genuinely popular to the extent that it was against them.

Although they were not really united, the leaders of the Cultural Revolution were therefore not faced with any real enemy on a nationwide scale. They gained confidence when the Wuhan affair appeared to have been cleared up without difficulty, and the most dangerous ultra-left organization had been crushed by the public security forces.

Of the three elements mentioned above, the military one remained the most dangerous. These incidents, instead of giving the army a sense of its own supremacy, were a source of humiliation to it. Wholesale self-examination was prescribed, and it would be foolish to believe that the army accepted this without considerable efforts by their leaders. Moreover, the Wuhan events had repercussions in the Northeast, Sinkiang, Chekiang, Honan, and, above all, in Canton, where developments took a potentially more serious, because more confused, turn.

However, one of the advantages of the self-criticism policy was that, albeit for different reasons, it satisfied both elements in the army.

The Rebels in the army saw in the self-criticism the conditions for the purge they wanted to make; while the Central Committee's Military Commission believed that the soldiers would be moved by their self-criticisms to pull out of political struggles and revert to their role as a disciplined army, at present obedient to the Centre and at a future date to the Party. Unlike the first group, the second publicly commended the official Mass Line. The serious contradiction between the two was finally brought into the open, although the Centre decided that the events of the summer did not provide sufficient grounds for a purge of the army.

The new attack by the extremists

In May of last year militant pseudo-left tendencies appeared, sometimes taking an extreme leftist form—left in appearance but right in reality. . . . These people did not keep us informed and did not ask our advice; they wanted to keep us out so that we would be in the dark about the plots they were hatching behind our backs. They have done a great deal of damage. Some of them tried to exploit certain events in order to deny the successes of the Cultural Revolution and the achievements of the revolutionary masses. . . . They were able to deceive some of the people. At that time we took some precautionary measures against them to prevent them causing any more trouble. We separated Wang Li from Kuan Feng. We acted differently with regard to Ch'i Pen-yü. This was why we intensified the measures we took against him; he had always been a problem.[2]

This was what Chiang Ch'ing had to say in March 1968, giving in a deliberately simplified form the story of a faction that had for a time seemed triumphant until the Centre sacrificed it. A simplification it must be, for it is hard to believe that the Centre had early adopted a united policy towards the group. Ch'i Pen-yü, Wang Li and Kuan Feng were all members of the Centre's Cultural Revolution Group. The position of these three men at the head of the editorial board of the theoretical journal *Red Flag* and, in the case of Kuan Feng, of the editorial board of the *PLA Daily,* gave them not only great scope for action but also widespread popularity among the revolutionary masses. This carried them away to the point where they believed that their policies would succeed both with the people and with the leading group. The Centre was careful to avoid the appearance of any splits within itself during the political interregnum, so that the ultra-radicals

[2] Speeches by leaders of the Centre on March 27, 1968, at a rally in the Peking Workers' Stadium, according to the paper *Tungfanghung* of the Geological Institute's Tungfanghung group, special issue of March 29, 1968.

were as much the leaders of the revolution as those who worked with them then and later claimed to have been suspicious of them at the time. The top leaders had shown a certain weakness for them on account of their revolutionary popularity and Chiang Ch'ing, who condemned them in 1968, had herself come under their influence in 1967.

In May and June splits could be observed in the alliances that had made the formation of Peking's revolutionary committee possible, and which were embodied in 'congresses.' In the provinces, similar dissensions among revolutionaries were making a great deal of trouble for the leaders on whom the Centre was counting to bring about the formation of alliances. Sung Jen-ch'iung,[3] the leader responsible for the Northeast of China, somewhat discouraged at the failure of his appeals to the revolutionary organizations, had tried to take a tougher line by cutting off all subsidies to Red Guard bodies, thus making himself the target of virulent abuse from extremist groups.

The Centre had made a tactical decision to concentrate criticism in mass rallies, aimed at such targets as P'eng Chen, Lo Jui-ch'ing, and the old Peking Municipal Party Committee, all 'ghosts and monsters' at whom revolutionaries could rage without causing any new splits in their own ranks. This policy was doubtless the best way of uniting revolutionaries of good will in alliances from which a movement to support and rejuvenate the Party might emerge.

The ultra-radicals, however, aware that these mass rallies were not arousing a fighting spirit, wanted action in small meetings at unit level, to 'deepen the criticism' and 'take the Cultural Revolution forward.' The victims were to be the ordinary cadres that the Centre wanted to win over *en masse* for the revolutionary committees. Chou Ching-fan,[4] one of the ringleaders of rebellion in the uni-

[3] A cadre who had come over in January and kept his position as First Secretary of the Central Committee's Northeast Bureau.

[4] A leading member of the Institute of Philosophy and Social Sciences of the Chinese Academy of Sciences, secretary of the

versities, and a deputy chairman of the Peking revolutionary committee, wrote that there should be many small struggle meetings.

We have already seen in Chapter 5 how some liberal interpretations of the Liu Shao-ch'i criticism had been made from March onwards, and how Lin Chieh demanded the totalitarian application of the proletarian dictatorship in June. The criticism of Liu Shao-ch'i remained an activity in which the most left-wing politicians involved Red Guards and Rebels, hoping that the Centre would itself be obliged to exclude all moderates from it.

On June 3rd demonstrators from the Institute of Architecture established themselves outside the west gate of Chungnanhai, and announced that they were going to keep up their struggle until Liu made a public self-criticism. They put up an awning, under which they displayed the slogan, 'Drag Liu out and burn him!' They claimed to have 'very strong support from over seven hundred revolutionary organizations,' most of which had been affiliated to the old Third Red Guard Headquarters. Working in shifts, they held out for thirty-one days and nights until, at 3.30 a.m. on July 4th, Ch'i Pen-yü came to see them under their shelter. According to what they later wrote,[5] he told them that the Standing Committee and Premier Chou had agreed that Liu Shao-ch'i should be ordered to bow his head and confess his crimes before them.

The Red Guards were exultant at the decisive step Ch'i Pen-yü had taken: 'What Comrade Ch'i's presence has given us is the unmatched interest and support of the Central Committee and its Cultural Revolution Group for the struggle to drag Liu out.'[6] But there was nothing to show

---

Institute of Philosophy's Party committee, member of the Institute's unified Red Guard detachment, secretary-general of the Peking Revolutionary Committee, and head of its political bureau.

[5] See *Hsin Payi*, no. 13, July 15, 1967. A special self-criticism for the Institute of Architecture may have been thought justified by the close interest Liu Shao-ch'i had shown in the Work Team there.

[6] *Ibid.*

unambiguously how the Centre, and Chou En-lai in particular, had given their consent. What mainly reassured the Red Guards was that Ch'i Pen-yü, a member of the Central Committee's Cultural Revolution Group, had joined them and started to direct their action.

Ch'i had been a leading exponent of the struggle against Liu Shao-ch'i from the beginning. An article he wrote on a historical theme in 1963 had been, according to Cultural Revolution tradition, one of the first attacks on those responsible for the renunciation of the arrested Communists in 1936.[7] When the Central Committee allowed criticism of the works of Liu Shao-ch'i, he was the one who opened the firing on April 1, 1967, with the article, 'Patriotism or National Betrayal?'[8] Ch'i Pen-yü was much admired by the young revolutionaries. The Centre was still allied with the *avant garde* of the Cultural Revolution, and it could not easily end its solidarity with him even if he had gone a little too far.

Another self-criticism was successfully demanded from Liu Shao-ch'i as a complement to the inquiry that was being made into his case. On July 9th he wrote a letter to the students of the Institute of Architecture that was published on posters on July 12th. The next step was to have him 'dragged out.' In his letter he explained briefly his position on the matters that, in his view, concerned the students. The Rebels and Red Guards were speechless with rage and the papers of the Peking and Shanghai revolutionary committees fulminated:

> This grandiose intriguer reckons that he can totally deny his crimes. He has not a word to say about his counter-revolutionary activities over several decades. He is silent on his opposition to the dictatorship of the proletariat and his criminal activities to restore capitalism. He merely condescends to say in pointless terms that during

[7] And thus against Liu Shao-ch'i and some of his political friends. This article had been reprinted in the *People's Daily* on July 24, 1964, although Ch'i Pen-yü was not a well-known historian at the time.

[8] See Chapter 5.

a period of some fifty days he made some mistakes of line and orientation.[9]

The leaders of the Centre met around July 17th and continued in session until the first news arrived from Wuhan.[10] Nothing suggested that their tactics *vis-à-vis* Liu Shao-ch'i had altered. There may have been a new alignment of the left and the moderates against the more right-inclined members of the Political Bureau. Lin Piao declared that the 'small handful' constituted a danger because of their 'important political potential.'[11]

There was talk about the 'reactionary line in the Cultural Revolution.'[12] This stressed that the Centre was making a deep analysis of the opinions of people with whom it had been allied until then. This was no doubt the time when decisions were made after the 'February counter-current,' given the inevitable delay in procedures. In addition to obtaining the formal condemnation of T'an Chen-lin, the radical leaders also succeeded in having several of the deputy premiers, including Ch'en Yi, warned.

So, while the leftist militants were beginning to put the Centre to the test, thus presenting it with its most serious challenge to date, the Centre itself was preoccupied with regulating its right wing. But Ch'i Pen-yü's success was superficial. Now that the reactionaries in the leadership had been identified, it would be possible later on to denounce the extreme leftist line in the Cultural Revolution.

The first time the central press used the term 'extreme left' in this context was in August after Sunama, the permanent representative of the Japanese Communist Party, and Konno, the correspondent of *Akahata*, finally left China. They were both very violently treated by Chinese

[9] *Wenhui Pao*, July 17, 1967.

[10] See the following section.

[11] These remarks by Lin Piao quoted by 'Red Pioneer,' a revolutionary mass organization of the air force, must be attributed to this meeting at the Centre. See New China News Agency release for July 22, 1967.

[12] 'Proletarian revolutionaries unite in the struggle against the Chinese Khrushchev and his agents,' New China News Agency, July 19, 1967.

and Japanese Red Guards at Peking Airport. The *People's Daily*, however, wrote on August 6th: 'We have noticed that some people have, for their own ulterior motives, adopted an ultra-leftist position on the presence of Sunama in China, taking our Party to task for not having expelled him.'

The article concluded that extremists had wanted to push the Party into a trap by giving the leaders of the Japanese Communist Party, who were already hostile to the Cultural Revolution, arguments to back their anti-China case.

The Wuhan affair

At the end of the first week in July some of the leaders of the Centre were sent on a mission to the cities of southwest China in which serious quarrels between revolutionary organizations were leading to bloody confrontations. Hsieh Fu-chih, the Minister for Public Security and a deputy premier; Wang Li, a member of the Central Committee's Cultural Revolution Group; and Yü Li-chin, the political commissar of the air force, went with some Red Guards from the Institute of Aviation to Chengtu and Chungking in Szechuan, and then to Kunming in Yunnan, before arriving on the afternoon of July 14th in Wuhan, where the military command was ruling with absolute power. In the triple conurbation, whose inhabitants included about half a million industrial workers, Rebel organizations had almost been silenced and forced to yield to organizations more amenable to the army. Fighting caused such heavy casualties that the Peking wall-papers printed the figures: over thirty dead on June 23rd, over forty the next day. The army had arrested over three thousand people in May and June.[13]

The envoys of the Centre made enquiries about the recruitment, conduct, and real beliefs of the revolutionary

---

[13] See Konno, *op. cit.*, pp. 161–62, for all the figures he collected from notices in Peking on casualties at Wuhan before July.

organizations. They visited the group which had the army's backing in Wuhan, and which bore the striking name of the 'Million Heroes' Army,'[14] and cautioned its leaders over their taste for violence. On the morning of July 19th they went to the headquarters of the Sankang (the 'three steel organizations'), a grouping of workers that claimed persecution from the local military authorities, but which was at the heart of the Rebel movement in Wuhan.[15] The same day they held a meeting for these workers at the local stadium, and the orators from Peking stirred up their revolutionary ardour.

During the afternoon they stopped at the regional military command, and explained to the army that it had failed to recognize where the left wing lay in Wuhan. This reveals the extent to which the Centre had let things ride until then. Wang Li handed over a directive from Chou En-lai ordering them to support the Sankang forces and ordered that it should be published in the town. Those of the revolutionaries who felt thwarted by this were soon accusing Wang Li of having written the directive himself.

In the small hours of the morning of July 20th the 'Million Heroes' and some of the regular troops occupied the civil and military airfields, stations, docks, main roads and key buildings.[16] The soldiers involved belonged to an independent division, Unit 8201, which had been entrusted with running the Cultural Revolution in the Wuhan Military Region by the local military command. A battalion of this unit surrounded the guest house where the envoys

[14] The name *Paiwan Hsiung Shih* is taken from a Mao Tsetung poem and refers to the PLA forces that crossed the Yangtse in the spring of 1949 (translator's note).

[15] These forces comprised the Sankang, the Sanlien ('Three allies') and Sanhsin (The 'Three New,' including the students of the New University of Hupei).

[16] The Wuhan affair was described in detail in several Red Guard publications, especially the Aviation Institute's *Hungch'i*, published by an organization several of whose members were there with Wang Li (*Hungch'i*, no. 55, July 29, 1967); and in *Wuhan Kang Erhszu*, no. 38 (published in Huichou on August 22, 1967), a paper brought out by workers in one of the Wuhan steel companies.

of the Centre were sleeping. Ch'en Tsai-tao, the officer commanding in Wuhan, refused to intervene, on the pretext that he had been instructed to avoid confrontations. He even withdrew the sentries from the army staff offices, and allowed some of his troops to hunt down Rebels in the streets of the city.

The 'Million Heroes' forced their way into the hotel. Hsieh Fu-chih was locked in a room. Wang Li was taken away by men of Unit 8201, beaten up, and some of the Red Guards with him were wounded.

Peking did not conceal its wrath. The naval forces stationed at Wuhan (a nodal point for inland waterways) came out against Ch'en Tsai-tao that afternoon. Another army unit demanded that Wang Li be handed over to it, and Unit 8201 had to yield. But the local army command, which wanted to make him withdraw the directive, would not permit his release. The Sankang forces then took the offensive in the city. Armed with any weapons they could lay their hands on, they invaded one district of the city and arrested the provisional revolutionary committee. The growing risk of civil war persuaded other units to apply pressure for the release of the Peking envoys. On July 22nd the air force took their side. When the 'Million Heroes,' having discovered Wang Li's hiding-place, prepared to attack the camp where he was being kept, the commander arranged his escape through the woods. Hsieh Fu-chih and Wang Li were able to return to Peking late that afternoon, where they received a triumphal welcome.

A film was shot of their return. It was called *Peking Supports You* and was dedicated to the isolated revolutionaries in the provinces. The scene of their arrival in Peking showed Chiang Ch'ing taking Hsieh Fu-chih and Wang Li by the arm, the latter with a black eye and staggering across the tarmac. But this passage had an air of gaiety to it: it made one feel that the leading group, whose few members were nearly all present, were happy to have their lost brethren back again. For a moment nothing else mattered, and their joy came over clearly.

The film's chief aim was to show that the Centre was united; but it was also intended to bolster the determination of Rebels suffering in the provinces by showing them the strength of the revolution in the big cities. It showed enormous demonstrations against Ch'en Tsai-tao in Peking, and an important mass meeting by the armed forces in Shanghai in which the troops were told about the crisis and the risks that had been involved. The units decided to help the revolutionaries in Wuhan, and climbed into their lorries as if going into battle, to the delirious enthusiasm of the audience at the army taking sides in this way.

For the sake of propaganda, Hsieh Fu-chih and Wang Li were treated as conquering heroes, but in the eyes of the nation their adventure faded away somewhat by comparison with the ordeal of the Wuhan Rebels, formerly oppressed and now fighting back. The army tried to make up for the reactionary part it had played in Wuhan by recognizing the courage of the Rebels.

The affair was built up to epic proportions. But Wang Li's mistake was to think that he, rather than the Sankang, was the hero of it. The Shanghai troops were ready to set out to their rescue as soon as the word was given. On July 25th the command of the Eastern Fleet proclaimed:

> Our great leader Chairman Mao has given us rifles, artillery, boats and aircraft. We must be ready to crush the class enemies *at home* and abroad. . . . We are resolutely determined to support the proletarian revolutionaries of the Wuhan region.[17]

However, from July 21st booths had been set up in Peking for volunteers to enlist, offering their lives if necessary to defend Mao Tse-tung and the Cultural Revolution Group. This movement showed that youth was prepared to accept the possibility of civil war.

For in Wuhan the fighting continued. The 'Million Heroes' did not accept their condemnation, and they drew reinforcements of peasants into the city. The army, which the day before had been using its tanks and lorries to defeat the Sankang, was now patrolling the streets to drive

[17] *Wenhui Pao,* July 26, 1967. Author's italics.

back the 'Million Heroes' or, if necessary, to crush them. This switch of alliances was bitterly resented by some of the military, and a quarrel went on among the army's top men between those who believed that the mistakes should be paid for and those who tried to excuse them.

Ch'en Tsai-tao and his political commissar Wang Jen-chung, one of T'ao Chu's barons, were replaced. Was this enough? The Rebels in the army were not satisfied with dismissals. 'Those responsible must be completely overthrown politically and ideologically, as well as organizationally,' they wrote in the *People's Daily* on July 22, 1967. In other words, they wanted a purge.

The article quoted in the previous paragraph was written by the *avant garde* of the air force staff, probably Yü Li-chin, one of the Centre's envoys in Wuhan. The *People's Daily* hesitated to print it, frightened perhaps of taking the initiative for a purge that the Centre had not yet approved. 'This article has raised an important question,' wrote the editorial board.

But the Centre was taking its time to decide its policy. Meanwhile, the movement for a purge in the army was growing in strength. However, when the oracle finally spoke, it ruled against purges. Apart from the dismissal of a number of leaders, the Centre chose self-criticism—a very different matter—for all who had been implicated in the affair. The only punishment for the troops was that they now had to do their utmost to help the very people they had been fighting.

'We must have the courage and the breadth of spirit needed to emancipate the deceived masses.'[18] The self-criticisms were actually carried out, and the new political commissar at Wuhan made one on behalf of the troops.[19]

---

[18] Point 4 from the 'urgent notice of the proletarian revolutionary command of the Wuhan region,' July 31st, printed in the *People's Daily,* August 2, 1967. This urgent notice followed a five-point letter to the command from the Central Committee, State Council, Military Commission, and Central Committee Cultural Revolution Group.

[19] Liu Feng, 'Remain faithful to our great commander-in-chief, Chairman Mao,' in New China News Agency's Chinese-language bulletin *Chinjih Hsinwen,* July 31, 1967, p. 14 ff.

But the fighting still had to be stopped. The Wuhan Proletarian Revolutionary Headquarters urged Rebels to bury
the hatchet.[20] Only the leaders of reactionary organizations were to be dealt with strictly.

But Wang Li maintained his position that drastic
changes would still have to be made in Wuhan.[21] Part of
the army staff was with him: they wanted such changes
throughout the army. The *People's Daily* had to protest,
and it did not mince its words.

> If comrades in the army have made mistakes, they are
> still sound, provided that they have corrected them.
> These mistakes should not be treated as if they were of
> irremediable political gravity. One should not prevent
> others from making revolution too.[22]

Why was it necessary for the paper to spell this out? It
became known later that Yang Ch'eng-wu, the acting chief
of the general staff, was himself committed to the extremist tendency.

'Beating the dog in the water'

August was a month to remember for the Cultural Revolution. In 1966 it had brought Mao Tse-tung's *tatzupao*,
the Eleventh Plenum of the Central Committee, Lin
Piao's elevation to the position of successor, and the introduction of the Red Guard to the country.

In 1967 the enlistment of volunteers in Peking went
hand in hand with the growing demand for a public trial
of Liu Shao-ch'i. In June and July the Red Guards of the
Institute of Architecture had installed themselves in the
road to the west of Chungnanhai, and in August over five
hundred other organizations were copying their example.

[20] Urgent appeal from the Rebel headquarters, broadcast on
the morning of August 1st.
[21] Remarks by Wang Li and Yao Teng-shan on August 7th,
according to a leaflet published in October 1967 by the Tientsin
Hungch'i Ping t'uan organization.
[22] *People's Daily*, August 4, 1967.

This road, which a year earlier had been the site of joyful processions celebrating the return of Mao Tse-tung, was now full of open-air political forums. It was as lively as a fairground.

On August 1st, Army Day, the papers reprinted Lin Piao's article on people's war. This may have been an indirect invitation for the people to take to the streets for a final assault on the 'authorities.' The next day Peking was in ferment. Revolutionary organizations erected hundreds of stalls in the road to the west of Chungnanhai and the southern gate. Lorries brought workers and peasants in from the suburbs shouting, 'Down with Liu Shao-ch'i.' The road was resplendent with colours: red flags with the names of different organizations sewn on them, open-air posters, and countless caricatures. At every stall leaflets, sometimes printed on the spot, were being distributed. The richer groups had loudspeakers blaring out proclamations. There were hunger strikes, brilliant orators, singers. Organizations had pickets out at the gates of Chungnanhai, making it difficult to go in and out. Rumours flew around: T'ao Chu and Ulanfu had escaped. They were with Ho Lung, who was leading a counter-revolution with some insurgent soldiers. This mood of panic pressed the revolutionaries to demand death penalties.

August 5th was the anniversary of Mao's *tatzupao*, 'Bombard the Headquarters,' and the revolutionary organizations demanded that Liu be handed over to him before midnight on the fourth. They wanted to organize a great confrontation with him, for which they believed that they had the consent of the revolutionary committee of Peking. This put the Centre in a dilemma. The persistent pressure of the extreme left was widening the gap between its leaders and the Centre, which would have preferred to form closer links with them in order to unite the left. If the Centre had allowed itself to be provoked by the agitation into using its power to repress the extreme left, it would have lost the confidence of many of the revolutionaries. The Centre therefore adopted the tactic of banning all mass trials, thus avoiding the problem of how to ensure Liu's personal safety.

Three hundred thousand people had already assembled in the huge T'ienanmen Square. The revolutionary committee persuaded them to disperse by making the false promise that Liu would be handed over at midnight, and notice was given that the criticism meeting would take place the next afternoon at 4 p.m. Liu Shao-ch'i would not be leaving Chungnanhai, but he would be criticized by his colleagues. The crowd outside were to follow the meeting as it was relayed over the public address system in the square. Liu himself, wherever he was, could hear the reactions of the crowd over loudspeakers.

At the set hour Chou En-lai, Ch'en Po-ta, and Chiang Ch'ing had taken their place on the T'ienanmen rostrum, overlooking the multitude. The crowd adopted a resolution that they would carry the struggle against Liu, Teng and T'ao Chu through to the end. Then the debate inside Chungnanhai was relayed, under conditions that a small group at the Centre had arranged by themselves. But from then on the leaders who belonged to this little group, and who had until then marched in a line at the head of the rebellion, now appeared separated from the tribunes of the extreme left. There was now a split between the Party's real chiefs, the promoters of the revolution, and the majority of the militants in the Central Committee's Cultural Revolution Group. The latter doubtless felt that they were being discriminated against by the old Party hands, who in the last resort seemed to be showing more solidarity with Liu Shao-ch'i than with the revolution.

The slogan: 'beat the dog in the water,' went up louder than ever from the Rebels. The government, and the surviving group of Party leaders, arranged that their differences with the extreme left should not be too apparent. But press, radio, the New China News Agency and even the national papers often gave the impression that they had sold out to the militants. Official information media were no longer like those normally found in Communist countries. They avoided holding a monopoly, and made themselves available to a proletarian dictatorship which wanted total power for rebel organizations. To deduce the government's policy from the press at that period was to risk reaching the mistaken conclusion that power lay further to the left and in more revolutionary hands than was in fact the case.

On the other hand, the Red Guards were unable to mark a triumphal celebration of their official birthday, August 18th. They made a lot of noise, but nobody in power called the rally on which they had been counting. Nobody spoke up in favour of it in the Centre, surrounded as it was by all the din. On the contrary, a number of rather severe articles, inspired by the Centre, began to appear in papers that had hitherto been overflowing with enthusiasm. One of their themes was that, compared with Red Guards, who were full of fire but short on experience, revolutionary cadres who had both were 'national treasures.' For the time being the Centre needed to loosen the Red Guard hold on Peking. It let it be known that the students should learn to criticize themselves and reform themselves according to the Thought of Mao Tse-tung.[23]

In the provinces the army was going through a crisis of confidence in the leaders at the Centre after its setback, and was in danger of going over to the Rebels; and in the capital, control was impeded by extremist pressure. News from Canton, Hangchow and Urumchi was full of accounts of growing anarchy and army repression. In Canton especially the troops were taking sides to such an extent that the command was suppressing the Rebels in the army.

Canton was a battlefield for two factions: that of the 'Red Flag,' of which the 'Revolutionary Workers' Alliance' and the Third Red Guard Headquarters were the kernel, and that of the 'Red Defence Brigades,' which included paramilitary organizations (as in Shanghai) such as the well known and still operational 'Joint Action Committee.' One of the unusual aspects of the situation was that all the organizations of the poor and middle peasants of the suburbs had joined the second faction. They made their choice not on ideological ground, but in order to throw their weight by force against any development in the revolution that was not in their interests. Both factions had obtained

[23] *People's Daily*, August 18, 1967.

arms and entrenched themselves in strategic positions. Peasants dug trenches and laid ambushes in which even the army lost men. But the latter held its hand, perhaps because the peasants had joined the wrong side: the 'elect' of the masses had gone astray. Instead of preventing conflict between the factions, the army allowed it under certain conditions: state inquests on street violence, no reinforcements to be sent in, and neutrality of the peasants, according to the seven-point agreement reached by revolutionary organizations on July 26th, and signed in the presence of the army. But in August the military commander, Huang Yung-sheng, suppressed the Revolutionary Rebels in the army, whom he described as 'delayed action bombs.' See the Canton leaflet *Kungan Chanpao*, August 11, 1967.

In Chekiang a mob of real gangsters seized control of the railways during July. In Sinkiang a movement in the Production Corps repressed workers affiliated to the Second Headquarters in the way the 'Million Heroes' had tried to do in Wuhan.

In the absence of any encouraging sign of progress, the political leaders of the revolution needed rare patience to persist in their plan to rebuild the Party.

In this time of great crisis all they asked of the people was to keep cool and rational. Rather than parrot the slogan, 'everything is contained in the Thought of Mao Tsetung,' which the militants had improperly used to demand absolute obedience, they stressed the need for reflection.[24]

Hsieh Fu-chih, the minister in charge of the police, made no mention of the forces under his control in his frank announcements of these reverses, or the suppression of Maoists in the provinces, or the sporadic uprisings of peasants who had been incited to surround some towns. The lessons he drew from these events were expressed in purely moral terms.[25] Ch'en Po-ta said that Peking was

[24] 'Excel not only in fighting but also in thinking. Keep a cool head in all circumstances, and carry out ideological and political work among the masses with all diligence.' *People's Daily*, August 8, 1967.
[25] Speeches by leaders of the Centre, August 10, 1968.

becoming so intolerably noisy that it was impossible to work there, and he would have to go to the countryside.[26] Everyone needed some time to reflect and consider. After all, why should the left-wing groups not settle down and resolve their differences with less trouble than had accompanied the incorporation of the revolutionary organization?

This call for reflection brought on a kind of renewal for the revolutionary masses. 'Comrades who have gone wrong must rid themselves of their burdens,' wrote a Shanghai paper,[27] incidentally using a Buddhist expression. It would now be possible to make a fresh start in the Cultural Revolution with all men of good will who had now come over, with Red Guards prepared to abandon the pursuit of their own glory, and with these 'national treasures,' the true revolutionary cadres.

Polycentrism

A number of the leaders of the extreme left did not politically survive August. But for the Centre to have been able to discredit and eliminate them, they must have made mistakes.

The best known of these were journalists who, as members of the Centre's Cultural Revolution Group, themselves had the responsibility for censuring others. They abused this charge when they succumbed to the temptation to urge the masses to launch fresh attacks. Without the approval of the Centre's leaders they wrote contentious articles that stirred up civil strife. But they could not be condemned except by a meeting of the leadership that was not, in the circumstances, feasible.

These men were mistaken over the role of the revolutionary committees. They thought that they should be local revolutionary governments. As they saw it, the committees and preparatory groups for committees could rapidly

[26] *Ibid.*
[27] Editorial in the *Tachung Jihpao*, reprinted in the *People's Daily*, August 10, 1967.

have achieved the aims of the Cultural Revolution if they
had been given their heads. They would have represented
new and pitiless regimes, ceaselessly attacking their opponents and chastising the half-hearted. Beyond that, they
had in mind ideological links with all revolutionary movements through civil war and even, perhaps, uninterrupted
revolution.

They did not see that the revolutionary committees were
not so much governments as schools of government. Cadres, soldiers, and ordinary people were there to learn to
know themselves rather than to share in local government.
The main component in the committees were cadres, and
it was they who benefited from having soldiers and ordinary people with them. From these crucibles good new
Party cadres were to be cast. It was an article of faith
that there could only be one guiding and apostolic party.
In trying to prolong the autonomy which the 'provisional
organs of the proletariat' had had to be given, the leftists
were guilty of the heresy of propagating polycentrism.

It was not, of course, until much later that the Party's
defenders identified polycentrism explicitly.[28] The term
itself was not much used, and it did not refer to a fully
worked-out political programme. It was only used in criticizing the phenomenon after the event.

Ch'i Pen-yü, Wang Li, Lin Chieh, Kuan Feng, and Mu
Hsin were acting as if they constituted an independent
Centre. They exercised arbitrary control over news. They
established close links with an organization known as the
'516' (May 16), which the leaders of the Centre did not
like. Without referring to the Centre they decided that
the Rebels in government departments should take the
initiative, which was tantamount to new and opportunist
seizures of power. 'For some time . . . small groups have
been in existence . . . which no longer operate through
the Centre or seek the authorization of the Prime Minister,'
said K'ang Sheng in September.[29]

[28] Polycentrism was condemned in the slogans put forward
by the Centre's Cultural Revolution Group for October 1, 1968.
[29] See the excerpts from K'ang Sheng's speech at the September 1, 1967, conference of the Peking Revolutionary Com-

In acting thus, they were trying to enforce a system by which revolutionaries did as they wished in the sectors where they had power. This was virtual polycentrism, tending to increase pressure on the Centre just when it was being threatened with splits.

The career of the '516' organization may have begun on August 3, 1967, the day on which the 'Metropolitan 516 Red Guard Corps'[30] was inaugurated, but all its detractors included in its record the criticisms that had been levelled at Chou En-lai since January. This *a posteriori* version of the story was intended to give the impression that the authors of the insidious attacks that had harassed the Prime Minister for short spells during the Cultural Revolution had now all been unmasked, and that his loyalty to the revolution was unimpeachable.

'Ambitious' revolutionaries were determined to overthrow Chou as he had too much of a tendency to support men who wanted order, at the cost of satisfying the immediate demands of the revolutionaries. When they did not dare to attack Chou En-lai himself, they took on men in power in the provinces and members of Chou's own team in Peking, especially the Foreign Minister Ch'en Yi, who had never shown much respect for the Red Guards, and had once asked them, 'Who are you rebelling against? Against me! How is it that you haven't gone to Vietnam to rebel against the Americans?'[31]

He was a perfect target. His accusers presented him as an actor playing his role, indifferent to the conflict between the proletarian and the capitalist ways, and unwill-

---

mittee, together with those of other leaders from the Centre in *Hungch'i Ping'uan,* October 1967, p. 5 (published by the Hungch'i Printing Works, Tientsin).

[30] This was an amalgamation of groups recruited mainly among intellectuals, especially at the Further Education College, whose leading lights were the 'Group of Seven' in the Institute of Philosophy and Social Sciences of the Chinese Academy of Sciences. One of these was the Chou Ching-fang, mentioned above as the author of an article in favour of small struggle meetings and the revival of the Cultural Revolution in the units.

[31] Quoted in *Hungwei Chanpao,* April 8, 1967.

ing to be converted to the Cultural Revolution. Ch'en Yi had even been criticized in important public meetings,[32] but Chou En-lai had always defended him, even at the risk of his own popularity.

At the head of the '516' organization was a group of power-hungry and probably unscrupulous intellectuals.[33] They believed that a critical examination of the Foreign Minister would expose his weakness, and that if the extreme left brought him down this would be a shock for Chou En-lai, who was now being indirectly charged with toleration of the army in Wuhan and delay over the formation of new revolutionary committees.

A combination of circumstances, some of them deliberately provoked, brought the struggle against Ch'en Yi to a particularly virulent level at the beginning of August. There was the new wave of revolutionary attempts to seize power in the British-ruled territory of Hong Kong; the influence in the Foreign Ministry of diplomats who had been withdrawn from Indonesia after the anti-Chinese riots in Indonesia; and the sudden rise of the '516' organization that was leading the Rebels in the Foreign Ministry. The Rebels claimed that they had new evidence against him, and were successful in demanding that Ch'en Yi be obliged to explain himself to them. There were tumultuous meetings at which his critics used every demagogic trick against him. It was impossible to prevent the suspending of the Foreign Minister for a fortnight.

Enquiries made later by other revolutionaries led to the charge that Wang Li had coveted the post of Foreign Minister for himself during this period of anarchy. During an important conversation which the 'hero' of Wuhan held with the Rebels in the ministry on August 7th, he had

[32] E.g., in front of 10,000 people on January 24th. See Konno, *op. cit.*, p. 176.

[33] Before the inauguration of the '516' organization, those who were to become its leaders conceived the notion of establishing, in conjunction with the Further Education College, a body to investigate the organizations of the Central Committee in March 1967 (according to a pamphlet published in September 1967 by the 'Steel Industry Revolutionary Rebels' Commune').

encouraged them to seize power boldly.[34] The details of what happened between then and Wan Li's fall are not known, but a climax was reached with the burning of the British Legation on August 22nd after a Chinese ultimatum had expired without reply. The Chinese news media said nothing of these reprisals except that 'angry demonstrators undertook vigorous action against the office of the British Chargé d'Affaires.'[35] Nor was there any reminder that there had been an ultimatum demanding complete freedom of action for the Hong Kong revolutionaries. The Centre acted as if there had been no diplomatic activity during the enforced absence of Ch'en Yi.

The only way the Centre expressed its disapproval of what had happened at the British mission was to publish a six-point list of prohibitions governing demonstrations against foreign diplomatic missions.[36] But there was a more vigorous reaction against organizations of the extreme left. Mu Hsin, the chief editor of the *Kwangming Jihpao*, and Lin Chieh, editor of the *Red Flag*, were arrested in the last days of August. Chao Yi-ya, chief editor of the *PLA Daily*, was also arrested, which sheds a confused light on the influence of the Central Group's extremists upon the army. After it was legally proscribed, the '516' organization was searched, and as a result Wang Li, Kuan Feng and Chou Ching-fang were put under surveillance.

The case of Ch'i Pen-yü was a more difficult one to establish, as he had tried either to involve Chiang Ch'ing with him or else used her to save himself. Despite advice not to associate too closely with Wang Li and Kuan Feng, Mao Tse-tung's wife was rather too much in sympathy with them. In November, when the storm was over, she decided to take a rest.

[34] 'Important Speeches of Central leaders at the September 1, 1967, Meeting of the Peking Revolutionary Committee,' Tientsin, September 10, 1967, p. 10. On the strength of August 7th, Wang Li was given the nickname Wang Pa-chi, which also carries an insulting reference.

[35] New China News Agency, English language series, no. 082225, 1967.

[36] See *Asahi Jyanaru*, vol. 9, no. 52, December 17, 1967, pp. 21–22, Minoru Takeuchi, 'Shūonrai no yakuwari.'

The methods Mao Tse-tung had recommended to show a change of policy—a notice, a directive, an editorial in the papers—have been mentioned above. This was the period when the workers and peasants were being drawn into the revolution too hastily, as a result of Red Guard provocation. During the ascendancy of the extreme left Mao Tse-tung himself was absent on a journey to central and east China. A warning was given by Chou En-lai and K'ang Sheng in their speeches of August 30th. Directives were issued by the Peking and Shanghai revolutionary committees. The Centre—the Central Committee, State Council, Cultural Revolution Group, and Military Commission —only issued a purely technical order forbidding the seizure of arms.[37]

It would have been difficult to call a meeting of the Political Bureau in Mao Tse-tung's absence for the lengthy discussions that would be needed to resolve a number of delicate questions. The main directive came from the Peking Revolutionary Committee on September 1st. It dealt with many other problems[38] and many other organizations besides the '516,' which it banned. It amounted to a reprimand for the extreme left in stronger terms than for the masses who had gone astray. Could it have been that the directive was intended to avert civil war at the calculated risk of coups against the minority groups. At all events, while many organizations could be saved, the '516' was not one of them.

There was also the publication of an article by Yao Wen-yuan attacking 'two books by T'ao Chu,' and in this indirect indictment it was implied that behind the '516,' there were other top leaders who had not yet been exposed.[39] The Central Committee's Cultural Revolution Group had been set up at the time when T'ao Chu was in charge

[37] Mentioned by Chiang Ch'ing in her talks at the third reception for delegates from Anhwei on September 5, 1967.

[38] E.g., the maintenance of salaries (see Chapter 6) and the ban on all arming of revolutionaries (see Chapter 8).

[39] *People's Daily*, September 8, 1967. See also 'Comments on T'ao Chu's Two Books,' *Peking Review* no. 38, September 15, 1967, pp. 7–17.

of propaganda, and he had put some of his own men into the Group who now had to be eliminated. People in the know now understood that those who had come to power with T'ao Chu were to be weeded out.

All the staffs of the main papers and the journal *Red Flag* were abruptly purged of the intransigents who had too often printed their incendiary pieces alongside the ones demanded by the moderate Centre. *Red Flag* ceased publication for a time, and all editorial initiatives were restrained in the *People's Daily*.

However, at a time when the crisis appeared to have deeply undermined the Cultural Revolution, the Centre was declaring with more assurance than ever that the revolution had won.

The crisis in the army

Until the Wuhan affair, the measures taken to limit the army's involvement in the Cultural Revolution had, on the whole, worked. With the exception of a few specified units, the soldiers were under orders not to interfere. An ordinary incident will illustrate the caution they were asked to observe. One day that August a foreigner's car broke down in a remote part of Peking. The driver, who spoke Chinese well, asked two soldiers who were passing to help her push it. They insisted that they did not understand. Then some local people came over to help her start it again, and briefly explained the situation: 'It's quite simple. They're under orders to stand aside. You only need to ask the people.'

Since the Wuhan incident impatient voices had been demanding changes. 'The big new development is that the army has participated in the Cultural Revolution in the civilian sphere,' declared a *New China* editorial of August 2nd.[40] In the style of the Central Group's extrem-

---

[40] In a note accompanying quotations from the military works of Mao Tse-tung, published by the press on August 1st (Army Day).

ists, the advocates of action in the army turned a deaf
ear to the Centre's attempts at calming the situation by
amnestying the troops and dismissing only a few senior
officers.

On August 16th the Centre published excerpts of the
resolution condemning P'eng Te-huai in 1959.[41] While
this clearly had contemporary significance, there were several possible interpretations, and everyone tried to draw
the most advantage from it.

The *PLA Daily* preached a crusade against all the old
friends of P'eng Te-huai and Lo Jui-ch'ing,[42] but we have
already seen what side it was on—its editor-in-chief was
eventually arrested. Following the familiar routine, by
which one article replied to another, and an authoritative
source refuted a pamphleteer, the theoretical journal *Red
Flag* spoke in its turn. One of its leader-writers wrote that
all the army cadres who had come under the influence
of rightists and militarists had now rectified themselves.
The wise reader would have taken this as meaning that
the *PLA Daily* had been wrong to call for a purge in the
army.

But when two such well respected publications disagreed
over a subject like this, the situation was serious. We saw
above how the general staff vacillated over whether
armed militiamen should take part in revolutionary action,
and then came out in support of the local commanders
who had mobilized them.[43] This happened on August
18th, the same week. The general staff definitely seemed
to be strongly in favour of an active Cultural Revolution,
both with and in the army. Its acting head was actually
meeting with Rebel elements in the high command. The
Chinese learned from their papers on August 24th that
'under the leadership of the general staff Party committee

[41] *Red Flag*, no. 13, August 17, 1967. See *Peking Review*,
no. 34, August 18, 1967.

[42] *PLA Daily*, August 16, 1967, editorial on the 1959 resolution. See New China News Agency (English language series),
no. 081613, 1967.

[43] See above, Chapter 8.

formed around Yang Ch'eng-wu,' proletarian rebels in the
offices of the general staff were acting in the spirit of 'beating the dog in the water.'[44]

Very different was the mood of the Centre, for whom
the reference to P'eng Te-huai probably meant that soldiers who put the army before the Party would have to be
relieved of their duties. The first victim was Hsiao Hua,
who had advocated a straightforward, strong army, though
perhaps rather a high-handed one. He was the first to dis-
appear of the medium ranking officers who seemed des-
tined to succeed the original marshals. Yang Ch'eng-wu
followed him six months later, but he may have been destroyed by ambition, while Hsiao Hua was the victim of his
belief that soldiers were a race apart and the army should
stand alone.

From this point onwards Lin Piao gave the impression
that he was no longer trying to protect his subordinates.
In this case, when his aim was to return to the mass line,
he used the stratagem of 'destroying a position on the right
when under pressure from the left.' By dismissing Hsiao
Hua he decapitated the Cultural Revolution Group in the
army, which was then completely reorganized, and Lin
Piao's wife, Yeh Ch'ün, was given a place on it.[45] In order
to reassert control of the air force, its commander-in-chief
took his place beside them. The air force had been a
source of worry ever since its political commissar, Yü
Li-chin, had been involved at Wuhan in the same incident
as Wang Li. He shared the latter's views, and had demanded a purge of 'the small handful in the army.'

It remained to declare categorically that this misleading
slogan should be repudiated for, as we have seen, the criticism of P'eng Te-huai had not succeeded in doing this.
Chou En-lai and Chiang Ch'ing declared in September that

[44] 'Establish with the greatest energy the absolute authority
of Chairman Mao and Mao Tse-tung's Thought,' published in
the *People's Daily* and *Kwangming Daily* on August 24, 1967.
[45] Posters in Peking, September 9th. The army's new cultural revolution group consisted of Wu Fa-hsien, the air force
chief of staff; Ch'iu Hui-tso, director of the general logistic
department; Chang Hsiu-ch'uan, the director of the political
department of the naval headquarters; and Yeh Ch'ün.

the propaganda demanding that the 'small handful in the army be thrown out' was 'a mistake.'[46]

But how could the plans of the general staff, who wanted to make the army 'beat the dog in the water,' be thwarted? One effort was the attempt to make self-criticisms into a ritual bringing officers and men closer together. Classes in the study of the Thought of Mao Tse-tung were held at all levels in the army. Papers that reflected the wishes of the Centre explained that the classes should be organized 'with the participation of the servicemen'[47]— i.e., the rank and file. After these meetings, which ended with criticism and self-criticism, it became hard for the partisans of purge to arrest men who had publicly admitted the error of their ways.

Under Lo Jui-ch'ing the army had discontinued the system by which it was possible for men to talk to their officers in the Party committees. These committees were proletarianized. Company cells and regimental committees received the soldiers in their study meetings.[48] It must be remembered that the Party committees in the army had not been criticized. Their members who took places on revolutionary committees fell into the error of confusing leadership (i.e., with the people) with command (for the people). The return of soldiers to the Party organizations

[46] Chiang Ch'ing was given the job of being the first to criticize this slogan and the demand for an army purge. This was because she had been the first to demand the right for the revolutionaries to use arms in self-defence in her speech of July 20th (reported, but without attribution, by *Wenhui Pao* on July 23rd). The dangers of this slogan had been demonstrated by the events of August in the provinces. Now she withdrew this right, bringing back the old rule that persuasion must be the weapon in defence as in attack. She did this in her September 5th speech to representatives from Anhwei, in which she also condemned the theory that there was a 'small handful' in the army. This speech was thought important enough for tapes of it to be sent to revolutionaries all over the country. Chou En-lai also told Red Guards of the Peking 'Red Congress' that after July 20th mistakes had been made in the propaganda over the 'small handful in the army.'

[47] *PLA Daily* editorial, December 12, 1967; New China News Agency (French language series), no. 121209, 1967.

[48] *People's Daily*, December 12, 1967.

revived the simple ideal of the Party's social and political
role in the country that was incompatible with any rivalry
for power.

Although this policy was based on a desire for unity,
it was not applied flexibly. It was carried out very strictly
towards military cadres, and the projects of the extremists,
whose power extended as far as the general staff, did not
leave much room for freedom of action. If some dismissals
were to be a substitute for a purge, they had to be real
ones. The Centre approved the dismissal of military commanders in Peking, Wuhan, Lanchow, Chengtu and
Huhehot. A conference of delegates from seventeen military regions was held in Peking in the second half of September. At the cost of a certain amount of criticism and
self-criticism, the conference strengthened the unity of
the People's Liberation Army and confirmed its support
for Mao Tse-tung.

The revolutionary committees in the balance

After the first revolutionary committees had emerged in a
somewhat brief burst of enthusiasm at the beginning of the
year, only one more had come into being—for Chinghai—
by August.[49] Two others appeared belatedly, one in Inner
Mongolia and the other in Tientsin,[50] but these were not
very significant achievements. The movement to which the
Centre attached such importance was stagnant, and therefore a matter of concern for the leaders and contention
for the extremists.

According to some on the extreme left, the 'institution'
was already corrupt. Discarding even the arguments which

[49] On August 12, 1967. Chinghai is a sparsely populated,
mountainous province on the borders of Tibet and Sinkiang,
crossed by key lines of communication. The founding of its
revolutionary committee was regarded not as a revolutionary
event but the renaming of an organization intended to ensure
the control of a strategic province.

[50] Inner Mongolia, November 1, 1967; Tientsin, December
6, 1967.

had led others to polycentrism, certain of these maintained that the revolutionary committees had already fallen into the hands of 'bourgeois usurpers.'[51] Chiang Ch'ing referred to this school of thought in her famous speech of September 5th to the Anhwei delegates.[52] Malcontents, she said, were even demanding the reorganization of all the revolutionary committees that had been approved by the Centre.

One of the reasons why so little progress was being made in setting up committees was probably because the masses, at one time passionately involved in politics, were now to some extent standing aloof. The man in the street was becoming disillusioned with the embittered quarrels between revolutionary groups (nearly always the same ones), the decay of the 'Peking congresses,' and the violent excesses in almost all parts of the country during the summer. Revolutionary organizations were not attracting new members, and although they were much spoken of, they were not sufficiently representative of the masses to give the revolutionary committees any balanced support.

Hsieh Fu-chih drew up a table of revolutionary workers' organizations of Peking in a speech on October 16th. He told members of the 'Workers' Congress' that they should have won the support of a tenth of the capital's 1,100,000 workers. The delegates replied that they represented 17,-000 of them. He pointed out that in the railways and the metal and textile industries two rival preparatory groups were trying to set up different congresses. Above all, he condemned 'underground or semi-clandestine organizations' that cut across the boundaries of occupations or companies . . . 'You cannot possibly give secret support to such things. What about organizations like the one in

---

[51] According to a document published by the Hunan ultra-leftist organization *Shengwulien,* even a reformed Party emerging from a conference would inevitably have been 'a bourgeois reformist party in the service of the bourgeois usurpers of the revolutionary committees.' Quoted by John Gittings, 'Student Power in China,' *Far Eastern Economic Review,* June 27, 1968, p. 649.

[52] See previous section.

Sinkiang whose boss calls himself "Hu the Battler" (Hu Luan-ch'uang)? Can organizations with such people in them be Marxists?'[53]

However, the instructions that Mao Tse-tung had given after his journey to Central and Eastern China were now beginning to be distributed. They were strict, and stated more or less that 'We have a very simple rule—whoever attacks his neighbour will have to face the consequences.'[54] They were also optimistic, and the Chairman's words, as always, had a magical power to calm tempers and inspire confidence. A few brawls should not be taken seriously. Even if there were fights going on, there were also things happening backstage, and 'the people backstage have something to say. The disorder is only temporary, and it can be turned into something good. Individuals have to be allowed the right of free speech: the heavens will not fall in if people are allowed to speak. Sometimes it is no bad thing to let things rip.'

These instructions hinted at the role the people would have to play, after the crisis of polycentrism, in putting the final touches to the revolution. 'All aspects of the movement must be transformed gradually. . . . with special attention to the transformation from quantity to quality.' Once the predominance of a single centre—the one of Mao and his associates—over political polycentrism was assured, the masses must be allowed the initiative in reform, criticism and management.

At the time a new movement to give the workers the foremost role among the people was being encouraged, a movement that culminated in the recognition of the leading role of the working class in August 1968. This helped to confirm that, once decision-making was restored to the Party, leadership (i.e., criticism and management) would

[53] Hsieh Fu-chih's speech of October 16, 1967, published in *Peiching Kungjen*, October 20, 1967.
[54] Point 1 of 'Mao Tse-tung's Latest Instructions' as published in the Red Guard paper *Harbin Thunder*, November 15, 1967. It was also here that the Chairman expressed his view that there were no serious conflicts of interest within the working class (Point 6). See Chapter 6 above.

be returned to the masses. What was new about this was that the masses were now to be led by the workers. This was the position that the Kweichow revolutionary committee had defended. Although Kweichow was a backward province, it was perhaps not surprising that it should have led the way in this. At all events, in the October 16th speech quoted above, Hsieh Fu-chih urged his audience to 'follow the example of Kweiyang and the Thirty-seven Instructions of Tientsin.'

A campaign was mounted to overcome the inhibitions of the masses and persuade them to stop withholding their support from the forces that were going to impose their hitherto contested authority. The Centre made it known, in a resolution of October 17th, that all organizations which overstepped companies and occupations would be suppressed; it wanted to bring the revolutionary organizations back to the framework of the 'units'—factories, offices, and people's communes.[55]

The whole story of the Cultural Revolution in Kweichow was one of a team of new cadres who had been transferred to the province after the 1965 purge, and of the leadership of the working class.

Soldiers seconded on Cultural Revolution duties were to bring together workers and peasants, and to get them to hold meetings and study sessions to combat sectarian tendencies. Although this was a new task for them, it was easier than what had been demanded of them when the order was to 'support the left.' Now the army was no longer required to choose between the factions: it simply had to get everybody together in every civilian place of work, and prevent dangerous contacts being made. This was how 'alliances' were to be formed. The soldiers sounded the call to arms, and the veteran cadres responded.

Everything could have worked out well if the army had not still been shaken by disturbances. It had been obliged

[55] This resolution, quoted in Chapter 8 above, also covered cadre policy and the Cultural Revolution in the countryside. See Takeuchi Minoru, 'Shūonrai no Yakuwari,' *Asahi Jyanaru*, vol. 9, no. 52, December 17, 1967.

to learn from its mistakes, and called Yang Ch'eng-wu to account for encouraging the spirit of revenge, agreeing to arm the militia, and taking the leadership of the Rebels in the general staff who wanted an army purge.[56] Yang Ch'eng-wu went through the motions of accepting this criticism, but wrote a somewhat aggressive article for the *PLA Daily*[57] in favour of the personality cult. This appeared in the same issue as the despatch of August 24th reporting his flamboyant action.[58] He was getting too big for his boots. Curiously enough, another article, unsigned, appeared in the same issue of the *PLA Daily* as an indirect reply to him. This said that absolute obedience was precisely the same exceptionable principle that 'China's Khrushchev' had been blamed for advocating, and that the slogan of 'unity' was not reason enough to have the spirit of criticism suppressed. How is one to account for the two articles appearing in the same paper, when one of them was by the chief of staff himself?

The general staff was not to regard itself either as oracle or arbiter. It was the army itself which had not yet sufficiently understood.

The *People's Daily* established this point conclusively in a leader on November 9th. It was necessary 'really to increase the army's political consciousness' and 'to eradicate the influence of all kinds of non-proletarian ideology in the army, whether from the Right or from the Left.'[59]

The main concern of the authorities was to bring about the emergence of revolutionary committees. Although there was as yet little visible progress, there was already a power structure in the preparatory groups and military

[56] 'Thoroughly establish the absolute authority of our great Supreme Commander Chairman Mao, and of his Thought'—see *Peking Review*, no. 46, November 10, 1967, pp. 17–24.

[57] See previous section.

[58] On 'The Spell of the Golden Circle'—an allusion to the 'monkey pilgrim'—see New China News Agency release for November 4, 1967.

[59] 'Make a good job of education on the current situation.' The text itself makes it clear that it is education within the army that is being referred to. See *Peking Review*, no. 47, November 17, 1967, pp. 7–8.

control committees, a structure almost entirely within the sphere of influence of the army, which had provided many of its leaders and controlled its communications. The army's behaviour in the revolutionary committees was being watched, and this was being done by the army itself, according to the Chinese method. The masses within the army, non-commissioned officers and men, who had been made to mix with their officers in study courses, could keep a check on the officers' loyalty to the revolution. At a conference of the Peking garrison troops, the deputy local commander insisted that units should 'conscientiously study the conditions in which the troops carry out Party directives.'[60]

It seems likely that the Party committees in the army were strengthened by the appointment of a representative of the ordinary soldiers. This was an early hint of the way the Party congress was to develop. First of all preparations were made to ensure that all the grass-roots organizations sent delegates with Maoist ideas to the congress. As we have seen above, the formula adopted for rural collectives was to purge the committees at *hsien* level. In the army, however, there was no purge; instead, committees were enlarged by co-opting proletarian revolutionaries with the elected members.[61] This was only a temporary arrangement, but it helped to ensure the loyalty of the troops when some of their leaders were being tempted to play politics.

The fifth round

The Centre had undertaken to unite with the revolutionaries by means of the 'alliance,' and to bring the army back to its role of 'serving the people.' It was now preparing to face a colossal task: restoring Party control over

[60] Peking newspapers, January 17, 1968.

[61] It was noteworthy that when Mao Tse-tung and Lin Piao received the participants in study classes for land and air forces of the Peking region on November 13, 1967, the Air Force Committee of the Party was present in full, enlarged by representatives of the revolutionary masses.

the revolutionary united front and the army. This problem had to be solved if the gains of the Cultural Revolution were to be conserved.

However, there were some circumstances that made this less difficult. To begin with, there was no dispute at all over the doctrine itself, for it was the Thought of Mao Tse-tung. Nor were there any economic interests that had banded together to bring political pressure. Finally—and the war on China's borders made this important—agreement had already been reached that the needs of defence in depth, Vietnamese style, took priority over the needs of economic development.

The tactics that the revolutionary leaders had been using since September were getting results. Each of the two forces that might have lured the Cultural Revolution under its own control, the extreme left and the army, had been cut in half. The extreme left had been decapitated. The mutilated Central Cultural Revolution Group clung more closely to the Centre than ever, so that the rank and file of the extreme left found no more protection from them. As for the army, it had not suffered drastic surgery, but the Centre had regrouped all the forces that were favourable to it in the units which it could influence. The study classes on the Thought of Mao Tse-tung for officers and men together were to be organized throughout the army. This movement culminated in big conferences in at least seven of the military regions before May 1, 1968.[62]

This activity, which we may call lateral, was complemented by a vertical approach in the different branches of the PLA, and all through the winter gatherings of activists in the study of the Thought of Mao Tse-tung were held, for the air force, the navy, the artillery, the engineers, and all command organs.[63] Finally the revolu-

---

[62] Chinghai, October–November 1967; Shantung, late 1967; Heilungkiang, December 1967 and January 1968; Kwangtung, March 1968; all the eastern provinces, April 1968 (a big rally in Nanking).

[63] Logistic services, some of the artillery, navy, and air force were in the first series; the rest of the artillery, railway

tionaries in the general staff, who had made themselves a
little too prominent with Yang Ch'eng-wu on August 23rd,
had to undergo a particularly intensive series of conferences.[64]

Up till then the army, as an active and uncriticized
body undertaking missions on behalf of the Cultural Revolution, had been supported by the Centre in almost everything it did. From its very formation it had been devoted
to the Party, but now the Party was discredited, and those
who were supposed to replace it, the Red Guards and
Rebels, were unable to mend their own quarrels. It was
too much to expect that, in the provinces far from Peking
where by force of circumstances the army was given a
great deal of authority, it should put itself at the service
of revolutionary groups unable to agree among themselves.
The disgruntled revolutionaries accused it of looking after
its own interests alone, and the leaders at the Centre recognized that this charge was not without foundation.

This was the time when the second group of revolutionary committees were formed. For almost a year most
of the country had been waiting for revolutionary committees that would be better united than the first ones.
Steps had to be taken to ensure that the new ones that
were about to emerge should not be permanently one-
sided under the influence of the army.

Yang Ch'eng-wu was dismissed between March 24 and
27, 1968. All sorts of accusations were made against the
acting chief of the general staff after his overthrow. He
was accused in particular of having been active behind
the scenes when Wang Li and Kuan Feng, the leaders
of the extreme left, were manoeuvring, and of having col-

---

corps, engineers, signals, chemical warfare, the PLA Political
Commissars Institute and the Higher National Defence Institute were in a second series that ended on March 7, 1968.

[64] In February 1968 the proletarian revolutionaries of the
staff departments attended their third conference since August
of the previous year. This was a 'Party-building' conference
and it lasted for over a month.

laborated with Ch'i Pen-yü.[65] He was, in brief, accused of being involved in a conspiracy with them. These accusations were given added weight by the blunder Yang had made in late August which, like their other actions, threatened to compromise the Centre. But at the time of his fall there were two criticisms that outweighed all the others: first, that he had tried to build up for himself a personal authority greater than Mao Tse-tung's, and, second, that he supported 'fragmentation.' Both charges were of course interrelated.

It is not unlikely that there may have been a clique in the army who had originally wanted a purge, and had resorted to conspiracy when the peaceful tactic of study classes was adopted instead. An article in the *People's Daily* on March 21st made clear that there were two conflicting views on the army's role in the revolution: one wanted criticism pure and simple, and the other wanted to combine criticism with attention to the army's other duties. Only the latter view was acceptable. From this it may be assumed that some of the soldiers maintained that the local commanders should be not subordinate to the revolutionary committees, but should give them orders and even criticize them.

The Centre's leaders lost no time in telling the masses why Yang Ch'eng-wu and other military leaders had been dismissed. As Ch'en Po-ta put it, this was the fifth trial of strength for the Cultural Revolution.[66] It was sparked off by a local problem over the Peking committee.

[65] 'The fifth stage of our Cultural Revolution was the unmasking of the counter-revolutionaries Yang Ch'eng-wu, Yü Li-chin, and Fu Ch'ung-pi, who were the protectors behind the scenes of Wang Li, Kuan Feng, and Ch'i Pen-yü,' said Ch'en Po-ta on March 27th. Chiang Ch'ing said, 'In November 1967 I criticized Ch'i Pen-yü without mentioning him by name. . . . He was collaborating with Yang Ch'eng-wu.' See *Tungfanghung* of the Geological Institute, March 29, 1968.

[66] Ch'en Po-ta mentioned five attacks; the first against P'eng Chen, Lo Jui-ch'ing, and Lu Ting-yi; the second against Liu Shao-ch'i, Teng Hsiao-p'ing, and T'ao Chu; the third against T'an Chen-lin; the fourth against Kuan Feng, Wang Li, and Ch'i Pen-yü; and the fifth against Yang Ch'eng-wu, Yü Li-chin, and Fu Ch'ung-pi. See *Tungfanghung*, March 28, 1968.

The Peking revolutionary committee was already an anachronism. The organizations represented on it dated from before the period of the 'grand alliance,' and some of them had not agreed to the formation of alliances with their rivals, even within the Units from which they had come. They also participated in the criticisms of the army being made by Rebels in the provinces. Those who had previously wanted a purge in the army naturally sympathized with the radical organizations.

Fu Ch'ung-pi, commander of the Peking garrison, deputy chairman of the municipal revolutionary committee, and a member of the Centre's Cultural Revolution Group, took sides with those of the Rebels who were unresponsive to the Centre's doctrine, and was accused of working secretly against it. There were a number of incidents,[67] and the upshot was that the leading group penalized Fu Ch'ung-pi together with Yang Ch'eng-wu and the air force commissar, Yü Li-chin, who had been with Wang Li in Wuhan.

As one purge followed another, it became harder than ever to keep together a group of people at the top to represent the Centre. The three last men to fall had, until the beginning of March, been present with Mao Tse-tung and his staff on the ceremonial occasions that served to show the country who were its real rulers. They were soon replaced by the former marshals of the Military Commission.[68] These latter were doubtless entitled to this position on the strength of their rank, but this switch was still

[67] Fu Ch'ung-pi had intercepted a letter to the Centre from Red Guard organizations in the universities, whose conflicts were threatening the existence of the Peking revolutionary committee, and had invaded the Central Committee's Cultural Revolution Group with lorries that were probably intended to take their records.

[68] They were present at the closing session of a conference of activists in the study of the Thought of Mao Tse-tung in the leading organs of the army on March 7th, the seventh of the sort since January 28th. The Central leadership now appeared to consist of Mao Tse-tung, Lin Piao, Chou En-lai, Ch'en Po-ta, K'ang Sheng, Chiang Ch'ing, Yao Wen-yuan, Li Fu-ch'un, and the five former marshals Yeh Chien-ying, Hsü Hsiang-ch'ien, Nieh Jung-chen, Liu Po-ch'eng, and Ch'en Yi.

significant politically. Instead of the Young Turks, veteran soldiers, the pillars of Party rule for over twenty years, were making a come-back. It was naturally thought that they were there to protect the very provincial regimes that the committed Rebels had accused of making military men into the new 'authorities.' Back in 1967 the Cultural Revolution would have been able to block the possibility of rigid and conservative local regimes.

However it seemed there was a need to rearrange the relationships between the revolutionary committees and the army. The army would always be competent to take control in times of crisis, but in normal times the soldiers seconded on Cultural Revolution duties would have to take the orders of the revolutionary committees of appropriate levels.[69]

The supporters of Yang Ch'eng-wu did not give in without causing some trouble. There were cases, notably in Anhwei and Nanking, when soldiers calling themselves 'models in the support of the left' wanted to impose their wishes in one way or the other on the rest of the army.[70] The Centre was worried, and for good reason, about the possible effects of the humiliation of the army on some revolutionaries who had not been well disposed toward it.[71] The best solution seemed to be to rid it of whatever had caused criticism. Thus the purge, which had previously been condemned in principle, now came about. A certain Ninth Company was given as an example, and it was made clear that it carried out 'small scale, limited operations for the regulation of attitudes.'[72]

Naturally, this purge was not aimed at the targets that Yang Ch'eng-wu would have chosen. The political power asserted its control over the army. The political leaders

[69] See the article on military support for revolutionary committees in Kweichow in the *People's Daily*, April 4, 1968.

[70] See *China News Analysis*, no. 710, May 31, 1968, pp. 6–7; this may also have happened in Kunming and Nanning.

[71] The *Peking Daily* published a threatening editorial attacking all who were trying to divide the army, or turn the revolutionaries against it, in a special issue on the evening of April 22, 1968.

[72] See New China News Agency release for May 12, 1968.

had been explaining for some time that soldiers sent to help the left would have to be rotated to prevent their new governmental powers from going to their heads. Had not some of them insisted on establishing a new order rather than awakening the masses?[73] What was really being done was to remove the final traces of ideas that had raised the spectre of polycentrism.

With the Centre restoring its authority over the army, and the army doing its utmost to earn its privileges, useful progress was being made towards re-establishing order in ideologically classic style. The last extremists turned their wrath on the army, which they now saw as an instrument of discipline. But they were no longer able to find allies for a new rebellion. There was a report that a group of students dressed in mourning were present at the inauguration of the Kiangsi revolutionary committee.

[73] On February 14th the Central press explained that study classes in the army should help to rotate the troops helping the left, because some of them with duties in the provisional institutions were forgetting to serve and educate the people, preferring to issue orders.

10. The Victory of Moderation

Mao Tse-tung was now running the Cultural Revolution with a much smaller staff. The group that gave guidance to revolutionaries throughout the country consisted only of a few of his companions. They made use of the press, radio, and the sensitive antennae of the Central Committee's Cultural Revolution Group. Brief talks by some of the leaders, reproduced in the few Red Guard journals that still survived, became the sources of inspiration. A few words or an observation by Mao Tse-tung were published as the 'latest instructions' for the revolution. By referring to a few principles he could, through reversing an urgent order or deflecting the pressure from the revolutionary masses, change a situation. The Central press then took up the theme, developing it at length and illustrating it with models culled from across the country, and from history, in order to show how it could be applied in practice. In the situation these models became very important.

The Centre had, by means of the revolutionary media and the press, called forth political action against divergent tendencies, and built up defences for the Cultural Revolution. Through these means the Centre was setting the building of socialism in China under way once more.

However, in keeping control over so big a country, this tiny staff was not alone in facing the revolutionaries. The Centre had been obliged to commit powerful machinery in order to direct the course of the revolution, and prevent its abuse by the violent idealists, the die-hards of the extreme lefts, and the soldiers who believed in the army's special mission. Even after the Party had been disrupted, the Centre had kept in being the government and army structures, although the problems of the Cultural Revolution within both of them threatened to develop into serious crises. Once these problems were overcome, the end of the movement was in sight.

The whole of the army, which was now back under control and accepting the discipline of the Military Commission, had been mobilized in order first to absorb and then to sublimate its own revolutionary liberation. The State Council, which had recovered its power after the power seizures, wanted a pyramid of revolutionary committees on which to rely to co-ordinate administrative tasks in the provinces. A comparable power structure had been missing for far too long, and in the spring of 1968 its re-establishment took first priority.

From January to August 1968 revolutionary committees mushroomed. As 'provisional institutions' their job was not to replace the Party but to establish themselves as the organs through which the government's authority was transmitted. Established under the army's wing, they contained a core of converted veteran cadres. This was too much for those who still regarded themselves as the true revolutionaries, arguing over the character of the veteran cadres and criticizing the government. 'Rebellion' still smouldered among the Red Guards, with whom the policy of alliance had failed. What was to be done with the groups of irreconcilables?

They could not be eliminated. Mao Tse-tung was against dissolving organizations in order to facilitate the 'grand alliances.' After all, the extreme left had its uses as a watch dog on the conservative forces' acceptance of the revolution. Mao Tse-tung believed in the value of opposition in general, and expected the revolutionary committees to cope with it. But conflicts among students almost destroyed the balance within the Peking revolutionary committee. Red Guard brawls were a scandal that everyone was talking about even though they no longer took place in the streets. They were an abscess on the Cultural Revolution that would have to be dealt with.

The solution was found in the doctrine that all enemy forces could be split. The 'good' rebels had to be identified within opportunist groups and insubordinate organizations, and turned against the others. This was an application of the Maoist principle that 'one divides into two.' Much of the year was needed to divide the Peking Red Guards into two. But the entry of philosophy into the debate did not prevent a number of bruises and wounds.

The creation of the provincial revolutionary committees emphasized the fact that a new stage had been reached. The slogan of the day was 'Struggle—Criticism—Reform.' Why the struggle and criticism when their parts had apparently been played? Apart from the students, the conflicts were apparently over. A bourgeois revolution would have proceeded to reforms, and the new committees would have become a political force. But the Cultural Revolution was working for the Party, and the pressing task was to refine and purify it. The behaviour of each of its members in the revolution had to be examined to see whether they deserved to stay in the Party.

During this singular period the revolutionary committees existed alongside Party committees that were resuming their political role, and the study classes in the Thought of Mao Tse-tung that were to form the basis of the new Party. It was clear that a complicated process was under way that would lead to a general meeting of the Party. But it may be asked which was the more important for those who had wanted the Cultural Revolution: reform of the establishment or the trial of the 'Resistance.'

Now, if a revolution in political attitudes was to be possible, it would have to reach down to basic levels. Who was to be a Party member, and how was he to become one? Although revolutionary organizations were a source of fresh blood, their members would have to undergo examination. Nobody was to be spared from 'struggle and criticism.' What had hitherto been a battle-cry now became a selection process.

A similar type of intrigue was applied to classifications of the people. The conclusion was reached that the workers were 'the main force of the revolution.' Till now the Centre had not said anything of this kind. Instead it had praised the students, who had launched the first assaults of the revolution with unparalleled courage. Then it had called the revolutionary cadres the country's most precious treasure. Had the workers deserved so much of the Cultural Revolution despite being tempted by their sectional interests? What in fact stood out clearest in the memory was the lesson of the Shanghai strike. At the end of a proletarian revolution, leadership should be returned to the labouring classes, among which the industrial workers had shown the most political awareness.

In August 1968 the workers were invited to enter the universities in order to reform the academic and teaching system. They achieved the apparently miraculous result of bringing the hitherto interminable struggles among students to an end. Their entry into the universities brought back a sense of respect. On the theoretical level the appeal to the workers solved one of the students' principal contradictions: how could one combine being a student, enjoying privileges, especially the privilege of learning, with being a non-privileged revolutionary constantly in the service of the people? Some students had believed before that they should give up their studies and join the masses. By bringing in workers alongside the teachers a new solution was being offered.

There were also practical considerations. China was short of cadres and technicians, and there was bound to be delay in training more. The existing ones had to realize that they should not hide away in their ivory towers, but should go among those less educated than themselves and spread their knowledge as widely as possible. Once revolutionary committees were established in all the provinces, educating the masses and committing oneself completely to the service of the collective became a matter of the first priority once again. Mao Tse-tung had been writing on the subject since September 1968.

Thus China headed towards the reform of its Commu-

nist Party, but it was borne in mind that the essential was
not structural reform. 'In the revolutionizing of state organs, the essential road is that of contact with the masses.
The revolutionizing of structures will adapt itself to contacts with the masses. There is no need to put the emphasis
on bureaucratic structures.'[1]

The only thing that really mattered was the small flame
of interest in public affairs that the Cultural Revolution
had kindled somewhere in the popular consciousness, and
which the people did not yet know how to maintain. What
was important was that they should be willing to think in
terms of China as a whole, and understand what had to
be done in common, and ultimately that they should have
enough faith in their mission to be able to criticize their
rulers. If the masses had not been sufficiently aroused this
time, a new Cultural Revolution would have to be undertaken. In the last resort organizations as such did not matter, nor did the extremism of some ideas. Criticism should
not be snuffed out: it was the tiny flame that had to be
kept alive, and had somehow to be transmitted to the vast
and complex meeting of the Party that was to come.

The political solution

In February 1968 the leaders themselves were explaining
that the Cultural Revolution would be different now from
what it had been the previous year. Those revolutionaries
who were still living on reputations acquired by criticizing
Liu Shao-ch'i and Teng Hsiao-p'ing had now to appreciate
that they had another job to do in depth. It was intolerable
to regard positions won in the revolution as personal conquests. The most thankless task now awaited them: rebuilding the Party and the state with elements that were
not of their own choice. The great majority of the cadres
had to be put back in harness on new principles, and it
was necessary to come to terms with them. As Chou En-
lai said:

The conflict between policies at present amounts to a

[1] Mao Tse-tung directive, issued November 1967.

conflict between public and private interest . . . a conflict between the spirit of Party and the spirit of faction-
alism. . . . This is why it would be wrong to apply the
criteria of 1966 and the beginning of 1967 to the present
situation. . . . Has not Chairman Mao told some veterans that one should not live on one's reputation, and
that one has to win new merits? In these circumstances
there can be even less question of any of you proletarian revolutionaries, whoever you may be, living on
your achievements in only eighteen months of revolution.

This tone was very different from that of 1967. Chou En-
lai added that it was time for the revolutionaries to make
room beside them for those of the cadres who were not
afraid of revealing their faults:

> We should be able to encourage a number of cadres to
> come forward and expose themselves to the criticism
> of the masses. . . . These are the conditions for the
> triple alliance.[2]

These instructions applied to the provinces as well as to
the backward sectors of Peking and Shanghai. But in fact
the movement was slow to take shape in the provincial
towns and the districts. The national press, for example, had to wait till January 27th before it could an-
nounce, in Anhwei, the formation of a revolutionary committee at unit level, the first to be created in that eastern
province.[3] But when the policy that had been ordered
began to be better understood, the regional leaders worked
hard to apply it. The revolutionaries had to be made rather
more tolerant of converted cadres. The preparatory group
for the Nanchang revolutionary committee won a mention in despatches for a decision that established the line
to follow: where there were still unresolved cadre problems, more of the cadres who had made mistakes had to

[2] Speech by Chou En-lai to representatives of committees in
government ministries on February 2, 1968.
[3] See New China News Agency release, *Chinjih Hsinwen,*
January 27, 1968.

be won over for the revolution. Proud cadres would have to be convinced through patient persuasion: they would come round when they knew more about successful examples of the fusion of cadres and revolutionaries.[4]

Revolutionary committees were finally established at the provincial level, something the Centre had long been hoping to achieve. They appeared at the rate of three a month from January to the end of May 1968.[5] Canton's province, Kwangtung, received its committee on February 21st; and Kiangsu, of which Nanking was the capital, on March 23rd. Although the Centre's wish that all the provinces and big cities should have their revolutionary committees by May Day was not realized, when Szechuan's was formed on May 31st only five remained to be formed, and these were in frontier regions where the army was in a state of alert.[6]

However, Chou En-lai stressed several points. First, the Cultural Revolution was not yet complete. There was no lack of revolutionaries to volunteer for criticizing Liu Shao-ch'i and Teng Hsiao-p'ing over their lines on the people's communes and foreign policy. But the current task, simplifying the bureaucracy, was far less popular. Revolutionaries should get closer to the cadres and find out more about the work they did.

What was in fact happening? 'Directors and heads of departments have not yet really been liberated,'[7] in other words, they had not yet made their confessions and been set back to work with a new set of ideas. They were simply sent back to their jobs so that the government could

[4] Resolution of an enlarged meeting of the preparatory group for the Nanchang revolutionary committee, February 20, 1968, published by the Central press.

[5] Kiangsi, January 5th; Kansu, January 24th; Honan, January 27th; Hopei, February 3rd; Hupei, February 5th; Kwangtung, February 21st; Kirin, March 6th; Kiangsu, March 23rd; Chekiang, March 24th; Hunan, April 8th; Ninghsia, April 10th; Anhwei, April 18th; Shensi, May 2nd; Liaoning, May 10th; Szechuan, May 31st.

[6] Yunnan, Fukien, Kwangsi, Sinkiang, and Tibet.

[7] Speech of Chou En-lai, February 2, 1968.

continue to function. The sovereign influence of the masses
had not yet touched them.

On the other hand, the Cultural Revolution gave positions of political responsibility to people of every stamp.

Light must be shed in order to reveal bad elements, should they exist among us—'black hands,' and groups exercising evil influences. This does not mean that most of the masses have been misled, but some of them are following leaders who must themselves be brought to political awareness. A distinction must be made between good and bad revolutionaries. We must drive them out ourselves. The besetting ill of our time is to hide our faults and to fail to make rigorous demands of ourselves.[8]

It was thus permissible to attack the leaders of revolutionary organizations who denied that it was their duty to form alliances, excluded cadres and other revolutionaries, and refused to accept the sincere alliances that were necessary if the proletarians were to be formed into a single Party. As K'ang Sheng explained, they were guilty of subjective idealism: they were so obsessed with their own motives that they forgot about the results to be achieved.[9] From now on the method to be used in consulting them was to split their forces from the inside: 'Alliance and unity go through struggle to division, and a new alliance is formed on the basis of the Thought of Mao Tse-tung. This is the dialectic of the Cultural Revolution.'[10]

Chiang Ch'ing gave some practical advice on carrying this out: exclude undesirable elements, put intellectuals into positions of responsibility, and bring together those who had proved themselves in the Cultural Revolution. Generations should be mixed.[11]

[8] *Ibid.*

[9] Speeches by Chang Ch'un-ch'iao and other leaders to delegates of Anhwei revolutionaries who had come to Peking to learn from the experiences of Shanghai.

[10] Red Guard organ *Hungch'i,* February 10, 1967, 'Long live the Peking People's Commune.'

[11] At the end of his speech of March 27, 1968, Chou En-lai discussed Chiang Ch'ing's instructions of November 1967.

This method got results. It was learnt that, in the army, several factions eventually dissolved themselves, including one that had once been connected with the proletarian revolutionaries in the general staff.[12] Yang Ch'eng-wu's supporters were thus weakened before his fall. Student Red Guard organizations appeared to be tougher. There was one success at the People's University, but in some other places the former followers of Lin Chieh and Wang Li held firm together against all attempts to convert them.

At Peita, the Cultural Revolution's model university, Nieh Yüan-tzu was under pressure from the Peking revolutionary committee to bring about an alliance. Had she lost heart after the frequent failure of persuasion? Apparently she refused to stop her own group from using their fists. There was fighting on the campus, and on March 29th Nieh herself suffered a knife wound. As a victim she could become a heroine once more. The Central leadership gave her their support, but it was necessary to send six hundred troops into Peking University. Even this did not prevent fighting between students from breaking out again at the end of April. The *Hsinpeita* and *Chingkangshan* groups each fortified a building in which they entrenched themselves, attacking each other from the rooftops, firing stones and tiles with huge catapults.[13] Their sentries, armed with red tasselled spears, tried in vain to invoke the peasant rebels of the revolutionary wars and to symbolize their loyalty to Mao Tse-tung, but most people mocked this distortion of the Cultural Revolution. Student organizations were soon to lose their political privileges.

The end of the Red Guards had an official date.

[12] According to the journal of the *Tungfanghung* Commune of the Peking Institute of Machinery, December 8, 1967, quoting the *Chingkangshan* organization of the Institute of Higher Defence Studies.

[13] The events of March 29th were described in Peking wall-posters, and those of April 26th in an *Agence France Presse* release from Peking. See Chapter 4 for the names of Peita Red Guard Organizations.

From July 27, 1968, powerful contingents of the working class entered places long dominated by leaders committed to the capitalist way, and to places where the
intellectuals were predominant.[14]

Workers were called in first to Peita, then to Tsinghua
University in the last part of July. During August they
appeared in most of the universities and colleges of Peking,
and they were called 'propaganda teams of the Thought
of Mao Tse-tung.'[15]

Chairman Mao apparently called a meeting of representatives from some of the city's most famous Red Guard
organizations[16] on the afternoon of July 27th, and told
them that their organizations would no longer be allowed
to take political initiatives.[17] They would now be, to some
extent, isolated. For the time being they had better accept
army control. Ten days later, Chiang Ch'ing referred to
Chairman Mao's July 27th instructions as the authority
for the working class to play the leading role in 'Struggle—
Criticism—Reform.' As we have seen in another context, the
students found the proletarian spirit hard to assimilate.
For the sake of peace and quiet they were even deprived
of their monopoly of the universities in order to amalgamate them with real proletarians.

While the entry of the workers was signifying the beginning of a new order in the privileged world of the students, a number of the latter were going to the wide open
spaces of the virgin lands to learn the realities of the
building of socialism. Already, after the neutralization of
the ultra-leftist wing, there had been an exodus of young
people and intellectuals from Peking for Inner Mongolia.

[14] Lin Piao, 'Report to the Ninth National Congress of the
Communist Party of China.' *Peking Review,* Special Issue, April
28, 1969.

[15] The groups and representatives included Nieh Yüan-tzu
for Hsin Peita, K'uai Ta-fu for Tsinghua's Chingkangshan, and
the Aeronautical Institute's Red Flag.

[16] See *Ajia Keizai Jumpo,* no. 736, Tokyo, November 1968.

[17] July 27th, according to the Hong Kong paper *Hsingtao;*
July 28th, according to a Peking Red Guard paper.

Ending one's Cultural Revolution in a camp on the steppe frontier, with the prospect of spending the rest of one's life as a pioneer, may not have been complete disgrace, but it was a harsh shock for those who had been dreaming of stirring political activity. Something of their condition may be guessed at from the remark by T'eng Hai-ch'ing, the Chairman of the Inner Mongolian revolutionary committee and regional military commander: 'In recent months we have organized activities giving revolutionaries the chance to live, work and study with the PLA. This has had a profound effect on their view of the world.'[18] The exodus of the beginning of 1968 was followed by a new one after the changes in higher education.

There was a purge in cultural circles. One incident which had considerable repercussions was that of the 'Congress of worker, peasant and soldier actors of Tientsin,' which performed satirical plays for private audiences. The most scandalous item in its repertoire was called, 'the Madman of the Twentieth Century,' and some press comments gave the impression that this play was an attack on Chairman Mao himself. From November onwards there was a series of investigations and prosecutions. T'eng Hai-ch'ing, the chairman of the Inner Mongolian revolutionary committee, who was involved in carrying out this purge as well as in the rehabilitation of the Red Guards, and perhaps for the same reason, said, 'After Comrade Chiang Ch'ing's speech of last November, the calm waters of literature and art began to move.'[19] Chiang Ch'ing had spoken on November 7th or 10th. It may well be that these were the investigations which led to the final downfall of Ch'i Pen-yü (see Chapter 9). At this time too the press purge began. But the most important purge was, of course, the one involving Liu Shao-ch'i, Teng Hsiao-p'ing and several others. The Central Committee originally appointed by the Eighth Party Congress held its twelfth

[18] 'Ideological work among proletarian revolutionaries,' People's Daily, January 15, 1968; New China News Agency, no. 011705, 1968 (French language series).

[19] T'eng Hai-ch'ing's remarks were published in the national press at the end of March 1968.

plenary session in October 1968, and ratified the 'Report on the examination of the crimes of the renegade, traitor and scab, Liu Shao-ch'i.' The session unanimously adopted a resolution to expel Liu Shao-ch'i from the Party once and for all, to dismiss him from all posts both inside and outside the Party, and to 'continue to denounce the crimes which he and his accomplices had committed in betraying the Party and the country.'[20] Liu had at last been exorcised by name, and he continued to oblige by acting as an excuse for later purges.

It was not surprising that those responsible for the ideas which the Cultural Revolution had risen up against should have been swept aside when the movement put its political programme into effect. It was also natural that the defenders of these ideas, such as T'an Chen-lin, should have been overthrown. The Cultural Revolution put forward its own conception of what the Party should be, and it was only natural that the chief exponents of the opposing line should fall with it. Apart from them, there does not seem to have been a systematic overall purge.

Some men of the right who had held to their conservative outlook and had been in total opposition to Mao Tse-tung on some vital questions (such as Ch'en Yün and, perhaps, Ch'en Yi) lost some of their importance, but remained in senior positions. They accepted democratic centralism, and did not conspire to bring a group of like-minded leaders into power.

As we have seen above, the revolution dismissed many men from its ranks, but from the middle of 1967 there was no longer any need for those who were loyal to the Party spirit to worry about this happening to them. The Cultural Revolution's victims were rightists, leftists and even enthusiastic Maoists who threatened the Party by representing a group that was too independent and powerful: such were P'eng Chen, T'ao Chu, Ho Lung, Ch'i Pen-yü, or Yang Ch'eng-wu.

[20] *Communiqué of the Enlarged Twelfth Plenary Session of the Eighth Central Committee of the Communist Party of China*, Foreign Languages Press, Peking, 1968.

Social change

Ever since the beginning of the Cultural Revolution the rebels had been asserting that what they had to do was 'destroy': destroy the 'Four Olds,' overthrow the authorities, make a clean sweep in the superstructure. Anyone who pointed out that they had nothing to put in its place was abused and vilified. For two years the rebels had denounced as reactionary the majority of local attempts at reorganization that appeared to be inspired by the spirit of reform.

An editorial which appeared simultaneously in the *People's Daily, Red Flag* and the *PLA Daily* on September 1, 1968, marked a significant change: 'Destruction comes first,' it read, 'but within it are contained the seeds of construction.'[21] While the terminology reveals the deep-rooted prejudice against 'construction,' the sense is clearly that the destructive phase was now developing into a new one. The revolutionaries were being assured that their work would continue—tomorrow's ideas would still be the ones formed in the struggle—but they were also being told that the forms of political struggle had now changed.

By the time it was accepted that 'the working class must play a leading part in everything' there was no longer any need to ask it to lead the political struggle. The Centre now held the reins once more, and the initiatives now required would be for the transformation of society rather than attacks on the political enemy. Thus it must be realized that the workers were now the 'principal force,' according to the role they were to play in the next phase of the revolution, which was to be social.

Leaving aside the question of the extent of their political awareness—a matter of some importance, as we have seen above—the role of the workers has to be understood by reference to two ideas: the simplification of the bureaucracy, and Maoist ideas on development. The first was based on the axiom that producers were better suited than man-

21 See *Peking Review,* no. 37, September 16, 1968.

agers for revolutionizing the relations of production, and the second carried with it the desire to achieve the 'proletarian industrial revolution'[22] that the Cultural Revolution had facilitated. Chou En-lai developed the first concept in these words:

> The revolution in the world of ideas comes first, with the proletarian revolutionaries seizing power from the advocates of the bourgeois line. Now it is up to us as economic revolutionaries to transform the economic system. An economic system is a matter not of power but of work relationships. . . . There must be revolution in every sphere of life, and the key question is the necessity of simplification.[23]

The second idea was emphasized in an editorial in *Red Flag* that may be attributed to Mao Tse-tung himself:

> What is the situation as regards the engineering and technical personnel in factories? . . . We must pay particular attention to re-education of graduates . . . so that they will integrate with the workers and peasants.[24]

The fight against bureaucratism, and the streamlining of the administration, were the basic themes in the building of revolutionary committees. Instead of a top-heavy administration maintained by the Party, and which the people

[22] This expression was used in the report of an investigation on 'The Revolution in Education in Colleges of Science and Engineering as reflected in the struggle between the two lines at the Shanghai Institute of Mechanical Engineering,' in *Red Flag*, no. 3, September 10, 1968, p. 13; see *Peking Review*, no. 37, September 13, 1968, p. 17. This was also published in the *People's Daily* of September 5, 1968.

[23] Chou En-lai, February 2, 1968, to delegates of committees in various ministries, *op. cit.*

[24] *Red Flag* editor's note on the report on the Shanghai Institute of Mechanical Engineering quoted above, of which Chiang Ch'ing said, 'This editorial represents the voice of our great leader Chairman Mao.' See *Peking Review*, no. 37, September 13, 1968, p. 8 for Chiang Ch'ing's speech, p. 13 for the editorial.

considered parasitic, the Units should be run by workers giving some of their time to public affairs.

> In order to remain an ordinary person as well as being an official, we need a drastic reform of the old methods of office and administrative work. Have a small leading body and a small staff. . . . so that there is no overlapping or redundancy in the organization and no overstaffing, so that bureaucracy can be prevented.[25]

Before the Cultural Revolution the Party had justified the growth of the bureaucracy by the increasing complexity of the economy and by the need to have a division of labour. Now it was necessary to reject any kind of technocracy and go back to Mao Tse-tung's 1942 teachings on frugality, on the availability of all people, on unity in work, complete equality of employments, and a turning away from anything which resembled technocracy.[26]

Discipline at work was now a matter for the workers themselves. We have seen above the strains under which discipline had been put, the worst being in the mines in February 1968. Meetings of workers in the various branches of industry were called, and the participants were asked to consider ways of improving output and the organization of work. The meeting for miners was held on May 22nd in the outskirts of Peking, and it passed resolutions on developing forms of self-management and making the best use of veteran workers in production.[27]

The principle laid down for teaching, 'in line with the needs of the proletarian industrial revolution, and proceeding from the realities of production' was to 'set up the required training courses, to learn whatever the work in

[25] *People's Daily, Red Flag,* and *PLA Daily* joint editorial, 'Revolutionary committees are fine,' March 30, 1968; see *Peking Review,* no. 14, April 5, 1968, p. 7.

[26] See the article by Yung Chung-tung, *People's Daily,* October 31, 1968; and *Ajia Keizai Jumpo,* no. 739 Tokyo, December 1968, p. 17.

[27] The conference, reported in the *People's Daily* of May 25, 1968, was held in the Muchengchien mine that had been the scene of bloody incidents during February.

progress may dictate, and to fill in the gaps.'[28] Links between universities and industry or between universities and agriculture were not confined to research workers. In order to integrate the institutions of higher education more closely into the development of the country, gifted workers and peasants would complement their technical knowledge with scientific training, then go back to their Units to share their new learning. Through this interchange the regime hoped to benefit the areas where knowledge would do most to achieve a new leap forward. This time there would be no attempt to triple output, but from the factories and communes 'innovations and inventions' would emerge to help production. The Cultural Revolution, now nearing its end, concentrated on sketching out a reform of education and careers for technicians, workers and peasants.

Interest was mainly devoted to technical and scientific universities as a result of a recent directive of Mao Tsetung:

> It is still necessary to have universities; here I refer mainly to colleges of science and engineering. However, it is essential to shorten the length of schooling, revolutionize education, put proletarian politics in command and take the road of the Shanghai Machine Tools Plant in training technicians from among the workers. Students should be selected from among workers and peasants with practical experience, and they should return to production after a few years' study.[29]

Following up this directive, the journal *Red Flag* opened its columns to an investigation of the factory and the institute that Chairman Mao had held up as examples. The questions of syllabuses, and the length of courses and personnel, were studied in detail. The barriers which existed between foundation courses, basic technical courses, and specialist courses would have to be destroyed. Courses

---

[28] *Red Flag*, no. 3, 1968; *Peking Review*, no. 37, September 13, 1968, p. 17.
[29] *Ibid.*, p. 16.

in scientific and technical colleges would now be limited
to two or three years, and a body of 'proletarian teachers'
would be formed. The main role of full-time teachers
would be:

> to arrange an organic link between colleges, factories
> and scientific research units, and to help the students
> raise their practical knowledge to the theoretical level,
> in order to redirect it again to the practical. The students
> may then go to the lecture platform to exchange the
> practical information they have. The present teachers
> should go among the workers and peasants in groups
> one after another and work towards integration with
> the workers and peasants.[30]

What about agriculture? The countryside was further
from the universities than were the factories. Would this
new emphasis on technical education, which had been
missing from the 1958 'leap forward,' bring about the
growth in agricultural output that China needed? It was
true that the countryside would produce more grain
through seed selection and above all through a diversified
use of fertilizers. But what was called for at the moment
was more work from the peasants in improving the land:
digging more wells and canals, and terracing more fields.
The example to be followed was that of Tachai.[31]

Poor and middle peasants devoted themselves to this
work and, as at Tachai, some of them rejected their sala-
ried status. At least, they rejected a system of set payments
for each kind of job. They said that peasants should be
mobilized for work in the fields as were soldiers for active
service. The members of each team should divide the
work among them, and each should declare afterwards
what he had done. On the strength of this everyone in the
team would decide how to share what they had to distribute.[32] This responsible attitude to work would com-

[30] *Ibid.*, p. 17.
[31] See Chapter 2.
[32] The peasants of the Tientsin suburbs, for example, passed
a resolution in these terms.

plement the new spurt of technical progress that the new
teaching system promised to workers and peasants.

A step had been taken towards simplifying the bureaucracy, workers managing their own work, and the reform
of teaching and pay. However, these measures were to be
regarded as projects, because they had not yet received a
general application. But at any rate they formed part of a
programme for greater autonomy in the people's communes and the Units. And the statement that workers were
to take over the traditional role of intellectuals was an
event of great significance to society.

An analysis of the provisional institutions

Before the Cultural Revolution, local and provincial government depended on a dual system of Party and people's
committees. Although political inspiration came primarily
from the former, the latter did something to give the
'united front' some reality alongside the Communist Party.
The Party and state leadership appeared to treat them with
equal respect, knowing the advantages to be gained from
well established local politicians. In a study on Party personnel published in 1967, F. C. Teiwes concluded that in
the previous decade Peking had shown great confidence
in the loyalty of provincial officials.[33] Then the Cultural
Revolution challenged the Party cadres to choose between
obedience to the old structure and rallying to the call of
the Thought of Mao Tse-tung. The shock this gave to the
committees made them unable to maintain their authority,
and the Centre instructed the revolutionary committees
to take their place.

The revolutionary committees seemed to have been invested with the authority of the Party committees, but in
their composition they were more like the people's committees in that they included representatives of the masses.
They had the 'widest revolutionary representation seen

[33] F. C. Teiwes, *Provincial Party Personnel in Mainland
China 1956–1966*, Columbia University, New York, 1967, p. 63.

since the Liberation,' wrote *Red Flag*,[34] and as it went on
to reaffirm that the committees had been invested with the
authority of the proletarian dictatorship, the view that the
revolutionary committees would become permanent rather
than transitional began to gather credence. Perceptive
observers agreed that they might last for a long time, replacing both kinds of old committees.[35]

In some places, however, Party committees co-existed
with corresponding revolutionary committees, and even
reconstituted themselves. There was the case of the Tachai
brigade.[36] Another important example was provided by
the Geological Institute, which created a 'provisional Party
committee' in November 1967. Its revolutionary committee met in special session to restore the Party organization
in the Institute.[37] Thus the new Party could be constituted
without the inevitable overthrow of the old.

But as a purge was taking place within their ranks—
which Lin Piao mentioned in his report to the Ninth Congress—the Party committees could not exercise leading
roles.[38] They seemed to exist in the shadow of the revolutionary committees, whereas another provisional institution played yet another role: the study classes of the
Thought of Mao Tse-tung. Party members and ordinary
people both took part in these classes, which were often
run by the military, and thus resembled the triple alliances

[34] *Red Flag*, October 15, 1968.

[35] See especially the Japanese-language edition of *Mainichi
Shimbun* of October 16, 1968.

[36] See *Ajia Keizai Jumpo*, no. 722, June 1968.

[37] On November 17, 1968, according to the official press
in Peking.

[38] 'In units where the work of purifying the class ranks
has not yet started or has only just started, it is imperative to
tackle the job firmly and do it well in accordance with the
Party's policies. In units where the purification of the class
ranks is by and large completed, it is necessary to take firm
hold of other tasks in keeping with Chairman Mao's instructions concerning the various stages of struggle-criticism-reform.' Lin Piao, *Report to the Ninth National Congress of
the Communist Party of China*, Peking, 1968, pocket edition,
pp. 57–58.

of these three elements in the revolutionary committees. The study classes, however, had no administrative or political control. They were to form the basis of the new Party, from which the delegates to the coming Congress were to be chosen.[39]

The revolutionary committees maintained themselves in existence right through to the end of the Cultural Revolution as the sole local organs with leadership power. How powerful were they in fact? The Centre certainly allowed them wide discretion in provincial matters. They were strong because they were founded on the principle of unified leadership. It will be remembered how the principle had been applied in the days when the Party's membership was reduced, and what part the army had played in those circumstances;[40] it was not therefore surprising that soldiers should be numerous in the revolutionary committees. Long ago in the bases, during the struggle against the Kuomintang, the army had disseminated the ideas of a small group of Communists to the Soviets. Now the Party, its numbers reduced by the tests it had imposed on itself, closed ranks around the leaders loyal to Mao Tse-tung, and used the unified leadership to pass on its counsels to the masses.

Comparisons have most often been drawn between the Party committees and the revolutionary committees, and this has generally been in order to highlight the army's new place in the power structure. With only about three exceptions, all the revolutionary committees heading the provinces and big cities had either a military commander or an army political commissar as chairman.[41] The concessions made to the military seemed quite exorbitant when the newly appointed leaders were not even commanders of local garrison troops but of troops only stationed in the

[39] See the good discussion of the role of the study classes in 'Kakumei jinkai ni miru kokka kikō kaikaku no hōkō,' *Ajia Keizai Jumpo,* no. 722, June 1968.

[40] See Chapter 1.

[41] The exceptions were Hopei, Shensi, and Tientsin Municipality.

area.[42] In cases when this was done it would seem likely that the army had been called upon to restore order locally.

But while it is true that the top leadership of all the revolutionary committees included generals, it must not be forgotten that at least one cadre from the former Party committee's secretariat was always with them. This is significant because it suggests that the precious records of the Party committees remained in competent hands. The files of confidential information on all the cadres who would have to be re-employed were neither seized by the people nor dispersed. In every case, one of the secretaries in charge of these records was won over to the Cultural Revolution.

The Party had long paid particular attention to ensuring the continuity of the teams which controlled the provinces. As F. C. Teiwes, already quoted above, has written:

> The top leaders, undoubtedly influenced by a deep belief in the power of indoctrination, seem also to have recognized that other methods were equally if not more effective for applying the right policy and achieving control in times of tension. . . . Large scale personnel changes were only carried out in specific situations that demanded radical action, as in Kweichow in 1965.[43]

The Cultural Revolution does not seem to have brought about any profound changes in this policy. All the documents needed for the appointment of cadres were closely guarded. They were kept, as far as possible, beyond the reach of revolutionary indiscretion.

Representatives of the people were, of course, included

---

[42] This was the case in Chekiang, Anhwei, and Ninghsia. See *China News Analysis*, no. 707, May 10, 1968.

[43] *Provincial Party Personnel in Mainland China, 1956–1966*, p. 63. The Kweichow purge in 1965 seems to have given that province a new administration that had few links with local interests and was highly responsive to ideological control. This doubtless explains the leading role played by the province in the Cultural Revolution, a role that its geographical isolation and backwardness of development would not otherwise justify.

in the revolutionary committees alongside the Party's representatives. The deputy chairman of the Inner Mongolian
committee included a lorry-driver,[44] Kwangtung included
a worker in a machine-building plant, and Shansi a peasant labour-hero.[45] Members of the Party learned to share
political work with the people they governed, beside whom
they made their careers. Moreover, propaganda insisted
that the members of revolutionary committees, including
the top leaders, should go down among the masses and
share their work.[46] There could be no doubt but that the
remoulded Party would include representatives of the
masses who had done a probationary spell in the Party.

Revolutionary committees maintained the situation in
the absence of Party committees, and served as a crucible
in which the cadres could be better fused with soldiers
and ordinary people. They did not seem to be intended to
become permanent institutions. In his report to the Ninth
Congress, Lin Piao only mentioned them in the section on
the phase of 'struggle-criticism-reform.'

The rebuilding of the Party

Popular revolutions always have songs. The Red Guards
wrote some, as did the propaganda media. The people
made their choice, for they sang the ones they preferred.
The favourites were undoubtedly 'The East is Red' and
'Sailing the Seas depends on the Helmsman,' both infused
with passionate feeling for Mao Tse-tung. But one of the
songs most often sung by revolutionaries was simply the
first quotation in the Little Red Book set to music: 'The
force at the core leading our cause forward is the Chinese

[44] 'Ōku no Jinzai wa hagukumu jidai,' *Jimmin Chūgoku*,
Peking, March 1968, p. 30 ff.
[45] Ch'en Yung-kuei, Tachai's leader.
[46] Most of the Kweichow revolutionary committee stayed in
their former jobs (New China News Agency, March 29, 1968).
Half of the members of the standing committee of the Heilungkiang committee compelled themselves to work in basic-level
Units while the other half did the committee's work (New
China News Agency, February 29, 1968).

Communist Party.' From start to finish, even when its leaders were falling to the pitiless attacks of the Rebels, the leading role of the Party was being celebrated in song.

The reconstruction of the Party was announced in a joint editorial of the *People's Daily*, *Red Flag*, and the *PLA Daily* on January 1, 1968, emphasizing the Party's leadership and announcing its reorganization.

> Alongside the rectification of the Party organization, the Communist Youth League, the Red Guards and the various revolutionary mass organizations should be rectified ideologically and organizationally.

In short, the same treatment was prescribed for the Party, infected as it was with revisionism, as for the mass organizations suffering from ultra-leftist tendencies. It was necessary above all to take what was good from all political bodies and give the Party everything it needed:

> In the coming year we should . . . purify and rectify the Party organization. A number of outstanding, advanced proletarian elements who have come forward in the great cultural revolution should be admitted into the Party; and the renegades, secret agents and leaders committed to the capitalist way, who refuse to reform themselves, should be expelled.[47]

Old Party members, whose positions had exposed them to public scrutiny, were still undergoing a series of trials. First they were suspended from their duties, but not expelled from the Party, and then made to undergo investigations into their public and private lives that dug right down to the roots of their personal philosophies.[48] Those who passed this test were allowed back to work, but they

---

[47] 'Forward to complete victory in the great proletarian Cultural Revolution,' *Peking Review*, no. 1, January 3, 1968, p. 12.

[48] See Ando Hikotaro, 'Bunkaku sannenme no kadai,' an excellent study of the situation of cadres relieved of their duties, *Asahi Jyanaru*, vol. 9, no. 52.

were not yet 'liberated.' The investigation was only an individual test, and collective agreement was needed before they could be set free. The cadre who wanted to be restored to his authority had to appear in public and try to make, with the help of the people, an analysis of the motives that had brought him into, or perilously close to, error. When the people accepted his analysis, which was generally self-critical and always ended with an attack on the 'bourgeois' leaders of the Party, the cadre was at last 'liberated' and allowed to resume his duties.

As far as one could tell, the point of holding these ceremonies was not to have show trials but to win as many as possible over to a unified way of thinking. The term *tuli ssuk'ao,* 'independent thought,' was used to denote the repeated process of profound self-examination and public adherence to the standard themes of revolutionary criticism. It is all too clear that the subject was under considerable psychological pressure; but he could not make a purely formal conversion as it would not have been accepted. The avowal had to be personal and backed up by evidence.

The cadres who underwent these tests without success were not usually threatened with anything worse than expulsion from the Party. Lin Piao himself guaranteed that, with regard to 'bad elements and suspects discovered in the course of the movement for purifying the class ranks, the policy of "killing none and not arresting most"[49] should be applied to all.'[50] Yao Wen-yuan declared: 'Men whose revolutionary thought has failed them, men who have lapsed, should be advised to leave the Party.'[51] The 'purifying of the class ranks' mentioned by Lin Piao was a movement on a much larger scale than a Party purge, extending as it did to revolutionary organizations that had to undergo the same treatment. But the significant fact about the latter was not so much their 'purifi-

[49] A quotation from Mao Tse-tung.

[50] *Report to the Ninth National Congress of the Communist Party of China,* pocket edition, p. 56.

[51] Editorial of October 1, 1968, which appeared simultaneously in *People's Daily, Red Flag,* and *PLA Daily.*

cation' as the incorporation of their members into the Party.

> We must take into the Party fresh blood from the pro-letariat—above all, progressive elements with communist awareness from among industrial workers—and select outstanding Party members who are resolute in carrying out Chairman Mao's proletarian revolutionary line for leading posts in the Party.

This was the conclusion of the Central Committee in the collective decision of its Twelfth Plenary Session.[52] The 'fresh blood' would therefore have to be taken from among the revolutionary organizations, especially from the in-dustrial workers, and, as Yao Wen-yuan wrote, 'a leading nucleus which resolutely implements Chairman Mao's proletarian revolutionary line will gradually be formed.'[53] This leading nucleus could no longer be the Party alone, but was now to be the unified leadership in the service of the Party.

The meetings, which consummated the work of the study classes, and which we have called conferences of activists in the Thought of Mao Tse-tung—or 'people's rev-olutionary congresses'—were used to select the progres-sive elements. Shanghai took the lead in this movement,[54] in which the purification of revolutionary organizations was combined with selecting delegates to the forthcoming Party congress.[55] In Shanghai the 'progressive elements of the proletariat' were principally industrial workers. This advance was a good sign of their political awareness at a time when the students in Peking were revealing nothing

[52] *Communiqué of the Enlarged 12th Plenary Session of the Eighth Central Committee of the Communist Party of China*, Peking, 1968, p. 7.

[53] *Peking Review*, no. 35, August 30, 1968, p. 6.

[54] 'Kyūzentaikai he Isogiashi,' *Asahi Shimbun*, morning edi-tion, March 15, 1968. The revolutionary leaders did not mind rapping Peking's knuckles in referring to the progress made by Shanghai at the great rally to criticize Yang Ch'eng-wu held in the Workers' Stadium on March 27th.

[55] On the study classes see the previous section.

but their quarrels. This and other evidence confirmed the 'leading role of the working class.'

Nomination to the congress was equivalent to admission to the Party. The revolutionaries who were nominated doubtless served a probationary period before the congress opened. Others who were not chosen as delegates served a trial term in the local organizations of the Party. The Party was preparing its blood transfusion. But the main scene was now being played in Peking, where 1,512 delegates were holding the main meeting of the Party's restoration.

The Ninth Congress of the Chinese Communist Party opened ceremonially on April 1, 1969, in Peking. It heard Lin Piao's report, elected a new Central Committee, and revised the Party constitution. The election of a new Central Committee was an event of great political significance. It marked a formal end to the revolutionary period. For over two years the leading organizations at the top had expelled those of their members they regarded as unworthy to participate in the revolution. The Central Committee's Cultural Revolution Group had played an exceptional part in this policy. Now the Ninth Congress restored the Central Committee to its supreme position, and put the various organs that had formed part of the Centre back to their jobs in government and propaganda.

The composition of the new Central Committee should have given a clearer picture of where power now lay; but examination does not reveal a great deal, except that a good number of its members were comparatively unknown.

The assembly, on which sat all the powerful figures in the Party who ran its apparatus in the provinces and the national ministries, lost its old sense of collective identity. Only a third of the members of the former Central Committee were re-elected. The new members were doubtless chosen on the strength of their attitudes in the Cultural Revolution. The lists of candidates were drawn up by commissions that attached more weight to reports of local events than to any other considerations. The procedure followed left much initiative to provincial delegates: the small leading group in Peking could not dictate the choice of members of an organ as large as the Central Committee.

The delegates to the Congress from the provincial revolutionary committees and those from other organizations that came with them were doubtless influenced by their idea of what sort of local order there should be at the end of the Cultural Revolution. The people they chose to represent them on the Central Committee were probably those who had distinguished themselves both by their local effectiveness and by their loyalty to the Centre. This would explain the large number of soldiers, whose representation in the central organization rose from 36 per cent to 45 per cent. At the same time the representation of senior administrative cadres was also increased. This may be explained by the role played by the ministries and the national services in keeping China functioning during so long a period of disorder. Those who lost out were the Party cadres, who gave way to revolutionaries from the people.

The new Party constitution adopted by the Congress obliged the Party to unite more closely with the masses in choosing its members and carrying out its duties. Party control over the army, the organs of state power, and the revolutionary mass organizations was doubtless strengthened, and the constitution stipulated that organizations of workers, poor and lower-middle peasants and Red Guards would have to submit to Party control.[56] On the other hand, applicants for Party membership would not be admitted without scrutiny by the people.[57] The Party initiated campaigns, but it could carry them out only with the people's representatives. The unified leadership, in which representatives of the people joined with those of the Party, would be reconstituted every time the latter sent out teams to carry out its policies.[58] In other words, the people were expected to play their part in the executive field.

In addition, precautions were taken to ensure that Party

[56] Article 5.
[57] Article 2.
[58] Article 7.

members should feel more free to argue with the leadership, make reservations on policies of which they disapproved, and make their criticisms known at the highest levels.

It is essential to create a political situation in which there simultaneously exists both centralism and democracy, both discipline and freedom, both unity of will and individual ease of mind and liveliness.[59]

The constitution thus insisted on the necessity of keeping a way open, so that the renunciation of individual sovereignty should not rule out the instinct of making up one's own mind.

Contradictions did of course remain dangerous. The individual spirit could rebel against discipline. Had not the Cultural Revolution itself been a 'rebellion?' Unified leadership might also, in practice, conflict with obedience to Party control. But the constitution's authors relied on discussion to resolve the contradictions, and their work was itself the product of a dialogue. In his report Lin Piao explained that the draft constitution had incorporated many suggestions from the masses and had been referred back to the masses for discussion.[60] If the revolution had indeed established a dialogue everywhere, particularly between the Party and the masses, this was a great achievement.

The old Party had put its organization above all other values. Now the new voices were demanding that the first priority be accorded to living ideology, affirming that henceforward it would be served by the 'progressive elements of the proletariat.' The Cultural Revolution opened the doors of the Party to many new members who had not undergone old training. The newcomers had won

[59] Article 5.
[60] The Twelfth Plenum drew up a draft constitution on the basis of several thousand suggestions submitted by primary Party organizations acting on Mao Tse-tung's suggestions of November 1967, and returned it for discussion among the revolutionary masses, the Party, and the army before the congress. See Lin Piao, *Report to the Ninth Congress*, p. 76.

their spurs through 'revolt,' and they would doubtless bring like-minded people in with them. The Ninth Congress insisted that they should 'be on guard against careerists' and become the pupils of the masses. In Lin Piao's words, 'The great proletarian Cultural Revolution is the broadest and deepest movement for Party consolidation in the history of our Party.'[61]

[61] *Report to the Ninth Congress,* p. 72.

Author's Note

The late date at which the Congress was called and the paucity of information on its work have made it impossible to make any profound analysis of the Congress's results. This book is, besides, based primarily on information gathered directly from the press by the author during a stay in China that ended in June 1968.

Conclusion

It is no longer possible to dispute that the Cultural Revolution really was a revolution. It was led by Mao Tse-tung and a few of his close associates who were convinced that the Party could not be regenerated without action by the people.

The movement thus called into being was so strong that it almost became another revolution, sweeping away the Communist Party. From January to September 1967 revolutionary detachments overturned the policies of the people in power. Ambitions arose to seize control of the revolution. Passions went beyond the level the leaders had encouraged in their desire to arouse the masses. At any rate, in the cities the sudden surge of interest in politics won for a time complete freedom of the press, of association, and of the right to run one's own place of work.

The Centre achieved the victory of the Party spirit over anarchic tendencies, and in this operation the army played an indispensable part. So many new political positions did the army control as a result of this that there were fears of a military regime. But there was a special relationship between the Chinese Communist Party and the People's Liberation Army.

The slogan that 'the working class should lead the way in everything' ensured that the army would have to hand over to others all the responsibilities that were not its own. But it proved easier to decentralize the state than to es-

tablish control over the political power that had to be
centralized. The Cultural Revolution had been launched
to bring about control through the Mass Line. In the last
resort, the continued existence of the people's organizations was more important than the revolutionary committees.

Few revolutionary organizations were disbanded. In
order that the reformed Party should have the popular
critics it deserved, Mao Tse-tung went to great trouble to
keep political enthusiasm alive wherever it had developed.
For a long time the main difficulty had been to stimulate
the activity needed to awaken political consciousness, while
saving the revolutionaries from their besetting temptation
to exploit the revolution for their own pleasure. 'It is too
easy,' Chiang Ch'ing had said. 'When you want to bite a
peach, you take a mouthful. But if you eat it all you lose
it.' The leaders of the revolution were trying at the same
time to give the Chinese the taste for peaches and to keep
all the fruit on the tree.

The outbreaks of violence reported in the Western press
often obscured the efforts that the revolution's propaganda
made to urge the masses not to lose interest too quickly.
The leaders' concern was to draw as many as possible
into the struggle from which a new alliance was to be
born. We saw it explained in these terms above:

Alliance and unity pass through struggle to division,
and a new alliance is formed on the basis of the Thought
of Mao Tse-tung. Such is the dialectic of the Cultural
Revolution.

Select Bibliography

Andō Hikotarō, *Chûgoku Tsûshin*, Daian, Tokyo, 1966.

Bettelheim, Charles; Charrière, Jacques; and Marchisio, Hélène, *La Construction du socialisme en Chine*, François Maspero, Paris, 1965.

Chen Po-ta, *Mao Tse-tung on the Chinese Revolution* (1951), Foreign Language Press, Peking, 1963.

———, *Notes on Mao Tse-tung's report on an investigation of the peasant movement in Hunan* (1953), Foreign Language Press, Peking, 1966.

Chesneaux, Jean, *L'Asie orientale au XIXe et au XXe siècles*, Presse Universitaire de France, Paris, 1966.

Dumont, René, *La Chine surpeuplée, Tiers Monde affamé*, Editions du Seuil, Paris, 1965.

Étienne, Gilbert, *La Voie chinoise*, P.U.F., Paris, 1962.

Faure, Edgar, *The Serpent and the Tortoise; Problems of the New China*. Translated by Lovett F. Edwards, Macmillan & Co., London and New York, 1965.

Gittings, John, *The Role of the Chinese Army*, R.I.A.A., Oxford University Press, 1968.

Guillain, Robert, *Dans trente ans la Chine*, Edition du Seuil, Paris, 1965.

Guillermaz, Jacques, *Histoire du parti communiste chinois*, Payot, Paris, 1968.

Konno, Junichi, *Pekin Kono Ichinen*, Shinnihon, Tokyo, 1968.

Le Duan, *On the Socialist Revolution in Vietnam,* Foreign Language Publishing House, Hanoi, 1965.

Lu Hsün, *Selected Works,* Foreign Language Press, Peking, 1956.

Mao Tse-tung, *Oeuvres choisies,* Editions sociales, Paris, 1955.

Myrdal, Jan, *Report from a Chinese Village.* Translated by Maurice Michael, Heinemann, London, 1965.

Nee, Victor, and Don Layman, 'The Cultural Revolution at Peking University,' *revue mensuelle,* Vol. 21, no. 3, New York and London, 1969.

Schram, Stuart, *Mao Tse-tung,* Allen Lane, The Penguin Press, London, 1967.

——, and Hélène Carrière d'Encausse, *Marxism and Asia,* Allen Lane, Penguin Press, London, 1969.

Schurmann, Franz, *Ideology and Organization in Communist China,* University of California Press, 1966.

Schwartz, Benjamin, *Communism and China. Ideology in Flux,* Harvard University Press, Cambridge, 1968.

Shih Nai-an, *Water Margin,* The Commercial Press Ltd., Hong Kong, 1963.

Shirono Hiroshi, *Chūgoku no hassō,* Shiwo, Tokyo, 1968.

Snow, Edgar, *Red Star over China,* Gollancz, London, 1968.

Teiwes, F. C., *Provincial Party Personnel in Mainland China, 1955–1966,* Columbia University, New York, 1967.

Wandermeersch, Léon, 'L'Orient rouge; de Confucius à Mao,' revue *Esprit,* no. 3, Paris, 1967.

Index